Security:
A MANAGEMENT
PERSPECTIVE

HARVEY BURSTEIN

Prentice Hall
Englewood Cliffs, New Jersey 07632

Library of Congress Cataloging-in-Publication Data

Burstein, Harvey
  Security: a management perspective-Harvey Burstein.

    p. cm.
  Includes bibliographical references and index.
  ISBN 0-13-150657-9
  1. Industries—Security measures—Management.   I. Titles.
HV8290.B875   1996   95-9241
658.4'7—dc20   CIP

Manufacturing Manager: *Ed O'Dougherty*
Acquisitions Editor: *Robin Baliszewski*
Director of Production and Manufacturing: *Bruce Johnson*
Managing Editor: *Mary Carnis*
Editorial/Production Supervision: *Editorial Services of New England, Inc.*
Cover Design: *Bruce Kenselaar*

© 1996 by Prentice-Hall, Inc.
A Simon & Schuster Company
Englewood Cliffs, New Jersey 07632

ISBN 0-13-150657-9

Printed in the United States of America

10 9 8 7 6 5 4 3 2 1

PRENTICE-HALL INTERNATIONAL (UK) LIMITED, London
PRENTICE-HALL OF AUSTRALIA PTY. LIMITED, Sydney
PRENTICE-HALL CANADA INC., Toronto
PRENTICE-HALL HISPANOAMERICANA, S.A., Mexico
PRENTICE-HALL OF INDIA PRIVATE LIMITED, New Delhi
PRENTICE-HALL OF JAPAN, INC., Tokyo
SIMON & SCHUSTER ASIA PTE. LTD., Singapore
EDITORA PRENTICE-HALL DO BRASIL, LTDA., Rio de Janeiro

To the memory of
Helen B. Sommer and Reverend Patrick G. Kelly, S.J.,
my English instructors at
Omaha Central High School and Creighton University respectively,
who taught me both the love and use of the English language

CONTENTS

About the Author

Harvey Burstein, Schulman Professor of Security at the College of Criminal Justice, Northeastern University, is a graduate of the Creighton University Law School. After admission to the bar, he served as a special agent of the FBI, and as chief, foreign and domestic investigations, surveys, and physical security with the U.S. Department of State.

His career in security has spanned more than forty years. As the security officer for the Massachusetts Institute of Technology, he was responsible for protecting all classified government research and established and managed MIT's first campus police force. He was also the corporate security director for The Sheraton Corporation, New England Life, and corporate director safety/security–staff attorney for Data General Corporation. Mr. Burstein has been a security management consultant to such businesses and institutions as Corning Glass, Monsanto, Schering, Intercontinental Hotels, Paul Harris Stores, Mallinckrodt Chemical, New York City's Beth Israel Medical Center, and the Hospital Department of the City of Boston. He has lectured to the Sloan Fellows Program at MIT's School of Industrial Management, and was a visiting professor at Fordham University's Martino Graduate School of Business Administration.

The author of seven books on security management, Mr. Burstein also has written numerous articles on security from both a corporate management and a legal point of view, for business and professional journals, among them the *Harvard Business Review*, the *University of Michigan Business Review*, *Hospitals*, *Journal of Applied Management*, *Stores*, *Insurance Counsel Journal*, *Retail Control*, *Food Engineering*, and *Best's Insurance News*. Mr. Burstein, a certified protection professional, has addressed meetings of the American

Hotel and Motel Association, the National Retail Merchants Association, the American Society for Industrial Security, the American Management Association, the National Restaurant Association, the Eastern Association of College and University Business Administrators, and the National Council on Crime and Delinquency.

PREFACE

In my years of teaching security and security related courses, whether as a lecturer or as adjunct or full-time faculty, my objective has been twofold. First, to help my students, both undergraduate and graduate, develop a greater appreciation of the significant contributions that truly effective security programs can and do make to the criminal justice and business communities. Second, to assist them in developing good overall managerial skills that can be applied to security department activities instead of having them focus on merely becoming better security managers.

In this respect my goal has its genesis in forty years of experience as either a corporate security director or security management consultant for a number of institutions and Fortune 500 companies representing a wide variety of industries. During that time I have encountered far too many security managers who have found it difficult to get the approvals needed to upgrade their programs, or have complained about their lack of input on matters related to their employers' security, notwithstanding their positions. Both situations possibly due in part to their own inability to make the transition from that of a security specialist to that of a business generalist.

Some of these complaints have been justified. However, in other cases their advice has not been sought, or their proposals for better protection have been rejected, not because of disinterested superiors but rather because they themselves lack the management skills that are essential if they hope to be listened to and have their recommendations accepted by executive management.

As businesses and institutions have become ever more aware of the need to provide for the protection and conservation of their assets, they have become increasingly mindful of the fact that if they want optimally effective loss prevention programs they need to employ security directors who truly are professionals in the field. With the passage of time they have come to realize that investigative, law enforcement, or military experience, once considered as the preeminent if not the sole qualifications for security directorships, are not necessarily the right credentials for dealing with the many, varied, and complex problems encountered in today's highly competitive business environment. Instead, whatever security experience is brought to the job now must be supplemented by good management skills and an understanding of the business world.

The most experienced investigators, law enforcement, or military personnel who cannot submit realistic budgets and work within their parameters are not good managers. Former members of the armed forces or quasi-military organizations, used to giving orders and having them obeyed without question, often find it hard to work with people, especially peers and subordinates, in a less disciplined environment. Even those who have held management positions in government may have difficulty adjusting to an environment where, for the first time, they find that more is expected of them than just getting a job done. Rather it is a matter of getting it done in those ways that will contribute most to the employer's profit picture.

Therefore, it is my hope that this text will prove helpful not only to those students who aspire to eventually become security directors and managers, but also to those who are interested in careers in business administration and to whom security managers some day may report. Perhaps even currently active security managers may find its contents useful.

In closing, I would like to thank Jacob Frank, vice president and general counsel, Data General Corporation, for permission to use as illustrations certain materials I either developed or helped to develop while employed as Data General's corporate director safety/security—and staff attorney, Jean Robertson, Esq., of Data General's Law Department, and Robert J. McBride, Data General's vice president and corporate controller, for providing a sample security department budget playback format. I would be remiss if I did not single out for special thanks Robin Baliszewski, the executive editor of Prentice Hall's Criminal Justice College Division, without whose interest, encouragement, and support this book might not have been written.

Harvey Burstein

Chapter 1

Introduction

A HISTORICAL PERSPECTIVE

The notion that one is entitled to protect one's property is ancient in origin. Historically speaking, the right to protect one's assets is an established, well-recognized principle despite variations in interpretation. In democratic societies this right is established as a matter of law. Its application extends not only to individuals but also to organizations. For example, the Fourth Amendment to the Constitution of the United States reads in part that people have a right "to be secure in their persons, houses, papers, and effects." The Fifth Amendment reads in part that no person is to "be deprived of life, liberty, *or property, without due process of law; nor shall private property be taken for public use, without just compensation"* (italics added). In other societies, such as dictatorships, virtually all property belongs to the state, and the state jealously guards what it owns or claims to own.

Even with the advent of so-called professional police agencies throughout the course of the eighteenth and nineteenth centuries, the primary responsibility for protecting private property against losses, whether attributable to criminal activity or otherwise, continued to rest with the property owner. This approach to protecting assets remained unchanged as the twentieth century dawned, and even as it now draws to a close owners still have the primary responsibility for preventing the loss of their property. This principle is reinforced by the fact that as a general rule public police agencies will not enter upon private property unless they are specifically asked to do so by the owner or tenant. Almost invariably such invitations are extended only after the realization that a presumably criminal act has taken place or is about to occur.

Individual rights and responsibilities vis-à-vis the protection of assets are well recognized, but from a security viewpoint the question arises as to whether these same principles extend to organizations. Certainly if a business is owned and operated by a person acting alone or by persons acting as a partnership, their individual rights and responsibilities for the security of their property are unchanged. By the same token, if a business is incorporated, the corporate entity is treated as if it were a person in matters of law. Therefore, corporations also have a legal right to protect their assets, and the protection of those assets is but one of many areas of management in which a variety of both state and federal agencies may take an interest. Not to be overlooked, and perhaps of even greater importance, is the fact that because of the special or fiduciary relationship owed by corporate officers to stockholders, there also is a mandated responsibility for them to protect the organization's assets.

Although the right to protect one's real and personal property is as old as humankind, it is interesting to note that an illustration of early concern for asset protection in relation to business needs occurred during the Middle Ages, when various guilds flourished in Europe. Equally interesting is the fact that while mutual aid and the protection of members were viewed as proper functions of guild membership in that long-ago era, it apparently was not until the early part of the twentieth century that using watchmen and guards to protect private property in Great Britain's highly industrialized society was considered acceptable.[1]

In contrast, even though the United States had not yet reached the same high level of industrialization, it proved to be more advanced than Europe with respect to the protection of business assets. An early example of one type of American business recognizing the need for security, and of another accepting the responsibility for providing it, occurred in 1855. In that year the newly developing railroads—expanding westward across the United States and seeing a need to protect their property, passengers, and freight—retained the services of Allan Pinkerton. He satisfied their needs by providing them with personnel under the terms of a contract. Two years later, realizing that other types of businesses also might be concerned with asset protection, Pinkerton expanded his contract security services by providing them with personnel to help protect their property.

Having no competition, Pinkerton for all intents and purposes remained the sole supplier of contract guards to business organizations until 1909, when William J. Burns founded the William J. Burns Detective Agency. In the interim a few isolated retailers, banks, and hotels occasionally employed men as "house detectives" to deal with shoplifting, robberies, barroom brawls, room burglaries, and prostitution, thus marking the beginning of proprietary security personnel. In 1858 a new weapon was added to the security arsenal when Edwin Holmes established the first central-station burglar alarm company. Holmes, very much like Pinkerton, had no real competition until 1874, when the American District Telegraph Company (best known today as ADT) was organized.

Although both Pinkerton and Burns provided their customers with personnel for the purpose of guarding their property against criminal activity, there was, nevertheless, considerable emphasis on detection. This was attributable to a theory that still exists in some quarters. It holds that one of the best ways to prevent crime is to be able to quickly identify, apprehend, and punish those responsible for committing crimes. The idea that from a business viewpoint there might be more efficient and cost-effective ways to prevent losses was nonexistent.

It was only natural that with the passage of time other companies would be organized for the purpose of providing contract personnel to businesses and institutions in the form of uniformed security officers or plainclothes investigators, or alarm systems, or both. Today a plethora of such agencies offers a wide range of security-related services:

guards, investigators, armored car services, alarms, and high-technology applications to help protect assets. They range in size from small, purely local companies serving equally small businesses to multinational organizations that provide personnel and equipment not only to large organizations but also in some instances to government and quasi-government operations.

Despite the availability of these services and notwithstanding the decision by some organizations to employ proprietary security personnel, the fact remains that even with the advent of World War II and heightened concern with possible acts of espionage and sabotage, security, as we have come to know it today, really had its roots in the post–World War II era. This is largely due to the security requirements imposed by the U.S. government on those businesses and academic institutions to which contracts still were awarded for the performance of defense-related work.

The cold war, which pitted the western powers (primarily the United States, Great Britain, and France) against the iron curtain countries (the Soviet Union and those dominated by it), increased the fear of espionage and put the major emphasis on the protection of information. However, because government contractors were reimbursed for the cost of security as part of their contracts' overhead, there also was increased concern on their part with regard to the risks of such things as fraud, theft of work in process and finished goods, and quality control. They feared that their contracts might be canceled, or worse still, that they also might be prosecuted. Despite the fact that the ability to deal effectively with these issues called for at least some understanding of business, many government contractors still saw their security programs as but an extension of public policing into the private sector and the organization's security director or manager as little more than the company's or institution's chief of police.

Although this perception was not necessarily correct, as long as this was how executive management viewed the security function, it seemed only logical to recruit security directors and managers from among the ranks of retired law enforcement or military personnel. Education and business experience received little if any consideration. College or university programs for the education of professional security managers were virtually nonexistent.

In the late 1950s and in the 1960s, Indiana University, under the guidance of Dr. Robert F. Borkenstein, chairman of its Department of Police Administration and Center for Police Studies, began to offer seminars on a fairly regular basis for active security managers. These offerings were also somewhat unique in that they did not focus solely on the needs of organizations doing defense-related work for the U.S. government. Other forms of business activities were given consideration, and their security managers responded.

Nevertheless, the practice of seeking former law enforcement or military officers for security directors' positions continued. As those recruited initially approached their second retirement, they helped perpetuate the practice when their advice was sought in the selection of their successors. However, as time passed, executive management began to develop a heightened awareness of the scope and magnitude of security-related problems and an ever increasing concern with shrinking profit margins. These factors caused some of them to reassess the qualifications for newly hired security directors and managers.

It must be remembered that for many organizations, if not most, security was a "necessary evil" that had to be suffered, albeit not silently, in order to satisfy insurance carriers, government agencies, stockholders, or possibly all three. Of course, if the organization was a government contractor, at least the suffering was less painful since the costs of the security program were considered a legitimate part of the overhead for which the government paid. Otherwise, security was strictly an "out-of-pocket" expense from which executive management saw neither tangible nor easily measured benefits.

Even those who firmly believed in the need for effective security programs became disillusioned when it seemed that their security director's response to every increase in security-related problems invariably prompted a request for still more personnel. Their disenchantment grew when it became evident that even as more people were hired for security and more and more money was being spent for security department operations, the problems did not abate. In reality this should not have come as a surprise since emphasis on the use of personnel was consistent with the practices of both police agencies and the military, even though on more than one occasion it has been found that numbers alone do not always decrease crime or cause enemies to surrender.

Consequently, slow as the evolutionary process has been, organizations in ever increasing numbers are coming to the realization that effective, efficient security programs require professionally qualified individuals as security directors and managers. Among the qualifications now being sought are skills in general and business management, human resources, and experience in integrating security programs into the rest of an employing organization's activities and goals. In today's business environment the emphasis is not only on the word *security;* the word *management* is emphasized equally.

THE NEED FOR SECURITY

Two questions inevitably will be asked of security directors or managers: (1) Is there really a need for security? (2) If so, why? That they may be asked these questions by senior executives who see security only in terms of overhead and expenses is not unexpected. However, frequently these same questions will be posed by senior executives who, while sympathetic to the basic concept of security, feel that they too need answers, since they may be put to the test by their peers in terms of justifying their support for the organization's security program. Such questions may be asked, and answers must be given, because even today many senior management people persist in viewing security programs only as cost centers that make absolutely no positive contribution to the business or institution.

Imagine then the importance to a security director of being able to answer such questions in a meaningful way. Obviously, if there is no need for security there is no need for either a security department or someone to manage it. By the same token, it is inadequate to answer the question merely by saying yes, there is a need for security, but without being able to justify that need. To simultaneously answer the question and justify the need, security managers must be able to use their appreciation of security's true role by putting things in proper perspective. What does this mean?

Like other professionals, security directors or managers must stay abreast of what goes on in their chosen career. Nevertheless, when having to justify the need for security within their own organizations, they must be capable of narrowing their focus and concentrating only on those issues that are important to their employers. Some people may be impressed by a security manager who can easily refer to a number of sources and cite losses that reportedly have been suffered by various types of organizations or have been caused by certain types of incidents. However, these data may not necessarily have any application, direct or indirect, to their own particular industry or place of employment. If this is the case, as far as senior executives are concerned the information is meaningless.

To a degree a comparable situation exists when security managers try to justify their needs by citing data that are related to other businesses or institutions of the same kind. When asked to justify the need for security within the framework of their own organizations, those who resort to citing problems encountered by competing businesses or institutions will in all likelihood be asked yet other questions, such as, what has this got to do with us, or how does this affect us? Therefore, providing general industry information may not by itself serve to justify the retention of the security program, department, or director or manager.

For instance, citing various publications that bemoan the fact that business losses due to inadequate security are unbelievably high, or that offer projections of losses in the billions of dollars normally will not prove helpful in terms of justification. Even when such data are broken down by either types of victims or types of losses, senior executives may not consider this a valid reason to keep spending money for their own programs, especially if the economy is tight or depressed. Instead they will be inclined to focus on what their security program is costing, and they may well be convinced that they already are spending too much on an activity that, even under the best of conditions, cannot guarantee tangible proof of success.

This makes it imperative for security directors to do two things. Initially, when trying to justify the need for security to their superiors, they must concentrate on the real and potential problems with which their employers are or may be faced. To do this effectively they must first have a good understanding of their employer's total business operation, not merely of the security department. With this as a foundation, they are in an infinitely better position to be able to analyze across-the-board risks, determine priorities, recommend ways to minimize both risks and losses, and point out that the most cost-effective security program is one that emphasizes prevention. This, in turn, will serve a dual purpose. It allows senior executives to better relate security's role to other aspects of the business or institution in terms with which they are already familiar. Also, by emphasizing prevention as the most cost-effective approach to loss prevention it avoids having to guarantee tangible proof of the security program's value.

Since security's objective is the protection and conservation of all of an employer's assets, even before trying to gain an understanding of the total business operation it becomes necessary to identify the assets of any given organization. It is relatively easy to think in terms of tangibles, whether in the form of real or personal property. Everyone can attach some value to things that can be seen and touched. It is not too difficult to appreciate the fact that employees are an asset since, as a practical matter, organizations cannot function without them. On the other hand, it may not always be that easy for either executives, security managers, or employees in general to accept the idea that virtually every business or institution also has certain intangible assets that need to be protected, including such things as reputation and data in other than hard-copy media.

Unless and until security directors or managers first identify their employers' assets, it is next to impossible for them to understand the relationship between those assets and operations. For example, if the employer is a manufacturer, raw materials are an asset. Suppose precious metals are among the raw materials used. They need to be protected upon receipt, while in storage, and while work is in process. In this situation security managers are obliged to find ways in which a very high degree of protection is afforded the precious metals at all stages of the manufacturing process. However, if the security procedures recommended are so tight or so rigid that they tend to interfere with or otherwise impede production, they become a hindrance rather than a help. Therefore, it becomes necessary to develop procedures that at the very least will minimize the risk of a loss or theft of precious metals but in ways that will not inhibit or impede production. If this is not done and the recommended security procedures are too restrictive, there will be a delay in the sale and shipment of the product. This may conceivably result in a loss of business and adversely affect reputation. At the very least it will defer income and the realization of any profit.

On the other hand, suppose the employer is a medical center. It has a food service operation for its patients and staff. Certain perishable foodstuffs are among the raw materials needed in order to provide service to its clientele. Therefore, the foodstuffs must be protected from the time of receipt until they are needed in the kitchen. In this case, unlike manufacturing, the security procedures must consider more than the risk of loss due to theft. They must also take into account the ways in which this category of raw materials are received in order to minimize losses due to vendors' short shipments, as well as their subsequent transfer to suitable storage facilities to prevent spoilage and waste. The suggested security procedures must reflect an appreciation of the fact that employee theft may not be the sole or even primary cause of the employer's food service operation losses.

Still another illustration may be helpful. A major manufacturer in a highly competitive industry has a policy for the protection of its information. It says, among other things, that the criterion for granting access to sensitive information is an "absolute need to know." An employee researching a new product encounters a problem and finds himself or herself in a dilemma. He or she is confident that a solution can be found, but it will take time. By the same token, there are coworkers who do not have an "absolute need to know" but who could help expedite the solution to the problem if only it could be discussed with them. To seek their help risks violating the security policy; if this cannot be done, there will be a delay in introducing the new product to market. Here interpreting the policy for protecting information must not be so rigid or inflexible that it will allow a competitor to introduce its product first.

A hotel's reputation undeniably is an asset, part of which depends upon the quality of its housekeeping and the skills of its engineering personnel. However, while neither department makes a direct contribution to profits, both contribute indirectly. Any hotel that downgraded these departments would find that its reputation, and ultimately its profits, would suffer. Knowing this, general managers would never consider doing away with the housekeeping or engineering functions or reducing the size and scope of their work on the theory that they, like security, are pure overhead but a necessary evil. This same logic can be applied to security's role. Like other departments that make no direct contribution to profits, security nevertheless does contribute indirectly, even though the results of that contribution do not lend themselves to precise measurement.

The various examples cited above serve a fourfold purpose. First, they illustrate the fact that organizations need effective security programs to protect all of their various tangible and intangible assets if they hope to be successful. Second, to protect those assets security directors or managers must be able not only to identify them but also to understand how they relate to the employer's total activity. Third, the protection that ultimately is to be provided has to be designed with a view to the employer's business objectives so that the security program can be consistent with them and contribute to rather than hinder operations. Fourth, these examples also suggest different ways in which security directors and managers can respond when asked to justify the need for security.

Above all, once justification is established, the program proposed for any given organization must be relevant to that specific employer's needs, not to those of other like businesses or institutions. That a competitor may use fifty security officers to provide protection for its assets does not automatically mean that all other like organizations, including those in similar neighborhoods and of the same size, require security departments of identical size to satisfy their own needs.

Finally, one question that should be uppermost in the minds of all security directors or managers before they submit proposals for improving their employer's security is, can my recommendations be implemented? In other words, are my ideas doable in realistic, cost-effective ways? Only if the answers are yes should the proposals be offered for senior management's consideration.

A DEMAND FOR INCREASED PROFESSIONALISM

The demand for increased professionalism, particularly at the director and managerial levels, has become more evident with the passage of time. This has been reflected in different and distinct ways. Among the first to acknowledge the need for a greater degree of professionalism on the part of active security directors and managers was the American Society for Industrial Security. From its inception the format for its annual meetings has consisted mainly of seminars dealing with a wide range of issues that its membership either has confronted or could expect to confront. The meetings have also provided members with opportunities to meet with suppliers of security equipment and services and view a variety of the latest products available for loss prevention purposes.

To further its efforts to help professionalize security, the society also inaugurated its certified protection professional program and established the American Society for Industrial Security Foundation. The former, which is not restricted to society members, requires those interested in certification to pass a written examination covering various security topics and to participate in certain society-approved forms of continuing education in order to maintain their professional certification, once earned. In addition, the foundation encourages professionalism by making grants available for research in the field of security.

A second indication of the increased demand for professionalism is reflected in the status of academic programs. Although in the late 1950s and early 1960s both Indiana University and Michigan State University were pioneers among institutions of higher learning by offering programs of interest to active security personnel, neither certificate nor degree programs in the field of security existed. In contrast, by the end of 1990 there were 164 certificate or degree programs in the United States.[2] Furthermore, some of the colleges and universities offering degrees have graduate programs in addition to their undergraduate curricula. The data indicate both the academic community's growing recognition of the demand for increased professionalism and student interest in security as a profession.

An examination of display advertising for security directors and managers is yet another indication of the extent to which the demand for professionalism has increased over time. For years the qualification most often called for in such advertisements was either law enforcement or investigative experience. While the preference was for persons who had worked for agencies of the U.S. government, police department retirees, especially those who had been officers of rank, were also considered. "Investigative experience" was extended to include service in the Central Intelligence Agency. Occasionally service in the higher commissioned ranks of the armed forces was acceptable in lieu of law enforcement or investigative experience. The latter were of particular interest to some government defense contractors who thought that employing retired military personnel could mean extensive Department of Defense contacts and an entree to further business. For all intents and purposes, there were no academic qualifications, although a minimum of a baccalaureate degree could be expected of most of those who had worked for civilian federal agencies or who held commissions in the armed forces.

The emphasis on this kind of experience was a reflection of executive managements' continued perception of security as but another form of policing and of their failure to recognize and accept it as a management responsibility and function. Too often a security director's success was measured by the number of errant employees identified, apprehended, and punished either administratively or by the criminal justice system. Even in cases where those ultimately hired as security directors may have had some prior exposure to managerial functions, their experiences were vastly different from what is normally encountered in private sector management. Few had been in positions where they were directly involved in either preparing budgets or managing expenses. None had ever found themselves in situations where their superiors' overriding concerns involved such diverse issues as competition, profit and loss, solvency, labor and customer relations, government regulation, and possibly fiduciary relationships to stockholders.

Granted, the law enforcement or investigative experience requirement has not disappeared completely from advertisements placed by businesses and institutions in search of security directors and managers. However, over the course of the last ten to fifteen years this requirement has become increasingly less frequent. More often than not the qualifications now set forth in advertisements are a combination of security and business management experience, and work in positions that provided the individual with progressively increased responsibility. Human relations skills and the ability to write and speak clearly are among the qualifications now included in advertisements. On occasion knowledge of a foreign language is helpful. A minimum of a baccalaureate degree, preferably in criminal justice with a major in security, or in business administration, now is a common requirement. Preference for a graduate degree is by no means uncommon.

The combined efforts of the American Society for Industrial Security and the academic community, and changes by businesses and institutions as evidenced by the qualifications they now seek for security directors or managers represent an acknowledgment of the continuing evolution of security. The demands confronting today's security directors and managers are not only many and varied but also are complex and in a constant state of change.

The wide range of organizational assets that need to be secured in today's world no longer can be protected adequately or cost effectively by continuing to adhere to relatively simple and more traditional approaches. Constant patrols, monitoring alarms and access control, parcel inspections, highly visible security officers, and the speedy identification, apprehension, and punishment of malefactors are but a small part of what is now needed to protect and conserve assets and prevent losses.

To fully appreciate the importance of security, one need only consider the contribution that can be made to the health of an employing organization by an effective, business-oriented program and understand how the well-being of a given business or institution in turn contributes to the overall economic health of the country. This becomes even more significant with multinational corporations, whose individual well-being can also have an impact on the global economy. Consequently, in order to do the job that has to be done and satisfy the needs of employers in today's highly competitive environment, security directors and managers are expected to do their jobs with a degree of professionalism previously unheard of for positions of this type.

WHAT IT MEANS TO BE A SECURITY DIRECTOR OR MANAGER

The preceding section clearly indicates that, among other things, being a security director or manager means being a professional. However, to leave it at that would be to oversimplify matters when so much more is involved.

First and foremost, being a good security manager differs from being a good manager only in that the former's focus is on the protection and conservation of the employer's assets, regardless of whether those assets are tangibles or intangibles, and unlike most other department heads, security managers' responsibilities, rather than being limited in scope, tend to cross all departmental, geographic, and divisional lines. However, security managers must also be able to apply good managerial skills to ensure that the department's objectives are met in efficient, effective, and economical ways. Good security managers, like all good managers, need to define their departments' duties, establish goals, determine priorities, control expenses, direct personnel, prepare appropriate policies and procedures when needed and oversee compliance therewith, and implement their programs. To do this also means being willing to accept total responsibility for all departmental operations and activities.

In many respects the skills needed to be a good manager, whether in charge of security or other functions, might be deemed generic. Despite this there are some qualities of a good security director that can be distinguished from those that might be needed to successfully manage another type of department.

While all good managers must be able to work well with their peers, the ability to do so is critically important for security managers due to their rather unique position in any organization. For instance, since their duties necessitate their interfacing with and relying on the cooperation of all other department heads, they must be consummate diplomats. Security managers learn quickly that no matter how effective their loss prevention programs may sound in theory or look on paper, their successful implementation will depend on the manager's ability to involve all employees generally and line managers and supervisors particularly.

Therefore, despite some differences between the roles of security manager and manager in general, the similarity that exists prompts one to ask, what does it really mean to be a security manager? There is neither a single nor a simple answer because in today's business environment the person holding that position has to be many things to many people. Among other things security managers are expected to be educated and to have a good understanding of the criminal justice system and its relationship to the world of business.

In addition to their diplomatic skills, they must be innovative, entrepreneurial, clear thinking, analytical, creative, and decisive. They need to be skilled educators, salespersons, and investigators. Successful security managers must have both credibility and good interpersonal skills, as well as the ability to make high-quality oral and written presentations. They need to be at least somewhat familiar with the various aspects of the law that have a bearing on security operations. Above all, they must be knowledgeable of the latest developments in the security field, including those related to technology.

Since being a security director or manager also means being an educated person, the ability to intelligently discuss a range of issues other than those of a purely security nature is essential if the security manager is going to be welcomed as a member of the employer's management team. It also means understanding and fully appreciating the organization's goals and how the security function can serve as a bridge between its business needs and the criminal justice system whenever criminal activity is involved or suspected.

Inasmuch as security represents authority, its role is not always fully understood or appreciated by persons outside of the department. This, in turn, can add to the difficulty of trying to involve everyone in the organization in the loss prevention effort. Impressing employees in general with the importance of properly protecting assets and minimizing losses is not always done easily. This is why security directors have to be more than mere managers in trying to get all employees involved, and why the very term *security director* or *security manager* also has to mean being a diplomat, educator, and salesperson. No matter how important the task of educating coworkers about security and how it can contribute to both the organization and the welfare of all employees, it must be done with tact and due consideration for the roles of other managers. To do otherwise risks alienating the very people whose help is so very important to the security program's success. Being a salesperson means convincing people that security is neither an enemy nor an impediment to good business. Most assuredly it is not a private police force that only represents authority. All employees have to be assured that security personnel can be trusted; they are not to be feared and resented.

Meeting the challenges confronting security directors in ways that are cost-effective and contribute to the employer's profits means that they must be innovators and entrepreneurs. To be successful, a good security manager must also be able to think clearly, analyze quickly, evaluate different types of situations, and offer meaningful solutions. Furthermore, being a security manager means accepting the fact that not all decisions can be made at leisure; there will be times when they will have to be made under stress and quickly.

Although the number of investigations that must be conducted may be low, the fact remains that security directors have to conduct internal investigations or oversee the work of investigative personnel. This requires more than investigative skills; credibility, good interpersonal skills, and patience are equally important. Once again, this means being able to work well with everyone in the organization, something more easily accomplished when credibility is respected.

Being a security director or manager also means being held in high regard for one's professional knowledge. This will happen only when it is apparent to everyone with whom there is contact that the security manager is always familiar with the latest developments in the field, including those legal issues and technological developments that can affect departmental operations.

It is extremely difficult to be an effective security manager without good oral and written communication skills. Once more, this is where education and professional knowledge add to a security director's stature and promote recognition by peers, superiors, and subordinates of his or her contributions to the organization. In other words, being a good security manager also means being able to express oneself clearly and concisely.

The demand for increased professionalism has added yet another dimension to what it means to be a security director or manager. Precisely because of the qualities executive management now looks for when assigning security responsibilities—namely, a combination of good managerial skills and an understanding of the employer's business as well as of its security needs—the ability to make decisions and deal with the unexpected in sound but expeditious ways is also required.

Security managers hired for (who clearly show) their professionalism in how they integrate the loss prevention program with all aspects of operations are respected members of the organization's management team. As such they are expected to do more than supervise their department's activities and provide guidance with regard to security-related issues. Like all managers, they obviously have to make decisions to ensure that their departments function effectively and efficiently.

However, there may be times, even if relatively few and sporadic, when something wholly unanticipated and unforeseen will occur. It may be an incident that requires security involvement but also has an impact on one or more other departments in terms of operations or the safety of personnel. Its very nature may require that decisions be made immediately under circumstances that deny the security manager the benefit of consultation with or approval of his or her superiors. At other times a superior may request advice in connection with a trip to a country where there is political unrest and terrorist activity. Stress exists not only in making a decision under pressure, but also because there is no guarantee that the decision will be the right one. Reportedly, a favorite saying of President Harry S. Truman was "If you can't stand the heat, you better get out of the kitchen."[3] There is no denying his statement's applicability to security managers.

These different attributes are representative of what it now means to be an effective security director or manager. It is obvious that today much more is involved than having good investigative skills and police contacts, being able to catch thieves, and making certain that uniformed security personnel always have a "spit and polish" look about them. To be a security director or manager today, especially in the employ of a sizable organization, means having the ability to think and act like an executive in every sense of the word, albeit one with a rather unique specialty.

SUMMARY

From a historical point of view, the very notion of a person's right to protect and conserve his or her property has not only been unquestioned but also has been acknowledged as a legal right and extended to businesses and institutions. Despite this, security in the form of an organized activity or function of any real significance was largely nonexistent in the United States until the post–World War II era. Even then, and for quite some time thereafter, it was used in only limited ways. The U.S. Department of Defense and other U.S. government agencies, concerned with protecting classified information, provided guidance for that purpose to defense contractors, many of whom recruited their security directors from the ranks of federal investigative, intelligence, or military agencies.

The very nature of these federally sponsored security programs was such that executives rarely, if ever, considered the additional benefits to be derived by their organizations if security was fully integrated into operations and administration. Nevertheless, the idea of security began to take root. Organizations that no longer did government work tended to retain their security departments, and others either expanded or developed theirs. However, for the most part their original orientation was such that they continued to either recruit or hire security managerial personnel from the same sources as before.

With the passage of time and an increasing awareness of just how competitive the business environment really had become, some organizations began to appreciate the fact that they needed more than the limited kinds of security to which they had become accustomed. The result was a grudging willingness to at least consider the added benefits to be derived from security programs based on cost-effective loss prevention measures and fully integrated into all aspects of a business's or institution's administration and operations. Equally important was the recognition that security was needed, and not just as a "necessary evil."

With increased recognition of the need for security came the realization that effective security management required a high degree of professionalism on the part of those who would be in charge of security departments. This meant recruiting persons who, in addition to experience in loss prevention, had some understanding of business and the business world's needs. This demand for increased professionalism spawned academic programs in the security field, fostered the growth of professional organizations, and made it necessary for security management personnel to keep abreast of developments in fields that affect security organizations and operations, such as technology, law, and business.

The demand for increased professionalism also made it necessary for security directors and managers to reconsider just what their positions meant. Since security evolved from a limited role, too often thought of and used as private policing, to a more expansive one in which security is increasingly recognized as both a management function and a management responsibility, today's successful security directors and managers cannot be content to think and behave like private sector police chiefs. Rather, they now have to assume roles as diplomats, educators, and salespersons in addition to satisfying the accepted demands of a security director's job. To be effective they have to be many things to many people. Above all they have to be seen and recognized by their coworkers as professionals and skilled managers in every sense of the word.

REVIEW QUESTIONS

1. In the United States, does the legal basis that allows persons to protect their property also extend to businesses and institutions? On what is the legal basis for protecting assets based?
2. Do the police or the owners have the primary responsibility for the protection of private property?
3. What was Allan Pinkerton's role in the development of private security?
4. From what sources did most organizations recruit their security directors and managers in the post–World War II era?
5. How should security managers respond when asked to justify a need for security?
6. When responding, what factors should they keep in mind?
7. Illustrate how a security manager can explain the need for security in a meaningful and convincing way.
8. Why is there now a need for increased professionalism?
9. How have academic programs been affected by this need?
10. What do good security managers have in common with other good managers, and in what ways are they different?

NOTES

[1] F. Oughton, *Ten Guineas a Day: A Portrait of the Private Detective* (London: John Long, 1961); R. B. Fosdick, *European Police Systems* (Montclair, NJ: Patterson Smith, 1969).

[2] *Security Letter Sourcebook*, 1990–91, pp. 305–310; *Journal of Security Administration*, December 1989, pp. 85–96.

[3] David McCullough, *Truman* (New York: Simon & Schuster, 1992), p. 584.

Chapter 2

THE SECURITY ORGANIZATION

THE NEED FOR AN ESTABLISHED SECURITY ORGANIZATION

The need for security should not be confused with the need for an established security organization. Every business or institution, regardless of size, location, or the nature of its activities, must protect its assets if it hopes to survive, let alone be successful. While this is a fundamental principle of good general management practices, not all businesses need an organized security department.

For instance, both a "mom and pop" neighborhood convenience store and a supermarket have assets that must be protected, but neither can justify having a full-blown security department. An old-fashioned drugstore that once served over 1800 people a day at its fountain, in addition to its high volume prescription and sundries sales, definitely needed to protect its assets, but no one could argue that it also needed a security department. In fact, except for the supermarket (part of a large chain), these businesses would be hard pressed to justify even having a corporate security director or manager.

In contrast, both a 600,000-square-foot manufacturing plant and a 600,000-square-foot insurance company's corporate headquarters, because of their size and the value of their assets, definitely needed more than a security director or manager; they also needed security officers and support personnel. The security officers were necessary to patrol the premises, control access, and monitor alarm systems, parking facilities, and shipping/receiving docks. They also handled emergencies and received and recorded complaints when losses or other security-related incidents occurred. Some secretarial and other support personnel were needed to ensure that the department could function efficiently.

Regardless of the differences noted above, one thing is clear. What each of the foregoing needed, and what every business and institution needs if it is to protect its assets, prevent losses, and minimize the dollar value of any losses that may be inevitable, is a focal point—one person who has been assigned the responsibility for security.

People within and without organizations have to know who to contact when security-related incidents occur and when they have questions about security matters. This person is the one who should determine the employer's physical security needs and ensure that suitable equipment is bought, installed, and used properly. He or she should develop security policies and procedures, be responsible for their implementation, and provide the leadership necessary for effective loss prevention programming. This person should also serve as the employer's liaison with local public safety officials.

That the smallness of a business or institution militates against creating a security department also will mean that this person, regardless of a job title of security director or manager, will probably have other duties and responsibilities that may have nothing at all to do with asset protection. That fact in and of itself is unimportant; the critical issue is that one person must be in charge of security regardless of the program's limitations.

There also are other cases where a security program's scope and magnitude are such that the one person in charge cannot possibly discharge all of the assigned duties without help. The employer's size or the number of square feet of space occupied should not be the only criteria employed in deciding on the need for an organized security department. Of greater importance in making this decision is the nature of the employer's activities, the value of its assets at any of its locations, and the extent to which the neighborhood in which each individual facility is located may increase or decrease the risk of loss.

For example, in proportion to its size, a 75,000-square-foot research and development facility with only 200 employees in a highly competitive industry (such as computers, biotechnology, pharmaceuticals, or automobile manufacturing) may require more protection than would a much larger manufacturing or warehousing site. On the other hand, a large multinational hotel chain with 100 or more properties worldwide would find it prudent to have a corporate level security department consisting of a security director and a secretary, but with security managers, security officers, and at least a minimal support staff at individual hotels.

In other words, employers must recognize the fact that there are times when, despite excellent relationships with and the cooperation of line managers and supervisors, security directors or managers must have help in protecting assets and preventing losses. Circumstances may dictate that that help must come from a select group of employees whose sole function is to provide security. When these conditions exist, an employer must give serious consideration to establishing a security organization. This is true whether businesses or institutions are organized as centralized or as decentralized management models, a subject to be discussed more fully later in this chapter.

DETERMINING THE SECURITY DEPARTMENT'S SIZE

Once senior management acknowledges the importance of and need for security and agrees to the establishment of a security organization, a question that must be answered is what size organization is needed. For the answer employers will turn to their security directors or managers. In this respect it is only logical to assume that if a new department is to be created, one of the first steps taken by executive management will be to either hire a professionally qualified security director or manager or at the very least assign the security responsibility to an existing managerial level employee. This person will be asked to determine how large a security department will be needed to provide the level of protection required to secure all of the employer's assets adequately.

Security directors or managers who in their haste to provide an answer think first and foremost in terms of the department's personnel requirements are thinking more like bureaucrats than good managers. They may also be guilty of wasting what financial resources their employer has allocated for the security department's activation. It was once said that "Whatever is produced in haste goes hastily to waste."[1] This adage applies to security department management when security managers react to questions of size by focusing primarily on numbers instead of taking other equally important factors into account.

The need for security personnel may not be subject to challenge, but the question of whether they alone can best serve the employer's interests should not go unchallenged. Good private sector managers, ever mindful of the importance of balance sheets and profit and loss statements as proof of an organization's financial health and success, are expected to be cost conscious. Consequently, one of the ways in which security directors show their professionalism is by how well they manage their financial and human resources. To think that the management of one can be divorced from the other is unrealistic. Without funds there can be no staff; if the entire budget is spent on personnel, there can be no implementation of other integral parts of the security program.

Almost without exception the greatest allocation of funds in security department budgets is for salaries and fringe benefits. To illustrate, a multinational Fortune 500 company using a decentralized management model had as its corporate headquarters security organization the security director, a support staff of two, a site security department consisting of a manager and supervisor, twenty proprietary and contract security officers, and a secretary who serviced both the corporate and site staffs. Eighty-five percent of the combined corporate/site budget was for salaries and fringe benefits for proprietary personnel and fees for contract personnel.

In addition to the fact that so large a percentage of a department budget may have to be allocated to pay personnel, whether proprietary or contract, there is the realization that these costs will not be constant. If nothing else, there will be periodic salary and wage increases for proprietary employees. Furthermore, even in times of economic hardship when wages and fringe benefits may be frozen, one dare not ignore the likelihood that the employer nevertheless may have to pay more for whatever benefits it does provide.

Even if contract personnel are used, either in whole or in part, it is almost certain that there will be cost increases. If the agreement with a provider is for more than one year, it most likely will contain a provision for a rate increase at year's end. If it is for only one year it is almost certain that a new agreement, whether with the same or a new agency, will cost more. While for years increases of at least ten percent were not unusual, the continued growth of the contract security industry, and the competition that has resulted, mean that although increases still occur they tend to be at a lower rate. This is even more the case where large contracts are involved. However, as discussed later in this chapter, costs alone should not be the sole or even primary criterion when choosing a contract agency.

What, then, does the cost of personnel mean to those who are called upon to establish a security department and determine its size? It means that before they project numbers they must assess the employers' needs to see to what extent, if any, they can substitute technology for personnel.

Technology Versus Personnel

Initially, one needs to understand what security managers mean when they refer to *technology*. A dictionary definition of the word itself is rather vague, but perhaps a definition of *technological* can provide a somewhat better understanding of its meaning. *Webster's New World Dictionary* has as one definition of *technological:* "due to developments in technology; resulting from technical progress in the use of machinery in industry." Used in a security sense, technology refers to the use of equipment and systems, such as hardware and possibly software, and includes but is not necessarily limited to closed circuit television, different types of locking devices and computerized access controls, and alarm systems, among other things.

When considering the many possibilities offered in the field of technology, it is imperative that security managers remember that its use is not necessarily a panacea for all of the real and potential problems that will confront them. Technology also costs money— in some cases more than in others. However, since the expense occurs but once, it can be amortized to spread its cost over a period of time, and it can also be used for tax purposes. If the manufacturer is reputable and well established, the equipment's quality is good, and the engineering and installation are done by competent people, then the maintenance charges should be minimal.

However, when considering technology, security managers need to be aware of four possible pitfalls.

1. That something new and state-of-the-art is on the market does not necessarily mean it is right for their particular situation and therefore should be bought.
2. Even if a product has application to a particular security need, there is still the risk of allowing oneself to be oversold.
3. A fear of things new and different should not prevent an objective evaluation of a product's ability to satisfy an employer's needs.
4. Technology is not necessarily a complete and satisfactory substitute for security officers.

To expand on this, when new products become available, security managers must be able to relate a product's practical application to their organization's security needs. Some security directors may think it is a sign of professionalism to buy state-of-the-art equipment largely because it is new. For instance, in some cases robots can now be substituted for security officers in making patrol rounds. This may be a realistic and cost-effective way to cover a warehouse or possibly even parts of a manufacturing plant where everything is on one floor and there is a lot of open space. However, could robots be used with equal effect in a multistoried office building with little or no open space?

Of course, simply because something is new does not necessarily mean that it should not even be considered, but in doing so one must not forget that even the newest and best equipment has to be monitored. Furthermore, security managers also need to remember that if the monitors see or hear anything questionable and no one is available to respond, the technology serves no real purpose and the money spent has been wasted.

Then, of course, there are still some "old school" security directors whose earlier careers were in policing; they feel that security problems are solved only by adding personnel. Therefore, there is a marked contrast between security managers who buy products because they are new, not because they necessarily have application to their needs, and those who reject a product despite its possible usefulness only because it is new. If it is something with which they are unfamiliar, they feel uncomfortable. Perhaps these points are best illustrated.

A major medical center was the victim of an attempt to oversell a product. Wanting to organize its first-ever security department, it retained the services of a security management consultant who recommended that the security officers on patrol be equipped with two-way radios. A cost-effective way to do so would be to use a handheld unit as a base station. The center's administrator agreed, and this was done even though every vendor of such systems tried to sell a full-blown base station. The installation chosen worked well. In this particular situation, which admittedly occurred in 1965, if the vendors' proposals had been accepted, not only would they have increased the hospital's cost considerably, but they also would have required going through the Federal Communication Commission's licensing process.

Another example of technology's use to cost-effectively satisfy a security need concerns a manufacturer that used its own fleet of trailer trucks to transport components and finished goods among its various U.S. plants. The trucking operation's focal point was one particular facility where loaded trailers often were parked overnight awaiting the arrival of a cab and driver. Posting a security officer in the parking lot around the clock to prevent the theft of a loaded trailer would have cost more than that officer's wages and fringe benefits. It also would have involved spending money to provide a lighted, heated shelter for the officer's protection in bad weather. Instead, a closed circuit television camera monitored by the same security officer who already monitored other cameras and the site's alarm systems, provided the necessary protection. On the other hand, at this same location security officers were assigned to the shipping/receiving area. Their job was to reduce the risk of losses that might result from either thefts or shipping errors when any vehicles were being loaded or unloaded. Under these circumstances closed circuit television alone would not have been effective.

Since the exclusive use of personnel is expensive and technology alone is often inadequate, it is incumbent upon security managers to carefully evaluate both the employer's needs and the most cost-effective options available to satisfy them. Certainly they should not base their decisions on the premise that the use of personnel and technology are mutually exclusive. The best approach often is a balanced one, with a combination of security officers and technology proving to be the most effective and least expensive solution to a host of problems.

Personnel Assignments

Once the foregoing evaluation process has been completed, security directors or managers must identify those assignments, such as fixed or patrol posts, that require hiring a security officer. They also need to decide upon the extent of coverage for each post. In other words, for how many hours a day and for how many days a week does each post have to be covered? It is important to understand that providing high levels of protection and service does not necessarily mean that all security department positions require the same number of hours of coverage. Just as a balance must be struck between the use of personnel and technology, so must there be a balanced approach to deciding on a department's size. Failure to take this into account may well cause problems of either over- or understaffing, neither of which is desirable.

Like all good managers, those in security soon learn that a department's personnel needs cannot be based on the idea that there always must be enough people at their disposal to deal with all possible contingencies. At the same time they know that unlike other departments, security is the one most likely to be confronted with unforeseen or unanticipated situations. As a result, security managers are aware of the fact that while they want to avoid overstaffing, they dare not allow staffing levels to fall so low that the department cannot even discharge its normal responsibilities. Simply put, overstaffing is wasteful; understaffing can be dangerous and can lead to criticism, possibly lawsuits, and probably questions about the department head's managerial skills.

To deal with this issue, one might divide the department's staffing needs into three categories: the number of persons required (1) to support the department's work, (2) to cover all assigned posts, and (3) to provide supervision to ensure a high level of job performance by security officers. Remember, while the labor costs for any department are subject to scrutiny, there is an even greater tendency to examine those for security departments. This is due to the false impression held by so many people that security personnel are unproductive and therefore are nothing more than a drain on profits.

The Support Group

Even as we approach the end of the twentieth century, with an ever increasing demand by employers for professional security directors and managers, there are still some "old-timers" who tend to be more concerned with the number of people they supervise and the size of their budgets than they are with what they accomplish. They feel entitled to personal perquisites and relatively large support groups as evidence of their importance. This attitude, which is counterproductive, wins neither friends nor supporters.

As an example, a plant security manager for a manufacturing company had a private secretary, office manager, secretary for his supervisory staff, file and general clerks, and three supervisors, for a total of eight people. Since this particular facility used contract guards, he also approved the agency's assigning three of its own supervisors to the account. In contrast, the corporate security director (who was also responsible for safety and environmental matters corporate-wide) shared a secretary with four people—two safety engineers and the headquarter's site security manager and supervisor, all of whom together constituted the corporate security department's support group. Eventually, and more appropriately, the plant support group was reduced to one secretary, one proprietary supervisor, and the three agency supervisors.

Still others, apparently enamored of bureaucracy, advocate the following for a security department's support group: an office manager; executive secretary; at least one other secretary; receptionist; and file, mail, and records clerks. Without doubt the functions represented by these jobs must be performed, but are seven people really needed to do the work?

Rarely is a department's support group so large as to require an office manager. If support personnel above and beyond a secretary are needed, there is no reason why the latter cannot oversee their activities. As for the secretary, although there may be exceptions, security managers rarely have so much work that they themselves will keep one secretary busy full-time. This tended to be true even when they gave dictation to secretaries or machines, after which the secretary transcribed the material. Today, with the use of computers, there may be even less to do for a secretary assigned for the department head's exclusive use. Computers allow security managers to handle many of their own communications and even to keep their own calendars. Consequently, many secretaries now find that in addition to handling a manager's calendar, appointments, and business travel arrangements and possibly overseeing a clerk, their work consists largely of formatting, printing, and mailing hard-copy correspondence. This is not to say that support groups should not include secretaries. Rather it is to suggest that unless the work load is unusually demanding, one secretary for a department might well be enough.

People always come to security offices. They may be departmental employees, other company personnel, salespersons, or visitors. Nevertheless, the volume of such traffic generally is rather low. By strategically locating the secretary's desk, it is possible that he or she can also function as a receptionist. This, too, reduces headcount.

Most organizations of any size have a staffed mail room for the entire facility. Its personnel receive, sort, and distribute incoming mail to all departments; they also collect, stamp, and otherwise handle all outgoing mail. Since logging mail in and distributing it at departmental level is neither particularly time-consuming nor difficult, it is a task usually performed by a secretary. Therefore, to add a mail clerk to a department's headcount, for no apparent reason other than to have a large support staff, is wasteful.

The very nature of security department operations requires record keeping. For purposes of operating efficiency, all records and other communications should be filed in a timely fashion. The question is, is the volume of this work so great that each function requires adding a full-time clerical employee to the support staff?

Occasionally, there may be times when a department's size and the volume of its work are such that these additions are warranted. On the other hand, good managers, familiar with the skills and work habits of their subordinates, may be able to satisfy the department's record-keeping and filing needs without having to add more people to the organization.

For instance, a security manager had a receptionist at each of two building entrances, primarily to help visitors and control employee access, but one processed far fewer people than did the other. Both receptionists had access to computer terminals. Since a good deal of the department's record keeping involved entering hard-copy data into computer files, the receptionist handling fewer employees and visitors was able to help with the record keeping without reducing her effectiveness. In fact, she welcomed the opportunity to be productive when things were otherwise slow.

As another example, a security department's secretary was responsible for filing all sensitive hard-copy materials, but other hard-copy records also had to be filed. Since after-hours access to the building was computer and card reader controlled and all security and life safety alarms were audiovisual, security officers who worked in the security control room from midnight to 8 A.M. were able to take care of the general filing.

Thus while all security departments need a support group, they do not necessarily need different employees for each different task. Assessments of what needs to be done and by whom it can be done best and most economically must be realistic. It is not a matter of overloading individuals. In the illustrations used, those given some additional work to do during the course of their regular shifts found boredom was minimal. A chance to be productive made them feel that they really were contributing to the department's success.

In this respect the possible risk of boredom cannot be ignored. Security directors should recognize that not all of the department's work is challenging or stimulating. When they can give employees opportunities to avoid boredom, they should take advantage of the situation in ways that can benefit both the staff and the department. When morale is high, greater efficiency results.

Security Officers

Of course, determining how many security officers have to be employed in order to cover all positions effectively and ensure proper protection of the employer's assets can be one of a manager's greatest challenges. Again, there is a need to strike a proper balance in order to avoid problems of either over- or understaffing. This involves more than merely ensuring that there will be enough people to cover the required number of hours for each post. Allied issues that can have an impact on costs, morale, and the efficiency of the staff cannot be ignored.

Some department heads will first determine the number of posts requiring a security officer's presence on an around-the-clock basis. Since such coverage mathematically calls for 4.3 security officers, they multiply the number of posts by 4.3 in deciding on how many bodies will be needed. Using this formula might seem to be an easy solution to the problem. However, in and of itself it does not always take into account either the number of hours each person would have off between shifts or the number of consecutive hours that that person should have off at the end of a scheduled work week. Nor does it necessarily take into account or provide for coverage of those posts that do not require an around-the-clock presence.

Without careful consideration and examination, this hoped-for solution to the staffing problem may in fact lead to other types of problems, all of which are best avoided. Among them are overstaffing, failure to allow for a minimum of sixteen hours off between each shift worked, and less than forty-eight consecutive hours off at the end of a work week. It goes without saying that an overstaffed organization is also an expensive one. By the same token, not allowing enough time off between shifts or at the end of a scheduled work week can be bad for morale and adversely affect operating efficiency.

In order to avoid problems of this kind, some managers take a different approach. They total the number of hours to be covered in a week, and divide each day into two twelve-hour shifts. With a degree of care in scheduling personnel, they may be able to provide all of the required coverage, including that for posts where a constant presence is unnecessary, in ways that minimize the risk of overstaffing and avoid paying overtime. Some security officers welcome this type of schedule because they have a large block of time off each week; their managers accept it as good for morale. However, adopting this formula blindly, despite what may appear to be certain benefits, can prove to be counterproductive in the final analysis.

Without minimizing the importance of good morale, managers nevertheless must ask themselves to what extent each officer's efficiency will be reduced by working a twelve-hour shift. Even when officers only work eight-hour shifts, and their physical presence is needed at several posts, the activity level at many of them can be rather low and cause boredom. This, in turn, can foster a degree of inattention, however unintentional, thereby further reducing efficiency.

With this in mind the risks inherent in having personnel work twelve- instead of eight-hour shifts, need to be considered carefully. Even if managers feel reasonably certain that their people can be sufficiently attentive in terms of observing things, a critically important question remains: Should any of those officers be confronted with a situation that calls for action on their part, will they still be able to respond both promptly and properly? Managers know that people tend to be less effective even as an eight-hour day draws to a close. As a result, any manager who has even the slightest doubt or hesitation about answering the question affirmatively needs to reconsider the wisdom of twelve-hour shifts and ask if the possible benefits either outweigh or are worth the possible risks.

There is yet another way of trying to determine just how many officers are needed to provide a desired level of coverage. Admittedly, it requires more time and effort on a manager's part since he or she will have to study the exact needs of each specific post in relation to the needs of the department as a whole. Instead of relying on a formula, it means charting personnel assignments on a post-by-post basis.

Despite the added effort, using this method to determine the number of officers needed to adequately staff the department offers certain benefits. Being able to visualize post coverage in terms of persons rather than on the basis of a mathematical formula, or one that divides days into twelve-hour shifts, allows managers to make assignments in ways that will still provide a minimum of sixteen hours off for each officer between shifts and a minimum of forty-eight hours off at the end of each five working days. This method also makes it easier to identify posts that do not necessarily require around-the-clock coverage, a factor that must be considered in terms of personnel requirements. It even may highlight some posts, however few, that call for a security officer's presence, but for less than eight-hours.

The willingness to expend this extra effort in the best interests of the staff is evidence of leadership on the security director's part. Soliciting feedback from security officers themselves, in terms of what they see as necessary to secure each post or do each job, can also be helpful and is another sign of leadership. Such displays by managers often help motivate subordinates, and in the final analysis the ultimate beneficiary is the employer.

Prudent managers are keenly aware of the fact that their job performance is closely intertwined with that of their departments. Officers perform best not only when they are well trained and morale is good but also when they are healthy and rested. Making certain that they have adequate time off between shifts and work weeks contributes to their physical and mental well-being, factors worth considering. These same managers also know that their performance is measured in part by how they manage their financial resources. Even if only one or two posts can be covered adequately by using part-time employees, there are savings to be realized.

Therefore, it is evident that in determining how many officers are needed to adequately protect and conserve an employer's assets, directors or managers should consider the alternative methods available to them for that purpose. Relying on seemingly simplistic solutions to what can be somewhat more complicated problems ultimately may prove to be shortsighted and costly.

Supervisory Personnel

It is a mistake for any manager to say categorically that he or she needs to have a minimum of four supervisors: one for each shift and one for relief. In some cases this may be true; in others it may not. It is unwise to decide on the number of supervisors that may be needed to provide proper oversight before knowing how many officers are to be employed, their working hours, and the level of activity on each shift. Nor should it be a foregone conclusion that every manager must have supervisory assistance.

In deciding on the need for and size of a supervisory staff, a factor once again to be considered is whether the department head is more bureaucrat than manager. The same managers who advocate large support organizations, as was discussed earlier, are also among those who envision having managers or supervisors for virtually every different function or detail handled by their departments. For instance, they would have a supervisor for personnel assigned to a computer room despite the fact that there may be only one security officer on duty for each of three shifts, or they would have a supervisor for investigators even if there are only two or three employed. This is wasteful, as is having a supervisory staff if technology can be used for that purpose.

To illustrate, a 650,000-square-foot corporate headquarters office building in an upscale business and residential neighborhood had around-the-clock security coverage. Between 4 P.M. and 8 A.M. daily one officer on each of two eight-hour shifts monitored all alarm systems and controlled access to the executives' garage; two others controlled access to the building and alternated making patrol rounds. On weekends and holidays there was a third shift. There were no supervisors.

A new director, authorized to hire three supervisors if he felt it necessary at a first-year cost of approximately $108,000, carefully examined the situation. Instead he proposed installing a card reader and two closed circuit television cameras to control and monitor after-hours access at the building's main entrance and in the main lobby. He also proposed the secure installation in his office of a videotape recorder and computer terminal, the latter to give him control of the alarm and card reader systems. The proposal was approved. The equipment enabled him to see quickly and easily if anything unusual occurred after hours. If so, he could then determine if the officers had submitted the required written reports covering the incident. This use of technology for supervision in lieu of personnel, with a one-time cost of about $25,000, proved to be both a very satisfactory solution to the problem as well as a less expensive one.

Of course, if there are practical limitations on technology's use for supervision, managers should look for still other possible alternatives that might prove to be feasible yet less expensive than supervisors. This requires careful consideration of how much authority and how much of a supervisory staff are needed to ensure proper job performance by on-duty officers. In some cases it may be possible to provide an adequate level of supervision for less than it would cost to hire supervisors in the accepted sense of the word, while simultaneously boosting morale.

To illustrate, this is how the matter was handled by a corporate headquarters security department working at a campus-like setting. There was a site security manager and supervisor; both normally worked days, but with staggered hours because of the volume of activity. However, there was a question as to whether the regular after-hours shifts, consisting of five officers (two proprietary and three contract), including one on duty in the security control room to monitor access via closed circuit television and all alarms, needed supervisors from 4 P.M. to midnight and midnight to 8 A.M.

In deciding, the corporate security director, site manager, and supervisor took various factors into account. Hiring two full-time supervisors at that particular time would have added more than $73,000 to the payroll for the first year alone. They also examined the nature and volume of work normally performed by officers working the after-hours shifts. After considering all of these factors, they realized that there had to be some form of supervision, but the question remained as to the need for supervisors as such.

At this juncture one more factor came into play—the proprietary officers' morale. The department's relatively small size limited their opportunities for promotion; so did the fact that none of them had attended college, let alone earned degrees. Limited opportunity also meant limited earning capacity. At the same time, some definitely were capable of assuming more responsibility than they had been given or could be given under the prevailing conditions. However, within the employer's table of organization there was an hourly job category of group leader available for a limited number of select hourly employees who could function in quasi-supervisory roles. For this they earned an additional ten percent of their hourly rate. Since the company also paid a ten percent shift differential to employees working second and third shifts, group leaders could realize a twenty percent increase in pay.

In this case the unanimous decision was to provide after-hours supervision by promoting a proprietary officer on each after-hours shift to group leader, accompanied by appropriate authority for that purpose. The reaction on the part of those not promoted was favorable. Now they felt that at least some chance for advancement existed and that in time they too might be considered. This approach to providing an acceptable degree of supervision saved the employer over $30,000 a year.

Inevitably, there will be circumstances that leave the department head with no viable alternative other than to consider hiring salaried supervisors. What remains is to decide on how many are needed to do the job properly. Again, managers have to strike a balance. As noted earlier, some security directors would urge that the number of supervisors be determined by the number of different functions within the department. Others, also with a bureaucratic bent or seemingly oblivious to either cost or reality, advocate employing one supervisor for every three to five security officers.[2]

The importance of the security function, and of those employed as officers, to a healthy business climate and economy cannot be overemphasized. This is especially true in organizations where security is fully integrated into all aspects of operations. Neverthe-less, most of the jobs performed by officers in a majority of security departments are not so complex that supervision based on function alone can be justified. Furthermore, the activities of the average site security department, as distinguished from one at corporate level for a large employer, are not so dispersed geographically as to warrant assigning multiple supervisors to the same shift.

In reality there is no single or simple answer to the question of supervision. All department managers must analyze the conditions with which they are faced at specific locations. A site security manager at a corporate headquarters, not involved with a lot of meetings or activities other than those related directly to managing the department, might need after-hours supervisors but none during the regular working day. On the other hand, a site manager who serves in both a staff and line capacity and who is thus involved with a range of activities not necessarily related directly to the department's management may find a need for supervisory personnel to help cover all shifts, including regular working days. Obviously, allowance must be made for exceptions, but having more than one secu-rity supervisor for any given shift should be an uncommon rather than a common practice.

USING PROPRIETARY OR CONTRACT PERSONNEL

The existence of a security department implies that officers probably are employed, but it does not automatically follow that they are direct employees of the organization at which they are found. They may be assigned there by a third party agency under the terms of a contract. Therefore, one staffing decision that has to be made deals with the source or sources from which officers will be hired. While support and often supervisory personnel, may be proprietary employees, it does not always mean that rank-and-file security officers will also be proprietary.

Some security departments are composed entirely of proprietary personnel; in others department heads and support staff are proprietary, but the officers and their immediate supervisors are assigned by a contract agency. Nor is it at all unusual to find a business or institution that uses a combination of proprietary and contract security officers. Notwithstand-ing the relative frequency of this arrangement, before deciding to proceed it behooves security directors and their employers to take into consideration various issues that may result from such co-employment.

For instance, from a legal perspective the differences between proprietary security officers (master and servant) and contract personnel (principal and agent) may be slight. Nevertheless, they may be sufficient to cause concerns in terms of liability allegedly attributable to their conduct or misconduct. States that regulate private security tend to dis-tinguish between proprietary and contract personnel, focusing more on the latter, while those that have passed or are considering legislation mandating minimum training require-ments may extend them to both categories. The point is that the decision-making process with respect to the use of a single or dual source of security officers, like all decisions, requires careful analysis; it is not simply a matter of numbers and direct costs.

In any event, in some cases a security manager's preference for one or the other is meaningless; senior management will have made the decision. In other cases executive management will seek the security director's opinion before deciding. Of course, there also are times when security managers are allowed to decide on the type of organization best suited for the employer's protection.

Regardless of how or by whom the decision is reached, directors and managers cannot divorce themselves from the process, nor should they want to. After all, as far as senior management is concerned, it is the director or manager who ultimately is responsible for the loss prevention program's execution and its success or failure, part of which depends on the quality of departmental personnel. Therefore, even if there is a policy decision to use contract personnel, security managers certainly have a role to play. At the very least they should be involved in identifying those agencies that in their opinion are best qualified for the job.

Some security directors undoubtedly may feel that the foregoing statements about their having a role to play, or at least being involved with the process, are unnecessary. However, the fact remains that their experiences are not necessarily universally accepted or typical of all organizations. In some the evolutionary process leading to security's integration into the employer's total operation has not yet been completed, and matters of this sort are considered to be a purchasing department function.

The important thing to remember is that being asked for advice on whether to use contract or proprietary personnel is a signal to security managers that their opinions are valued. This, in turn, gives them an opportunity to influence senior management's decision. However, if the decision is left to them, they have the burden of justifying their choice. Therefore, what should security directors or managers do when they must identify qualified agencies, give an opinion as to what kind of organization to use, or decide on whether to use proprietary or contract services or a combination of the two?

Pros and Cons

Oftentimes if there is some indecision on senior management's part as to whether their particular business or institution would be best served by having a proprietary, contract, or combined security organization, the first question asked of the security manager will deal with the pros and cons of proprietary versus contract personnel. Truthfully, arguments can be made to support or refute either position, and they are worth noting. However, it must also be pointed out that in today's business environment it is possible that some of the reasons that historically have favored employing proprietary rather than contract personnel can now be overcome by dealing with reputable contract agencies and insisting on using written agreements that have been prepared by the customers' lawyers. Among the principal arguments advanced in support of either position are the following.

1. A proprietary staff's loyalty is to the employer rather than to a third party. This is a fact that cannot be overcome by contract, no matter how well written.
2. It is also true that proprietary security officers are recruited, chosen, and screened on the basis of the employer's standards to minimize the risk of hiring unsuitable people. This is a matter of concern since a security officer's suitability and retention can have a bearing on liability in the event of litigation calling his or her conduct into question. However, unlike the loyalty issue, and without dictating its own standards to an agency, a customer can insist on having access to background investigation reports on agency personnel assigned to its facilities. A customer can also

reserve the right to have contract officers removed from its premises at any time without giving the agency a reason for the removal.

3. Proprietary personnel can be trained initially and also given in-service updates in accordance with the security manager's wishes. There is nothing to prevent incorporating into an agency contract the security manager's generic as well as organization and site-specific training requirements.

4. A proprietary staff will perform at a higher level than a contract one since the officers know that their salary increases and opportunities for promotion, whether within or without the security department, depend on job performance. No written agreement, notwithstanding a customer's right to background information and security officer removal, or training requirements, can ensure that contract personnel will discharge their duties at a particular level. Consequently, although there may be some relatively rare exceptions, it is generally true that the better performance will come from proprietary officers. In all fairness, however, leadership and the ability of security managers to motivate cannot be ignored as important factors in all subordinates' (proprietary or contract) job performance.

5. Those who favor using contract personnel will argue that agency services are less expensive. In some cases this may be true, in others it may not be. Geography may have a bearing on the subject since pay scales are not necessarily uniform throughout the United States. For example, the corporate security director for a Fortune 500 company with eleven major U.S. facilities that employed security personnel undertook a study of the costs. Some sites had a combined proprietary–contract staff; others only used agency personnel. Despite wages, fringe benefits, and uniform and other related costs, it became evident that for facilities in the Northeast and the West it actually would be cheaper to employ officers directly. At the same time, because the company's pay scales were constant at all locations, contract agencies' rates in the Southeast made their use less costly.

6. Another argument is that customers who use agencies can save money for administrative costs. Again, this is not necessarily true. Prudent senior management, realistically concerned with protecting and conserving assets, and appreciating the inherent value of fully integrated security programs, will want to ensure that their loss prevention efforts are directed by their own managers regardless of the type of security staff used. This, combined with the fact that security organizations tend to be relatively small compared with other departments, suggests that the cost of administering a proprietary staff need not be prohibitive, let alone a major expense. In contrast, some contract agencies may insist on assigning their own supervisory personnel, each of whom is paid at a higher scale than are its security officers. Regardless of how this charge is shown on invoices, the fact remains that it represents additional expense to customers.

7. If one uses contract personnel there is a saving in the costs normally associated with advertising, recruiting, and screening people. This can be significant if the turnover among officers is high. While this tends to be true, a question remains to be answered: What are the comparative turnover rates of proprietary and contract personnel? Depending on a contract agency's personnel practices, its turnover may be appreciably higher. If it pays its security officers minimum wages, offers little or

nothing in the way of fringe benefits or chances for promotion, expects them to buy their uniforms, or constantly changes shift assignments, that agency's turnover may be far higher than that of a proprietary department.

8. Presumably, officers are assigned to specific posts on the basis of a real need. Therefore, if one fails to report for duty, there is an increased risk that a breech of security will occur. Allegedly, under such circumstances the use of agency personnel serves a dual purpose: it relieves customers of the worry about coverage, and it saves them money by not having to pay proprietary employees overtime to cover an assignment. This is only partially true. Experienced security managers who have used or use contract personnel can attest to the fact that notwithstanding contract provisions there are times when posts are uncovered because officers fail to report for duty without notice and it is too late to hold someone over. If this occurs, the agency's size may be a factor in terms of its ability to provide a replacement.

9. Another argument offered as a reason to use contract staff is based on the assumption that rank-and-file proprietary security officers may be unionized. If so, and other employees should strike for any reason, the officers may refuse to cross a picket line in sympathy with the strikers. Should this happen, the absence of security personnel obviously increases the employer's risk. Contract agency advocates will say that this is a problem with which their customers would not have to be concerned. Again, this is not necessarily true. A customer's risk would be no less if agency employees belong to a union and either go on strike for reasons of their own or refuse to cross a picket line set up by the customer's striking employees.

10. Two other issues remain. First, to what extent are there inherent risks in using proprietary personnel who become familiar with and possibly develop close relationships with other employees? Second, is it possible that the morale and hence performance of contract officers may be adversely affected by their not participating in certain fringe benefits and programs that are available to proprietary employees? The saying "Familiarity breeds contempt," attributable to Mark Twain, may have a ring of truth to it. If so, its application is universal. Contract personnel are no more immune to becoming familiar and establishing personal relationships with people than are proprietary officers. Proper training and supervision can be a counterbalance in either case. As for agency officers' morale, it depends primarily on fringe benefits and opportunities afforded to them by their employers, not by what customers do. By the same token, it is not unusual for them to be invited to join in some social functions and activities in which customers' employees participate, much as if they fell into that category. Consequently, neither of these factors should be significant when deciding on the use of proprietary or contract personnel.

Choosing a Contract Agency

Assume that a decision has been made to retain a contract agency's services. One of the first things to remember is that the purchasing department, through which any agreement will have to be reached, has no security expertise. As a result it will need guidance and direction from the security manager in identifying prospective agencies and writing the specifications on which their proposals will have to be based. This must be done before any agency can be sent a request for proposal (RFP). Therefore, certain factors should be taken into account by both security and purchasing managers as part of the process of determining to which agencies RFPs should be sent.

The principal products of a contract security agency are its service and the people who perform those services. As with any other type of business, the quality of those products can and does vary from agency to agency. While an agency's size admittedly is one of several factors to be considered, the fact that it may be well known and operating nationally, or even internationally, is no guarantee that its products are of high quality. Conversely, smallness does not necessarily mean that its products are of poor quality.

The number of firms that now offer these services has grown to such an extent that asking all of them for proposals is impractical; therefore, the field must be narrowed. If so, what are some of the factors that should enter into the identification of contract agencies from whom proposals should be solicited and with whom agreements should be executed? Among the most important factors are the professional qualifications of the owners and management staff; the organization's financial strength; the ways in which it recruits, screens, trains, and promotes its employees; what it pays them; its general reputation in the industry; its size; and what references say about job performance.

It is hard to imagine anyone inexperienced in and unfamiliar with what security's role really is in a business or institutional environment being able to offer a high-quality product in terms of customer service and qualified personnel. An agency's owners may be able to satisfy a state's licensing and bonding requirements, but this does not always mean that they are experienced.

Just as nothing would prevent a recent liberal arts graduate from incorporating and going into the construction business, there is also very little to prevent a person from starting a contract security agency. However, just as it is unlikely that such a construction company would be hired to erect a $50 million high-rise building it should be no less important to make certain that a security firm is qualified to provide a high standard of performance for its customers.

Furthermore, as security functions become increasingly integrated into business operations, one also must remember that security in its broadest sense is neither an extension of policing nor a quasi-military activity. Therefore, one should not automatically assume that police or military experience per se is a sufficient indication that an agency's owners or management staff are in a position to deliver the type of service wanted. Nor can a security manager afford to assume that just because an agency has satisfied a state's licensing requirements its owners and managers are professionally qualified in the security field.

Financial strength is important. If an agency is not financially sound, there is the risk that on occasion it may have cash flow problems. That can mean trouble in meeting its payroll and other financial obligations. Prudent security managers should not knowingly elect to do business with contract agencies whose employees may refuse to work because they have not been paid or whose insurance policies could be canceled for nonpayment of premiums. Retaining such an agency on the theory that if either or both incidents should occur it can be sued for breach of contract is naive. If the agency lacks the financial resources to pay its employees and other bills, it is highly unlikely that a judgment for the customer in a lawsuit would mean anything more than legal expenses and a hollow victory. Then, too, the customer would have the added expense of finding and entering into a contract with another agency whose rates might be even higher.

Since an agency's employees are representative of how its services will be performed, the ways in which its personnel are recruited, screened, trained, promoted, and paid are important considerations. Some agencies are selective in their recruiting and as thorough as the law will permit in terms of screening; others do relatively little in either sphere in order to keep their overhead, and consequently their rates, low and their profits high. Similarly, some agencies put their employees through extensive training programs before assigning them to any client; others wait until they have a customer. They may then give officers from one to four hours of on-the-job training consisting mainly of walking them through the facility to which they have been assigned.

Questions about an agency's pay and promotion procedures are also valid. As with any organization, more often than not employees paid minimum wages will tend to put forth minimum effort in terms of job performance. Nor is there any incentive to improve performance if salary increases are infrequent and minimal, there are no fringe benefits, and promotions are based on seniority, friendships, or nepotism rather than merit. Many managers fail to ask about these practices, only to learn that agency personnel assigned to them are paid minimum wages and have no fringe benefits, and that their contract supervisor was given that job on the basis of his or her length of service with the firm. Wages paid to and promotions for agency personnel obviously are within the agency's province, but how those employees will perform their duties for a customer is critically important to the latter's security manager. Consequently, as part of the final selection process, it is not improper for security managers to ask what an agency pays and how it promotes its personnel.

Reputation in the industry, size, and references also should play a part in contract agency identification and selection. Although most managers know the general reputations of security agencies in their areas, this may not always be the case. An example might help. A manufacturer about to open a limited operation in a relatively small town more than 1500 miles from its corporate headquarters, and 75 miles from the nearest large city, heard about two local agencies in the town. Also, two nationally known agencies had offices in the nearest city. For several reasons doing business with one of the local agencies was preferable. To learn more about them the corporate security director contacted the local sheriff, who willingly provided information. The sheriff pointed out that from time to time there had been other agencies in the town, but of the two now there, one at least had been in business for four years, inferring some degree of stability.

Size becomes a factor in terms of an agency's ability to adequately service a particular client's needs. Oftentimes the answer will lie in what references have to say, and reputable agencies usually volunteer to provide them. If references are not given voluntarily, they should be requested and should be contacted by the security manager. One question to be asked of them deals with the responsiveness to customer concerns by the agency's management. It should make no difference if those concerns relate to personnel assignments, invoices, or anything else. Someone representing agency management should always be available to meet with customers in a timely fashion to resolve any outstanding issues.

Another question to be asked, yet sometimes forgotten, concerns any given reference's personnel requirements. Agency performance certainly is important, but realistically it cannot be separated from a customer's personnel needs. A reference may have the highest praise for an agency's performance, but unless its personnel needs are comparable to those of the prospective customer, there is no assurance that the same quality of service can be provided.

For instance, suppose that in contacting all of the references it is learned that none needs security officers for more than 400 hours a week. On the other hand, the prospective customer needs 1600 hours a week. Although the agency may have no trouble providing personnel in the 400-hour range, it may find it difficult, if not impossible, to staff a much larger account. If there are doubts about an agency's ability to satisfy a customer's staffing requirements, despite its reported responsiveness and high quality of service, it may be unwise to retain it.

The foregoing factors, used in identifying prospective agencies and in making a final selection, must be reviewed in connection with what each agency sets forth in its proposal. To ensure fairness in this regard, a copy of the specifications for the work to be performed, complete in every respect, should be included with the purchasing department's RFPs. This, too, is something with which security managers are involved since, as a practical matter, they know what is needed. To submit realistic proposals bidders have to know more than just how many hours of service are to be provided. If not, there can be confusion, wasted time and effort, a delay in implementing the personnel aspects of the security program, and unanticipated costs.

Suppose, for instance, that the specifications set forth general insurance requirements but fail to include either minimum levels of coverage or the fact that individual agency employees assigned to the customer must be bonded. The purchasing and security managers review the proposals and agree on an agency. When the agency receives the contract, it learns for the first time of terms and conditions of which it was unaware or that it cannot meet. The agreement calls for certain levels and kinds of insurance, including a fidelity bond, stipulates extensive training at no cost to the customer, and requires the agency to hold the client harmless in the event of a lawsuit prompted by an agency employee's behavior. Even if the agency can satisfy the contract terms, the fact remains that issues that could and should have been avoided were not, and the initial relationship between the parties is strained. On the other hand, if the agency cannot satisfy the terms, the time-consuming and possibly costly selection process must begin all over again; unless the mistake is corrected, it even may have to be repeated for a third time. One would like to think that these pitfalls are so obvious as to be avoided and that problems of this sort never occur. Unfortunately, they do.

Another thing to keep in mind is that purchase orders never should be substituted for formal, written contracts when agency security services are to be used, even if those services are for a period of not more than one year. Equally important, the contract document should set forth clearly what the buyer requires of the seller. It should include, without necessarily being limited to, such things as the agency's payment of wages and taxes, background investigations of and physical requirements for personnel, training, insurance, fidelity bonding, the use and carrying of weapons, uniforms and equipment, supervision, invoice submissions, dispute resolution, protection of information, police liaison, representation in cases of litigation, and publicity. Special needs, such as clearances that would be required for personnel to be assigned to defense contractor facilities, should also be included (Appendix 2A).

What has been said about contract services, based on the assumption that only agency personnel will be used, applies equally whenever a security department will consist of a combination of contract and proprietary personnel. Whether agency personnel will be used in whole or in part, one factor in the decision-making process undoubtedly will be cost. While it already has been noted that geography may have a bearing on differences between wages paid to proprietary versus agency personnel, it should not have an impact on wages offered by bidding contract firms. Without minimizing the importance of cost, buyers of contract services who base their decision entirely or primarily on cost may regret the day that they did since the lowest bidder also may be the least competent. In addition, to say awards will be made to the lowest "qualified" bidder also may be problematic, depending on the term's interpretation. An agency may be fully qualified on the basis of state regulations yet unable to satisfy a prospective customer's needs. To guard against this, contracts should be awarded to the lowest *responsible* bidder, which obviously includes qualification, not merely to the lowest bidder.

Using Proprietary Security Officers

Despite some of the significant benefits to be enjoyed by using proprietary personnel, including the fact that under some circumstances their use may cost less than contract services, security managers still may find opposition to the idea because they would add to the employer's headcount. Unfortunately, since those who feel this way are often an organization's ultimate decision makers, it is not easy to dissuade them even though their argument is illogical.

A detailed study of costs led a national corporation's security director to the conclusion that an estimated $250,000 could be saved annually by converting from a combination of proprietary and contract officers to an all proprietary staff. Nevertheless, the company's chief executive officer disapproved of the idea. He focused on the company's employment figures, viewing this proposal only in terms of headcount rather than as an opportunity to effect savings. He failed to see that in reality the actual number of officers on duty would be unchanged. The only change would have been one of uniforms and employers.

In trying to decide on whether to use a proprietary staff, either in whole or in part, security managers owe it to their employers and themselves to examine all of the pros and cons carefully and objectively. They must consider all of the financial and other factors that will affect the employer.

Approval to hire at least some proprietary officers for use in conjunction with contract officers is not uncommon. This practice occurs most often when there will be an appreciable saving by using agency personnel, although other reasons for doing so may exist. Since wages and fringe benefits combined are frequently the biggest items in security department budgets, the savings that may be realized by using a partial contract staff cannot be ignored. However, under these circumstances managers should be prepared to justify the assignments to be given to proprietary officers as distinguished from those to be given to contract personnel. Managers who have carefully considered their overall staffing needs should have no difficulty in this regard.

To illustrate, a newly hired corporate security director found that only agency personnel were used at major facilities. He was concerned about all after-hours communications, including what could be sensitive teletype and fax messages for key managers, that arrived in the security control room for routing to the addressees. Viewing these conditions as an unacceptable risk to the protection of proprietary information, he obtained senior management approval to hire enough proprietary officers to staff the various control rooms at all times.

Security managers authorized to hire proprietary officers in any numbers should remember that there is much truth to the cliche that one only gets what one pays for. Frequently, though, more is involved than the hourly rate of pay and fringe benefits, matters over which they have no control. Other important factors that to a large extent they can control are the atmosphere and environment in which the staff finds itself, elements that can contribute to the department's success or failure.

For example, if contract officers resign because they are dissatisfied with their working conditions, the agency has to provide replacements at no cost to customers. If proprietary security officers are unhappy and resign, their employer has unavoidable expenses. In all probability some overtime will have to be paid to those officers providing coverage until replacements are hired and trained. There will also be the costs involved in recruiting, screening, uniforming, and training the replacements.

This points up the need for managers to maintain departmental stability, something that can be helped or hurt by the atmosphere no matter how good the pay or fringe benefits. To a large extent a security manager's personality and ability to work well with superiors, peers, and subordinates are prime factors. Two critically important issues in this respect are evidence of fairness and consideration in dealing with subordinates.

Managers who show favoritism or bias in assignments and promotions do a disservice to their personnel, departments, employers, and themselves. The same is true of those who show no consideration for subordinates' needs. As an illustration, if a security director is aware of the fact that some security officers are attending school, they should be assured that despite the department's shift rotation policy their shift changes will not be scheduled so as to prevent them from completing any semester for which they are enrolled.

It has already been said that before embarking on a program to use proprietary personnel security managers have to weigh carefully all of the pros and cons. In doing so they also need to acknowledge that the principal pros for the use of proprietary officers are loyalty to the employer, the ability to screen and hire people of their own choice, and the prospect of better job performance. Therefore, they also need to be alert for circumstances that may enable them to hire better people for security officers' jobs.

For instance, better people can be hired as proprietary personnel if proprietary officers take home more pay than contract agency personnel. This possibility hinges on an analysis of the cost variables used to help decide on the type of security staff to be used in the first place. Remember, if a contract staff is to be used, the agency's hourly rate understandably includes a percent to cover its profit and overhead, something not figured in proprietary personnel costs. As a result, to remain competitive without cutting into profits and overhead, agencies may pay their officers a lower hourly rate than what customers would pay theirs. Thus since the latter actually get more money on payday, this can help attract better applicants for proprietary positions.

DEVELOPING EMPLOYMENT STANDARDS AND JOB DESCRIPTIONS

Human resources departments are involved with the structure, format, and terminology for employment standards and job descriptions. Nevertheless, developing actual standards and descriptions for security positions should be within the security manager's province since he or she is the one who best knows and understands what is called for in both cases.

Employment Standards

Managers must be realistic in developing employment standards, but this does not excuse failure to establish criteria for character, education, physical ability, and emotional stability. By the same token, it is important to acknowledge that rank-and-file officers' work is neither particularly challenging nor sophisticated, despite what good security programs can contribute to an employer's success. Consequently, with this in mind practical managers will not set standards that cannot be met.

Not to be overlooked in setting standards is the fact that all employees, including security personnel, are entitled to and have private lives. Their privacy must be respected; what security personnel do after working hours should be of no concern to employers unless their activities will directly interfere with or prevent them from doing their jobs effectively and efficiently.

Aside from the criteria noted above, employment standards should be based primarily on two factors: (1) an individual's ability to do the job for which he or she either is being or already has been hired; (2) compliance with any legal restraints imposed by government, such as the Civil Rights Act of 1964 and the Americans with Disabilities Act. In many respects all of these factors are interrelated. If ability is a prime consideration, as it must be, there is no reason to ask questions based on race, creed, color, religious belief, sex, or country of national origin. As for discriminating against persons with disabilities, by developing standards that distinguish among certain types of positions, it is possible to employ disabled persons consistent with their ability to perform specific duties. Unfortunately, despite these legislative enactments there are still some whose ignorance or prejudices prompt them to avoid hiring certain applicants. Managers in this category do a disservice to rejected applicants and their employers. They also risk adverse publicity, embarrassment, and litigation expenses if those discriminated against should elect to sue.

For instance, in one case a security manager, who boasted that he worked his security officers overtime to avoid hiring minority applicants, did not think like a manager. His prejudice resulted in needless overtime; hiring a minority as an officer at straight salary would have been less costly. In another instance, a hotel security director, asked about job opportunities for women, said that they existed but that it was hard for a woman to spend eight hours a day walking in high heels or dealing with drunks in a bar. Similarly, managers who try to avoid hiring disabled persons by arguing that all security positions are physically demanding are shortsighted and insensitive.

Complying with the Civil Rights Act of 1964 should pose no problems for security managers. A person's sex, race, creed, color, religion, or country of national origin has absolutely no bearing on one's ability to hold a security position. The principal qualifications for initial and continued employment should be character and the ability to satisfy any educational, experience, or other skills requirements needed to do the job effectively. Since nothing in the Civil Rights Act prevents their inclusion, incorporating such qualifications when developing employment standards is both proper and acceptable. On the other hand, not including them may conceivably cause serious personnel (and possibly legal) problems later on.

Educational criteria have to be included when developing standards. The years of schooling will vary for different positions, with more required of those seeking supervisory or managerial jobs. However, at the very least every security department employee should be able to read, write, and speak English. While other language skills may be helpful, this in no way alters the need for and importance of their being fluent in English; nor is this by itself discrimination against those who speak other languages. Of course, multinational organizations' security directors should set the same standards relative to local languages, with skill in English helpful for security officers and required for supervisory or managerial positions.

Complying with the Americans with Disabilities Act is not as easy as complying with the Civil Rights Act. Prudent managers are not so unrealistic as to insist that all personnel have 20/20 vision, perfect hearing, the ability to run a military-type obstacle course without difficulty, or carry objects weighing more than 100 pounds with ease. True, patrol rounds must be made, and occasional emergencies must be responded to, but the physical demands on most officers are not terribly taxing. Standards should distinguish between positions that require a degree of physical fitness and those that really do not.

Everyone should have correctable vision and good hearing, but being able to stand for long periods of time, walk up and down steps, or possibly carry a limited weight need not apply to all positions. Disabled persons can be accommodated. For example, if there is a security control room for monitoring closed circuit television and alarms or if there is a job for a receptionist or secretary, a person confined to a wheelchair but qualified in every other respect can be hired since mobility really is not a factor.

However, as part of the physical standards for employment, an effort should be made to try to ensure that all security department applicants are emotionally stable, whether they will be armed or not. There are three reasons: (1) occasional job stress, (2) an employer's dependence on security personnel in emergencies, and (3) the likelihood of public contact. For instance, a security employee who is immobilized upon receiving a bomb threat or when a fire alarm is activated creates problems rather than solving them. Officers overly impressed with their authority can adversely affect an employer's good labor or public relations.

In addition, thought should be given to other employment standards, important from a security manager's perspective. These should be thought of as the ground rules under which all departmental personnel work, but in applying them allowance should be made for those employees with disabilities or special needs.

To illustrate, rotating both shifts and posts serves a useful purpose but not if done with such frequency that rotation becomes disruptive. Changing shifts quarterly can avoid morale problems; posts can be changed more often at management's discretion. For instance, one director who initiated such a program assured those attending school that their shift changes would coincide with the end of semesters so as not to interfere with their education.

From management's viewpoint such rotation means that over time virtually all officers become familiar with every post, regardless of the time of day or day of week. This can be invaluable in an emergency. Shift rotation also enables the officers to equalize their pay; it is not uncommon for second and third shift personnel to be paid a shift differential. Thus everyone benefits when shift and post rotation are included among the employment standards, and implemented.

Job Descriptions

Human resources departments in large organizations usually create job families for all of the employer's personnel. For example, a job family for a multinational company's security department (which is also responsible for safety and environmental protection) from a hierarchical perspective might consist of the following:

❏ Corporate director of security and safety
❏ Senior corporate safety engineer
❏ Site security manager
❏ Junior corporate safety engineer
❏ Site security supervisor
❏ Site safety officer
❏ Site hazardous waste coordinator
❏ Security officer I
❏ Security officer II
❏ Secretary
❏ Receptionist

In addition, human resources normally assigns a grade for each position within the family for the purpose of establishing salary and wage parameters. Within each department's job family and grades there should still be job descriptions for each position. While the format generally is standardized throughout the entire organization, wise human resources personnel lean heavily on department managers for descriptive details.

Job descriptions include title, grade, and to whom the incumbent reports; they also describe particular positions. However, in describing the work to be performed by security personnel, it is best to avoid being too specific. There must be enough specificity for both job holders and their superiors to have something against which performance can be measured, but there also must be an allowance for some flexibility due to the nature of security work. This can be done by closing the descriptive part with a statement to the effect that the person may be expected to perform such other duties as may from time to time become necessary.

It also is worth noting that most job descriptions include more than what any specific job entails. As a general rule they also include such other elements as educational and work experience requirements for the position, with the job itself having a bearing on the amount of schooling required. It is not unreasonable to expect security officers and receptionists to have high school diplomas or to require a secretary to have acquired those skills normally associated with a secretarial position. It is reasonable to expect applicants for supervisory or managerial jobs to have at a minimum baccalaureate degrees, preferably in criminal justice with some business administration or possibly computer science electives.

Except for applicants for jobs as security directors or managers, or possibly as investigators in organizations where investigations are a primary function or their need occurs with such frequency as to justify employing people solely in that capacity, experience need not be a critical factor. In fact, insisting that applicants for jobs below manager level have experience often can be more hindrance than help. As one might expect, directors or managers have a good deal of experience. They have developed methodologies for their departments' operations, and they expect their staffs to perform accordingly. Therefore, by not insisting on experience for lower level positions, they can train new employees to do their jobs the way the department head wants them done. Otherwise they risk having to spend valuable time breaking new employees of old habits that do not conform with the new job's standards.

Job descriptions also will often include any special skills or qualifications needed for satisfactory performance. They could consist of such varied things as the ability to speak a foreign language or training in making keys. Parenthetically, managers working in an environment where there may be relatively frequent contact with people who are not fluent in English, whether they are employees, customers, guests, or hospital patients, are well advised to try to hire personnel who can speak at least some of the languages most likely to be encountered on the job. Depending on the nature of an organization's activities and its employees or invitees, thought might even be given to having someone capable of using sign language.

Job descriptions often include information about the extent to which job holders may be called upon to make decisions, sometimes without benefit of a superior's guidance or approval. They may also note the size of the staff and budget for which the incumbent is responsible. Decision-making responsibility obviously increases as one assumes supervisory or managerial duties. While security officers would rarely be called upon to make decisions without at least getting supervisory approval, department heads may have to exercise their independent judgment with relative frequency.

Regarding the number of people supervised, promotions bring increased responsibility. The average officer supervises no one; supervisors are responsible for overseeing shifts or particular functions. Department heads, in turn, ultimately are responsible for the entire security organization. Even though they may seek subordinates' input when preparing budgets, they alone are accountable for managing the department's finances and all of its other resources.

STAFFING AND OPPORTUNITIES FOR PROMOTION

Questions about a department's size, employment standards, and staffing really are inseparable. The first focuses on numbers; the other two on the quality of its personnel. At the same time it would be naive to deny that a relationship also exists between the quality of the staff and the availability of opportunities for promotion.

Staffing

As noted previously, when developing employment standards, managers must avoid those that realistically are unattainable. However, once standards have been set, they should not be compromised. Applicants for salaried positions at supervisory or managerial level usually will be persons interested in security field careers. Since they normally are paid salaries and are ineligible for overtime regardless of the number of hours worked per week, their jobs are referred to as exempt positions. Therefore, it is logical to set higher standards for these jobs than for hourly positions, and every effort should be made to staff exempt positions with personnel of the highest quality.

Jobs such as security officers, receptionists, or secretaries, for which employees are paid an hourly wage and are eligible for overtime, are referred to as nonexempt positions. Although standards for these jobs obviously will be different from those for exempt positions, it is no less important to make a similar effort to fill them with the best people. However, since security officer applicants often may not be career oriented, it is sometimes possible to staff those positions with persons whose qualifications will exceed the minimum standards.

This is most likely to occur under one of two conditions. During a recession when organizations may be letting employees go, many of whom are educated and have good skills, their financial hardships can result in creating a labor pool from which security departments can draw. Their unemployment may prompt them to accept jobs that they otherwise would not consider. Some will say that hiring such people is wasteful since once the economy improves many will leave for jobs more akin to those that they lost earlier. However, since the turnover rate for security officers generally tends to be high, this should not bar their being considered. Instead, their availability, even if of relatively brief duration, should be seen as a chance to improve the staff's quality.

Even so, a different problem may exist with an organization's human resources policies. Some businesses and institutions will not even consider holders of baccalaureate degrees, let alone graduate degrees, for nonexempt positions. For example, a person who was recently awarded a graduate degree in criminal justice and was willing to accept an hourly job for experience in a security department applied for a position with a large financial institution in need of a security officer. The application was arbitrarily rejected by the human resources department because of just such a policy. While these policies may have some validity, it is sometimes difficult to understand the rigidity with which they are applied. A policy of this type can prevent the temporary employment of a quality staff. As with the cited example, it also can deny recent graduates who want security careers and are willing to accept nonexempt jobs the chance to get some hands-on experience.

The other opportunity to improve staff quality presents itself when, in determining staff size, security managers see ways to cover all posts yet save some money by using a small number of part-time officers. Such positions frequently can be filled by hiring college or university students whose goals are jobs in the security field and who want some practical experience. They often can be assigned duties that will permit them to do some studying. They can add value to the staff as long as they understand that while at work their studies cannot interfere with their primary responsibilities as officers.

A factor that can affect staffing in terms of both number and quality will be the salaries and hourly wages that an employer is willing to pay for competent personnel. Security managers have some control over increases awarded in connection with performance reviews, but base salaries for all employees organization-wide are generally set by human resources departments when they develop job families. Even if they hope to set pay scales to avoid labor relations problems, this does not always result in equity. They often look at jobs in terms of required skills rather than their meaningful contributions to an employer. As a result, failure to appreciate fully what security can contribute to an organization adversely affects what security personnel are paid.

For example, in 1993 a retail specialty shop chain headquartered in New York City set an annual salary of $25,000 for its corporate security management job. The salary in relation to the cost of living in the area caused a person with a graduate degree in security, to whom an offer was made, to turn it down. On the other hand, some industries pay all of their security personnel, not merely managers, quite well.

Thus one can establish employment standards that are consistent with the Civil Rights Act of 1964 and the Americans with Disabilities Act. There is nothing in either act that prevents security managers from staffing their departments with the highest quality personnel. In the final analysis, if one wants to staff a security department with truly well-qualified personnel, high standards alone are insufficient. Salaries and fringe benefits need to be attractive, and chances for promotion must exist.

Promotions

Opportunities for promotion help make jobs more attractive and are good for morale and discipline. However, reality makes it necessary for security directors or managers to admit to two facts: promotions should be made only on the basis of merit; and opportunities for promotion within most security organizations are limited. Managers who give subordinates false hopes when asked about chances for advancement are either impractical or afraid to face the truth.

Regardless of how many officers are employed, the number of supervisors and managers needed to ensure that they do their jobs properly is limited. This, and employment standards for supervisory and managerial positions that require a certain level of education, usually prevent most security officers from being promoted to those jobs despite their experience. Experience is helpful but not sufficient. Seniority alone is no substitute for ability. It should only become a factor when a chance for promotion exists and there are two equally qualified candidates. Of course, if an opening does exist and a security officer fully meets all of the job requirements, he or she deserves to be considered for the position. For instance, a corporate security director, with a supportive headquarters site security manager, promoted to site supervisor a person who had been his administrative assistant once she received her baccalaureate degree. This was based on job performance and the fact that she then fully satisfied all of the requirements for the position.

These limitations do not necessarily foreclose all opportunities for advancement for security officers. For example, if the number of security personnel on duty after hours is insufficient to warrant having a supervisor, but someone may have to make an occasional yet rather routine decision, a "group leader" might be considered as part of the department's job family. It is a title that gives recognition as well as some added responsibility and income to a person not otherwise qualified for a supervisory or management position. Similarly, if the department has or needs its own locksmith, training and promoting a security officer to that job recognizes a person's ability and trustworthiness.

Knowing that these limitations exist, managers should not discourage subordinates from looking for other opportunities to better themselves within the employing business or institution. Quite often organizations will post openings for jobs before going outside to recruit. If so, and security personnel want to or do apply, doing so never should be held against them, whether or not they are selected for such a job. True, if this happens, a replacement will have to be found, possibly causing a temporary hardship. However, such unwilling or uncooperative managers will find that their attitudes have an adverse effect on departmental morale. If the person to whom this chance is denied resigns, the need to hire a replacement still exists.

Nonexempt security personnel are not the only ones for whom promotional opportunities within the department are limited. The same can be true for exempt employees. A department may need three supervisors, but in all likelihood it will have only one manager. Multisite corporations may have a security manager at each facility, but they will have only one corporate security director. As a result, any opportunities for promotion that may exist within the organization will not occur with great frequency. This, in turn, leaves the exempt staff in somewhat the same position as the nonexempt staff insofar as bettering themselves is concerned. They too can look for opportunities both within and without the employer organization.

Exempt employees interested in advancement often ignore the possibilities that may exist within the business or institution for which they are already working. Few other exempt personnel are in as good a position as those in security in being able to learn about an organization, albeit from a different perspective. Two illustrations are worth noting. In one, a person hired by a medical center as its security director later was promoted to assistant vice president and given the additional responsibility for safety and transportation. In the other, the person employed as security director by a hotel was promoted to rooms division manager with the new security director reporting to him.

However, those interested in advancement solely in security may find it necessary to seek work with other employers. As with nonexempt personnel, this involves recruiting a replacement and some temporary inconvenience until one is found. When this occurs, department heads should remember two things. They themselves probably went through the same experience before reaching their current positions. The best way to avoid this type of problem is to hire subordinates who have no ambition. However, one cannot hope to get optimal performance from such people. Too often those who lack ambition do only what is needed to avoid being discharged.

DUTIES AND RESPONSIBILITIES

A security organization's duties and responsibilities depend primarily on senior management's ideas of what they should be and the extent to which the heads of security departments actively participate in discussions of the subject. If executives think of security as private sector policing, security's role will be much more limited than if they accept the idea of security as both a management function and responsibility. Security as private policing tends to be more reactive than proactive, with more emphasis on deterrence than prevention. These concepts are not identical, although they need not be mutually exclusive. *Webster's New World Dictionary* defines *deter* as "to frighten, to keep (a person) from doing something through fear, anxiety, doubt, etc.," and defines *prevent* as "to act in anticipation of (an event or a fixed time);. . . to forestall; balk; frustrate."

These distinctions should be kept in mind in terms of deciding on security's duties and responsibilities and how they will be performed. Deterrence, by suggesting a focus on behavior, can be frightening and cause friction between security personnel and other employees, which, in reality, means friction between labor and management that does no one any good. Prevention, which focuses on conditions, need not be threatening to anyone. Of course, there will be times when security duties will require acts of deterrence, but if the emphasis is on prevention, problems between security and other employees need not have a negative impact on business operations.

The duties and responsibilities of individual members of security departments decrease as one descends the scale of jobs. They are greatest for department heads; they decrease for subordinate positions. Regardless of the breadth of the work agreed upon by senior management, the director's or manager's functions will vary depending on whether that person is at a corporate or other level. For instance, corporate security directors for multisite employers will find themselves in staff positions; managers at individual facilities have line jobs. Of course, it is not unusual for a corporate security director or manager whose employer has but one location to serve in both a staff and line function.

To try to delineate the duties and responsibilities of security directors or managers, and of other security personnel for that matter, with any degree of specificity could be misleading since so much depends on senior executives' wishes. That means that what all employees are expected to do, from the top down, can be expanded or contracted at any time. Nevertheless, duties at least need to be considered in general terms. Responsibility simply means that individuals are accountable for the proper execution of their assigned duties.

A first duty of directors or managers is to oversee the department's work and supervise those who report directly to them. However, their actions in doing so must be consistent with the advancement of the employer's business objectives, one of which is to make a profit. In staff functions they serve as in-house consultants on all security-related matters. This means advising senior management on all security-related issues, developing and updating organization-wide security policies and procedures, and ensuring the implementation of and compliance with those policies and procedures. Furthermore, security directors or managers should be involved with all new construction or major alteration projects to ensure that proper security measures are incorporated in the plans and specifications.

Another duty involves liaison with public law enforcement agencies, especially those at the federal level. Department heads participate in investigations—directly when the cases are complex or sensitive, indirectly when they are uncomplicated or unsophisticated. They also work closely with other department heads in finding cost-effective ways to protect and conserve the employer's assets. They develop educational programs designed to encourage full employee participation in the loss prevention effort. Corporate level directors or managers also set the goals for the entire security organization; help develop employment standards, job descriptions, and training programs for security personnel; prepare the department's budgets; decide questions regarding uniforms and equipment; and provide leadership and motivation for the security organization. Perhaps their duties are best summarized by saying they involve the management of all of their department's human, physical, and financial resources.

The foregoing duties also apply to corporate level directors or managers for single-site employers. However, since they function in a line capacity as well, they have to be involved with and responsible for daily activities such as recruiting and hiring personnel at and below supervisory level; training, supervision, and discipline; and developing and overseeing the maintenance of departmental records and communications.

In addition to these line duties, site managers for multisite organizations can be expected to conduct less complex investigations, either themselves or with corporate oversight. They also provide leadership and motivation at the local level. It should be noted that in some multisite organizations where security operations are decentralized, a subject yet to be considered, site managers may be called upon to perform some duties comparable to those required of single site corporate directors or managers.

The duties described, whether applicable to staff or line positions, deal primarily with security operations in a narrow sense. However, if the role is expanded to include other things such as safety or possibly environmental matters, the respective duties of corporate and site security directors or managers must be adjusted accordingly. Adding new areas does not alter their basic duties, but adding to their responsibilities will require senior management's permission to hire people with suitable professional or technical credentials to represent the department head in matters of oversight and implementation.

Supervisory duties can also be set forth in general terms. Supervisors are primarily responsible for overseeing the security officers for whom they are responsible, including their on-duty appearance, ability to perform, on-the-job training, discipline, and actual job performance. If contract personnel are used, proprietary supervisors should be involved with verifying agency invoices as they apply to their shifts to prevent overcharging. They may help with or conduct preliminary investigations of reported incidents, they perform other duties that may be assigned to them by their managers, and they ensure that any special manager's instructions are properly executed.

In many respects the job titles of other departmental personnel indicate the primary duties involved, but a detailed discussion could consume an entire volume since so much depends on where they work. Generally speaking, officers or receptionists on duty at buildings' entrances control employee and visitor access; managers' secretaries (other than the security manager's) also act as receptionists, but they are not security department members. Patrol officers make rounds to prevent security or safety incidents from happening and detect those that have occurred. If assigned to shipping/receiving docks, their job is to prevent thefts and minimize mistakes that can lead to losses. Those on duty in security control rooms monitor security and life safety systems.

To illustrate briefly how the workplace can influence the duties of other personnel, compare the work of security officers in retailing, hotels, and hospitals. When retail stores are open, their patrols focus on detecting shoplifters. In hotels they try to do more than prevent and detect incidents; they also provide assistance to and protection for guests. Hospital security officers help control access, but they often assist emergency room or floor personnel with unruly patients or visitors.

It can safely be said that the duties and responsibilities of security personnel at all levels flow downward. Senior executives set policy; directors or managers implement. However, all must understand that to assign duties and responsibilities but deny the authority needed to execute equals failure. Authority may be limited, but it must be granted. Certainly there can be no integrated program if the security manager lacks the authority to ask questions about operations and suggest ways to prevent problems, or if parking lot officers have no authority to tow illegally parked vehicles, or if receptionists have no authority to deny access to employees without their identification badges.

DEPARTMENTAL OBJECTIVES

Increasingly, businesses and institutions are adopting management-by-objective (MBO) programs to help measure job performance, among other things. Senior management sets objectives for department heads to meet; the latter set those for their departments. Setting departmental objectives that cannot be met is unrealistic and unwise.

Managers know what resources are available to them. Based on budget approval, they also know if those resources will be increased, decreased, or remain constant. Therefore, in setting departmental objectives there may be two simultaneous approaches: one somewhat specific, the other more general. For instance, improving performance to reduce the number of incidents reported and losses incurred is rather specific; finding ways to further improve the protection program is more general. Both are proper objectives.

Thus a department's more specific objectives might be to install new access controls and alarm systems, audit twenty-five percent of all facilities in the next fiscal year, and reduce the number of security incidents by fifteen percent. Generic goals might include protecting and conserving assets, minimizing the amount of loss in cases where loss is inevitable, and involving more line managers and supervisors in the security program. Before setting specific objectives and priorities, prudent managers will analyze what is needed to ensure their accomplishment in light of available resources. Although generic objectives usually involve only minimal resources, they still need to be analyzed to make certain of access to what limited resources may be necessary.

Even though specific objectives will vary from one organization to another and possibly from year to year, department heads must set the specific and general objectives that will determine the program's course. Without goals it is difficult to measure accomplishments, and their absence is often reflected in lackluster performance. Thus where objectives are concerned, two things should be kept in mind: they are both a measuring tool and a stimulus for program accomplishment.

CENTRALIZED VERSUS DECENTRALIZED ORGANIZATIONS

There are two basic business models, found particularly among larger organizations: centralized and decentralized. Although most businesses were centralized originally, some have switched. Some that had switched have reverted to the original. Still others have tried to combine the two. Regardless, the model used may affect both the security organization and its program.

In a centralized organization everything is controlled by the corporate headquarters staff. Security managers at various facilities report directly to the corporate security director and indirectly to the person in charge of the facility. An organizational chart would show a solid line connecting them to the corporate security director and a dotted line connecting them to the facility manager. If the organization is decentralized, local managers are more autonomous. An organizational chart would show a solid line from the security manager to the facility manager and a dotted line to corporate headquarters. Organizations that have combined the two models give local managers a good deal of autonomy, but at the same time certain specific functions continue to report directly to corporate headquarters.

As a rule the duties and responsibilities of corporate level security department heads, as discussed earlier, apply in both situations. However, directors need to understand that program implementation may be more difficult and effectiveness may suffer in decentralized organizations, largely due to their personalities and those of individual location managers and to the latter's attitude toward corporate headquarters.

As an example, one plant manager for a decentralized company forbade his security manager to have any contact with the corporate security director without first getting his approval. He did this despite knowing that the director had executive support. He also resented the director's plant audit in response to the manufacturing vice president's specific request. When the security manager needed the corporate security director's help, he called from off-site, knowing the plant manager would not approve the call. Implementing corporate policies was difficult; the plant's program was ineffective.

Later a new plant manager, who knew and worked well with the director, was appointed and wanted the security manager to report more directly to the security director. The plant manager also asked if the security manager could attend corporate security staff meetings and asked for the director's comments when preparing the manager's annual performance review. Policies were implemented with marked improvement in the program's effectiveness.

From senior management's viewpoint decentralization serves a purpose. Giving location managers a degree of autonomy, often with profit and loss responsibility, may encourage them to be more cost and quality conscious and thus be better managers. However, from security's perspective this autonomy can be harmful even if location and corporate security managers get along with and respect each other.

To illustrate, suppose a site security manager sees both a problem and a solution, but the location manager disagrees even though inaction may be costly. It is highly unlikely that security managers, dependent on location managers for performance reviews and salary increases, will pursue the matter any further with their superiors, and rarely will they risk their jobs by appealing to the corporate director. By the same token if location managers, lacking security expertise, make questionable demands on security managers, the latter once again have no recourse.

For the most effective loss prevention programs, decentralized businesses are better off centralizing authority and responsibility for security administration in their corporate security directors, just as many do with internal audit management. Only in this way can the security concerns of all locations be objectively assessed and acted upon to provide the best protection for the employer's total operation.

SUMMARY

One of the first things to be decided before considering a security department's management and operations, even when the need for a formal department is unquestioned, is its size in order to minimize the risk of over- or understaffing, since both can be costly, albeit in different ways. This applies to support personnel as well as security officers. Next, what is the best type of organization? The options, each with its pros and cons, are a proprietary, contract, or combined staff. If any contract personnel are to be used, what are the criteria for an agency's selection?

Regardless of a department's composition, employment standards and job descriptions must be developed. While the former are critical in recruiting and selecting the best available people, it is also important that they be realistic in relation to the nature of the work. With job performance a key factor in evaluating candidates for salary increases and possible promotions, there must also be something against which a person's performance can be measured. That yardstick is a good job description.

Prudent directors or managers, cost conscious and knowing that security's role is often misunderstood even in a friendly environment, avoid bureaucracies and excessive support staffs. Knowing also that promotions within security departments often come very slowly if at all, they will try to give some recognition to meritorious employees. They will not discourage or stand in the way of those who look for opportunities to better themselves, whether within or without the employer's organization.

Just as departmental duties and responsibilities vary from organization to organization, they do not necessarily remain constant within an organization; they may expand or contract. Regardless, personnel must be given that program's purpose.

In many ways departmental objectives, both specific and generic, are to the unit what job descriptions are to individuals; they are a tool against which performance can be measured. However, it is unwise to set objectives that, as a practical matter, cannot be met because the resources needed to accomplish them are unavailable, thus suggesting poor management skills on the department head's part.

Both centralized and decentralized organizations exist. The latter can be troublesome insofar as security program implementation and effectiveness are concerned, and one can only try to make the best of it. Doing so requires diplomacy, whether in trying to convince executives that the employer will be best served by centralizing security, or in maintaining good relationships with location managers.

REVIEW QUESTIONS

1. Does a need for security necessarily mean that there is also a need for an established security organization? If not, what does it mean?

2. What is the most practical way of determining a security department's size?

3. In making this determination, should the department be large enough to be able to handle all emergencies or contingencies without a need for overtime?

4. If contract personnel are to be used, what factors should be considered before selecting a particular agency?
5. Who should have primary responsibility for developing employment standards and job descriptions?
6. What are the principal factors to be considered with regard to their development?
7. Who really determines the duties and responsibilities of a security department?
8. Distinguish between responsibility and authority.
9. What are the two categories of objectives? Give an example of each.
10. What is the difference between a centralized and a decentralized organization?

NOTES

[1] Sa'di, *Gulistan* (1258), 8.36, trans. James Ross.

[2] Charles A. Sennewald, *Effective Security Management,* 2d ed. (Stoneham, MA: Butterworth Publishers, 1985), p. 59.

APPENDIX 2A
Sample Contract for Security Services

THIS AGREEMENT NO. _____ dated this _____ day of _____, 19____, by and between _____, a Corporation with its principal office at _____ (hereinafter referred to as Vendor), and _____, a Corporation located at _____ (hereinafter referred to as ABC. WHEREAS VENDOR is in the business of providing guard services for industrial concerns and desires to supply such services to ABC; and WHEREAS ABC desires to utilize such services under the terms and conditions set forth herein;

NOW, THEREFORE, in consideration of the mutual covenants specified herein, the parties hereto agree as follows:

ARTICLE I: AGREEMENT TERM

The term of this Agreement will be Twelve (12) months beginning on the date first written above and continuing thereafter in full force and effect unless and until either party gives the other ninety (90) days prior written notice of termination. Upon termination both parties agree to continue honoring their respective obligations hereunder for the ninety (90) day notice period or such shorter period of time as may be mutually agreed upon.

In no event will ABC's liability for payment hereunder extend beyond the number of guard hours actually provided by Vendor under the terms of this Agreement.

ARTICLE II: EMPLOYMENT

A. Vendor shall employ all persons necessary to perform its obligations hereunder according to the terms of this Agreement and ABC's requirements, which may be modified by ABC at any time, and Vendor will be solely and exclusively responsible for all acts or omission by its employees.

B. Vendor shall not discriminate against any applicant for employment or employee on the basis of race, creed, sex, color, country of national origin, or age, in violation of any federal or state laws or local ordinances.

C. No former ABC employees shall be assigned to ABC without ABC's prior written consent.

D. Guards will be solely the employees of Vendor and not ABC, and Vendor shall pay all of their salaries and related expenses, including but not necessarily limited to all taxes and employees' contributions.

E. Vendor agrees that all services provided by it and through its employees under the terms of this Agreement will be performed by qualified, careful, efficient personnel in strict conformity with the best practices and according to standards that ABC may from time to time prescribe. Vendor also agrees that it will remove from service any employee(s) if asked to do so by ABC, with or without cause.

F. All personnel employed by Vendor will be covered by a fidelity bond, the amount and terms and conditions of which are acceptable to ABC, and a copy of said bond shall be provided to ABC prior to the effective date of this Agreement.

G. ABC agrees that it will not make an offer of employment to any employee(s) of Vendor without having first obtained written approval to do so.

ARTICLE III: GUARD QUALIFICATIONS

A. All guards assigned to ABC will meet the minimum standards set forth below, the only exception(s) being guards on temporary assignment. For the purpose of this Vendor, any assignment of less than one week's duration will be considered temporary. ABC reserves the right through its authorized agent(s) to waive any requirements set forth herein, but only in writing and in individual cases. In no event is any waiver in any particular case to be construed as revising that standard as it applies to other guards.

B. Before assigning any of its personnel to ABC, Vendor will do the following with respect to each such employee:

1. Conduct as complete a background investigation of that person as is legally permissible, complying with all laws relating to the making of investigative reports and the disclosure of their contents.

2. Verify that the person is a high school graduate or has the equivalent of a high school education.

3. Verify that the person has no record of criminal convictions, minor traffic violations excepted.

4. Determine that the person has not had any credit difficulties within the past three (3) years.

5. Certify the following for each employee:

   a. That the person is in good mental health, and has no physical defects or abnormalities that would interfere with complete performance of all guard duties.

     b. That the person has binocular vision correctable to 20/20, is able to discriminate standard colors, and has normal hearing without the use of hearing aids.

     c. That the person's weight is in proportion to his or her height.

     d. That the person is capable of performing duties that may require moderate to arduous physical exertion including, but not necessarily limited to, standing or walking for an entire tour of duty, climbing stairs and ladders, lifting and carrying objects weighing up to fifty (50) pounds, running, and acts of physical self-defense.

  6. Provide ABC with a copy of the medical certification for each person as evidence of the fact that that person meets the prescribed minimum physical standards.

  7. Certify to ABC in writing that a thorough background investigation of that person has been completed, and that the qualifications set forth herein have been complied with.

C. Vendor will maintain the employment applications, or copies thereof, of all of its personnel assigned to ABC under the terms of this Agreement. They will be maintained in Vendor's office located at _____ and made available for review by ABC upon request for a period of three (3) years following the last appearance of that person at ABC whether permanent or temporary.

D. Vendor also will maintain at that office, or at some other location acceptable to ABC, records of all training and all disciplinary action provided or taken by it with respect to each of its employees assigned to ABC in the performance of this Agreement, and they will be made available for ABC's review upon request.

E. ABC reserves the right to review the employment application and/or resume, and to interview every person that Vendor proposes to assign to it. The final decision regarding an individual's acceptability for assignment to ABC will rest with ABC. Vendor understands that if the parties hereto agree to the assignment of supervisory personnel to ABC, those proposed for such assignment shall have had not less than three (3) years of increasingly responsible duties as guards.

F. Notwithstanding any of the foregoing, nothing in this Article or this Agreement is to be construed to imply employment of any guards by ABC, and guards shall be solely the responsibility of Vendor.

ARTICLE IV: GUARD ASSIGNMENTS

A. Hours and Posts to be covered are as per Exhibit "B," which is attached hereto and made a part hereof. Vendor agrees that no guards assigned by it to ABC will be permitted to work in excess of twelve (12) hours in any given twenty-four (24) hour period, or more than sixty (60) hours in any given week, and each guard will be off duty not less than twenty-four (24) consecutive hours in each work week.
For the purpose of this Agreement, the work week will begin at 12:01 A.M., Wednesday, and end at 12 midnight the following Tuesday. The provisions of this paragraph relative to time off may be waived only by ABC's authorized representative, and in writing.

B. A schedule of guard assignments in conformity with ABC's requirements will be submitted to ABC not less than seven (7) days before its implementation.

C. Inasmuch as certain guards assigned to ABC may have to get a United States Government Security Clearance, Vendor agrees that it will assign only personnel eligible for such clearances, and in the event that any guard assigned by it to ABC is denied clearance, that guard will be replaced immediately by one who can be cleared at no cost to ABC.

D. Guards assigned to ABC will remain at ABC for a period of one (1) year or the remaining term of this Agreement, whichever first occurs, unless (1) the guard's employment is terminated, (2) ABC agrees to the guard's prior transfer, (3) the guard is promoted by Vendor and no such position exists at ABC, or (4) the guard requests transfer.

E. In no event will Vendor assign to any ABC facility a guard who has been removed for cause or discharged from another facility.

F. A guard assigned to one ABC facility will not be transferred to another without ABC's prior written approval. If a guard's transfer is approved, all training requirements hereinafter pre-scribed shall apply to the transferred guard as if that guard had not been assigned previously to an ABC facility.

G. If it becomes necessary at any time for Vendor to provide guards for special duty it will be compensated for those special duty hours at the unit rates hereinafter set forth.

H. In an emergency Vendor may be required to provide up to two times the number of guards normally assigned to ABC under the terms of this Agreement. In all such cases the unit rate herein-after agreed upon will prevail, but ABC will reimburse Vendor for the actual cost of expenses incurred in providing such ser-vices that are in excess of those incurred in regularly furnish-ing guards to ABC under the terms of this Agreement, including premium wages, additional administration, and overhead, provided, however, that the total payment to Vendor will not exceed 150% of the unit rates times the number of emergency guard hours actually worked.

ARTICLE V: UNIFORMS AND EQUIPMENT

A. Vendor will provide each of its guards with all uniforms, equipment, including flashlights, and related materials as specified by ABC necessary for the performance of their duties. ABC will furnish all fire-fighting equipment.

B. THE USE OR CARRYING OF WEAPONS, FIREARMS INCLUDED, ON ABC PREMISES IS PROHIBITED. Weapons may not be stored on ABC premises unless first approved in writing by ABC's Vice President and General Counsel, or his or her designee, which approval will state specifically the terms and conditions under which such storage will be allowed by Vendor's employees.

C. At all times while on duty each guard will wear or otherwise openly display identification badges provided by ABC.

D. Immediately upon termination of any guard assigned to ABC, regardless of reason, Vendor shall immediately notify ABC in writing of the termination and reasons therefor, and it also will immediately recover and return to ABC the identification originally issued to that guard. If for any reason the ABC-issued identification is not available, Vendor will submit in writing to ABC its explanation as to why the identification cannot be returned, and the efforts made by it for recovery.

ARTICLE VI: TRAINING AND SUPERVISION

A. In addition to whatever general training Vendor provides to all of its guards, it also will provide, prior to assignment to ABC, a minimum of eight (8) hours of training covering the subjects set forth below unless such requirement is waived in writing by ABC, or temporary guards as previously defined herein are used in unusual circumstances.

B. The subjects to be covered in training will include, but not necessarily be limited to, the following:

1. Legal restrictions on arrests, searches, and seizures.

2. Detection, reporting, and control of fires; the use of portable fire-fighting equipment; the control of sprinkler systems; and the use of emergency breathing apparatus.

3. Appearance, attitude, and conduct as may be set forth in ABC's Guard Manual or otherwise prescribed by ABC's authorized representative(s).

4. General application of patrol routines (winds, rounds), activities, and reports.

5. Human, public, and employee relations.

6. Controlling entry to and exit from the premises.

7. Controlling the movement of ABC assets, and other property for whose protection ABC may be responsible, to, from, and between or among ABC facilities or premises.

8. Riot, strike, and emergency procedures.

9. Other topics selected from among those listed in ABC's Guard Manual or prescribed by ABC's authorized representatives.

C. Upon first reporting for duty at ABC each newly assigned guard will be given a minimum of sixteen (16) hours of "on-the-job" training, and Vendor will not charge ABC for the services of any guard until all training required under the terms of this Agreement, including on-the-job training, has been completed to ABC's satisfaction.

D. Vendor also will give each guard assigned to ABC a minimum of eight (8) hours of refresher or in-service training once every six (6) months.

E. Vendor will provide at least twice weekly, at random times to cover all shifts on a regular basis, unannounced inspections of each post to which its guards are assigned by one of its nonresident supervisors.

F. Vendor agrees to remove and replace any guard from assignment at ABC (a) if such employee is not properly performing his or her duties, or (b) upon request of ABC.

G. Vendor agrees that it will not knowingly hire or assign to any ABC facility any person who is or has been assigned, whether on a temporary or a permanent basis, to any entity that is a business competitor of ABC.

ARTICLE VII: GUARD RESPONSIBILITIES

A. Unless otherwise specifically instructed in writing by ABC's authorized representative, guards will be responsible for all aspects of protection, including, but not necessarily limited to, the following: monitoring shipping and receiving dock activities; guarding the premises against fire, burglary, theft, breaking and entering, pilferage, acts of vandalism, damage to or the destruction of property; preventing malicious injury to persons; and allowing only authorized persons to enter the premises. They will make regular tours of the property, report immediately all violations of fire and safety regulations, and when instructed to do so they will control traffic on and in ABC-owned roadways and parking areas. Guards also will carry out such special written instructions as may from time to time be issued to them by ABC's authorized representative(s).

B. Upon completing a tour of duty each guard will submit a written report to ABC's designated representative covering all activities, including details of all unusual or hazardous conditions encountered during such tour. Any guard who discovers an emergency condition will report it immediately, in person, by telephone, or by alarm, whichever is most appropriate, and will confirm both the discovery and action taken in response thereto in the written report submitted at the conclusion of his or her tour of duty.

C. Guards are prohibited from making arrests, detaining persons, or swearing out complaints on behalf of ABC without the express written consent of ABC's Vice President and General Counsel or his or her designee. In the event that a guard witnesses a crime being committed in his or her presence, on ABC premises or in one of its facilities, it will be reported immediately to either the ABC Site Security Manager/Representative, Supervisor, or Group Leader, if one is then on duty, and if not, to the guard's Contractor supervisor, and if the ABC representative or guard's supervisor, as the case may be, is of the opinion that immediate action is required, the ABC representative or guard's supervisor may notify the police directly with notification immediately thereafter to both the ABC Site Security Manager/Representative and ABC's Vice President and General Counsel or his or her designee.

ARTICLE VIII: LIABILITY/INDEMNIFICATION

A. Vendor will indemnify and hold ABC, its directors, agents, employees, and representatives, harmless against all loss and liability resulting from personal injury or death to its own employees or others, property damage, assault, false arrest and false imprisonment, slander, defamation of character, negligence, or any other cause arising out of or in connection with the services to be provided hereunder irrespective of whether performed on ABC's premises or elsewhere.

B. In the event a claim is made against ABC, its directors, agents, employees, or representatives, for which Vendor has undertaken to indemnify ABC, ABC or its legal representative will promptly notify Vendor in writing of such claim or lawsuit arising out of or in connection with the services provided under the terms of this Agreement, will forward to Vendor all related documents, and Vendor then will defend the case at its own expense. However, ABC reserves the right to be represented by counsel of its own choice, and at its own expense, at any proceeding or settlement discussions related thereto.

C. Vendor will procure and maintain a minimum of the following insurance:

1. Workmen's Compensation Insurance as prescribed by the laws of the Commonwealth of Massachusetts and Employer's Liability Insurance with a limit of $100,000.00.

2. Comprehensive Automobile Liability Insurance, including Automobile Non-Ownership Liability, with limits of $1,000,000.00 for bodily injury or death of each person; $1,000,000.00 for bodily injury or death for each occurrence; and $1,000,000.00 for property damage in each occurrence.

3. Comprehensive General Liability Insurance, including contractual liability, broad form property damage, and personal injury liability, with a combined $2,000,000.00 bodily injury and property damage limit in each occurrence.

4. Employee Dishonesty Insurance with a limit of $1,000,000.00 per loss.

D. Within two working days of this Agreement's execution Vendor will furnish ABC a Certificate of Insurance as evidence that the required coverage is in effect, and that ABC has been named as an additional insured under both the Comprehensive General Liability and Automobile Insurance policies.

E. Each of the insurance policies referred to above will include a provision that it may not be canceled without thirty (30) days' prior written notice to ABC of such cancellation.

F. Nothing in this Article will be deemed to limit Vendor's responsibility to the amounts stated above, or under any other provisions of this Agreement.

ARTICLE IX: PAYMENT

A. The services to be performed hereunder will be billable on an hourly basis at the rates shown on Exhibit A, attached hereto and made a part hereof (billable rate). All of the rates set forth in Exhibit A, with the sole exception described in paragraph B of this Article, will be in full force and effect for the duration of this Agreement, and they will include all of Vendor's profit, overhead, guard and supervisory salaries, administrative expenses, and all other costs related to the performance of this Agreement. The billable rate will apply to all guard services provided irrespective of the date or time of day when such services are to be performed. ABC will not be subject to any overtime or premium billings for additional hours or holiday rates except as provided for in paragraph B, below.

B. In the event that ABC, with less than twenty-four (24) hours' prior notice to Vendor requests additional hours of unscheduled service, Vendor will make every reasonable effort to provide such service to ABC without any charge for overtime. However, if the additional hours of service can be provided only with overtime, Vendor will advise ABC of that fact, the overtime rate that it will have to charge, and the number of hours to which it will apply.

C. Not until authorization has been received from ABC's Site Purchasing Manager, or his or her designee, will Vendor provide such additional hours of service, and the additional cost of the overtime will be paid by ABC within thirty (30) days from the receipt of a separate invoice referencing an ABC Purchase Order for the stated amount.

D. Vendor will maintain complete, clear, and accurate records of all guard assignments, hours of work performed by each, and actual direct labor hourly rates incurred in the performance of this Agreement. ABC reserves the right to inspect and audit, during regular business hours, Vendor's business records as they relate to the services rendered under this Agreement. Vendor agrees to make such records available either on site at the ABC facility where the guards are assigned, or in one (1) central location within a thirty-five (35) mile radius of the ABC location where the services are being performed, and to retain all such records for a period of not less than three (3) years from the date of completion of this Agreement.

E. Vendor will submit for payment one (1) invoice supported by all documentation required by ABC for the verification of the billing on a weekly basis for the preceding month, except that any overtime authorized by ABC, as set forth in this Article, will be invoiced separately against an ABC authorized Purchase Order.

F. If ABC disputes the billing, in whole or in part, it will process promptly for payment the undisputed portion thereof, and it will confer with Vendor relative to the disputed portion. ABC is not obligated to make any payment until the billing and documentation therefor are submitted in a form acceptable to it.

G. Within thirty (30) days following the receipt of a valid invoice and its supporting documentation ABC will remit payment.

H. The rates set forth in this Agreement are based on Vendor providing services to ABC's Corporate facility. However, if during the course of this Agreement ABC adds other locations under the same terms and conditions, Vendor then agrees to consider renegotiating downward the billings set forth in Exhibit A.

I. Vendor will be responsible for all sales, use, or other taxes, if any, applicable to the work.

J. If, in ABC's opinion, guard rates should be reduced to conform to any reductions in minimum wages, Vendor agrees to renegotiate its billing rates.

K. Vendor warrants that the billable rate charged ABC hereunder is as low as the Vendor charges any client purchasing such services in the same or greater quantity under similar terms and conditions, and in the event that Vendor grants any other client a lower rate for the same quantity of services under similar terms and conditions during the term hereof, then ABC's price shall be adjusted for the balance of the term to reflect the lower rate.

ARTICLE X: DEFAULT

A. If Vendor fails to perform any of the services called for by this Agreement, or if any proceeding is filed by or against it in bankruptcy or insolvency, or an assignment is made by it for the benefit of its creditors, or if there is a transfer of proprietary interest, and such condition or conditions are not remedied to ABC's reasonable satisfaction within fourteen (14) calendar days following written notice thereof given by ABC, ABC may without any liability immediately terminate all or any part of this Agreement by written or telegraphic notice to Vendor and seek similar services elsewhere.

B. If, during the term of this Agreement, Vendor for any reason is unable or unwilling to furnish ABC the number of guards required for the protection of the site or sites covered thereby, ABC may contract with another guard service of its choice, at the then prevailing rate, for such additional or replacement services as it may require.

C. In such an event Vendor will be responsible for all damages and expenses incurred by ABC prior to the replacement of such services, as well as for all additional expenses incurred by ABC above and beyond the rates set forth in this Agreement for the protection of the site or sites covered thereby.

D. ABC agrees to make every reasonable effort to pay all properly submitted and documented Contractor's invoices within thirty (30) days of their receipt. In the event that Vendor has not been paid within that time, provided Vendor has submitted correct and documented invoices and has otherwise complied with its obligations hereunder, it then may issue a written demand for payment to ABC, and if within fifteen (15) days of the receipt by ABC of such a demand Vendor still has not received payment, it then may notify ABC in writing of its intention to terminate this Agreement forty-five (45) days following ABC's receipt of such notice.

ARTICLE XI: CONFIDENTIALITY

A. All information obtained by Vendor from ABC in connection with
    this Agreement, its performance, or for any other reason, is
    received by Vendor in confidence, remains the property of ABC,
    and will be used by Vendor only to the extent necessary for the
    performance of this Agreement and in accordance with ABC's Pro-
    prietary Rights and Non-Disclosure Agreement, a copy of which
    Vendor has executed and which is attached hereto as Exhibit C.

B. All such ABC information and property will be returned to it
    upon the expiration, termination, or cancellation of this Agree-
    ment, or at any other time that ABC requests its return.

C. Vendor agrees that it will not disclose to others, advertise, or
    publish the fact that it is performing or has performed any ser-
    vice or work for ABC, whether under the terms of this Agreement
    or otherwise, unless it is expressly authorized to do so in
    writing by ABC. It also agrees that all information, data,
    results, analyses, and reports received, collected, developed,
    prepared or written by it, its employees, representatives, or
    agents in the performance of this Agreement will be maintained
    in confidence without restriction as to time, that disclosure
    will be made only to ABC, and that no such information or mate-
    rial will be used by it for any purpose other than the comple-
    tion of its obligations to ABC.

D. Vendor agrees that the provisions of this Article XI will sur-
    vive the expiration, termination, or cancellation of this Agree-
    ment.

ARTICLE XII: ABC-FURNISHED DOCUMENTATION

A. ABC will prepare written instructions, including a Guard Manual
    where deemed appropriate, setting forth specifically the days
    and hours of the week when guards are to be on duty, the number
    of guards required and the duties that they are to perform, and
    the location of guard rooms, and it will furnish guard logs. All
    materials provided by ABC, including but not necessarily limited
    to, Guard Manuals, post orders, copies of ABC's Safety/Security
    Policies and Procedures, and of ABC's telephone directory, will
    not be reproduced by Vendor or distributed to any of its person-
    nel other than those guards working on site at the facility cov-
    ered by the terms of this Agreement, and all such materials must
    be returned to ABC immediately upon the completion of this
    Agreement, its prior termination, or at any other time that ABC
    requests their return.

B. ABC may modify or revise these materials at any time upon
    twenty-four (24) hours' prior notification.

C. All guards will be required to sign in and out in the guard log
    provided by ABC.

D. If requested by ABC, Vendor agrees to assist with the preparation of written materials for guards, such as post orders, manuals, etc., at no additional charge to ABC.

ARTICLE XIII: GENERAL PROVISIONS

A. This Agreement and any amendments hereto will be governed by the laws of the ABC location where the services are provided. If any provision contravenes such law it will be deemed to have been deleted, but no such deletion will in any way affect any of the other portions of this Agreement.

B. This Agreement, and all exhibits referenced herein, or attached hereto and made a part hereof, constitute the entire understanding between Vendor and ABC and supersede all prior oral or written communications, agreements, representations, statements, negotiations, and undertakings relating to the subject matter hereof.

C. No representation, promise, waiver, modification, or amendment will be binding on either party unless made in writing and signed by an authorized representative of each.

D. ABC's failure to insist upon, or enforce in any instance, strict performance by Vendor of any part of this Agreement, or to exercise any of the rights herein conferred upon or reserved by it, will not be construed as a waiver or relinquishment by ABC to any extent of its right to assert or rely upon such terms or rights on any future occasion.

E. All notices required to be given by either party under the terms of this Agreement must be sent by Registered or Certified Mail, Return Receipt Requested, and addressed to:

> ABC
> Street Address
> Anytown, USA
> ATTN: Corporate Purchasing Director

VENDOR:

> _____
> _____
> _____
>
> ATTN: _____

F. Neither this Agreement nor any interest hereunder may be assigned, in whole or in part, by either party without the prior written consent of the other, and any such attempted assignment will be null and void.

G. Vendor agrees that without having first obtained ABC's written consent it will neither disclose to any person or persons outside of its employ, nor use for any purpose other than the performance of this Agreement, any information pertaining to ABC or ABC's affairs, including the contents of this Agreement. Furthermore, without having first obtained ABC's written consent, Vendor will not in any way or to anyone disclose, advertise, or publish the fact that it has furnished or contracted to furnish any services to ABC.

IN WITNESS WHEREOF the parties hereto have caused this Agreement to be executed in duplicate by their duly authorized representatives as of the day and year first written above.

ACCEPTED: ACCEPTED:

_____   _____ABC_____

BY: _____   BY: _____

TITLE: _____   TITLE: _____

EXHIBIT A

The cost to ABC for security services is as follows:

$_____.____ per hour for unarmed security officers and lead guard.

In the event that ABC, with less than twenty-four hours' (24) prior notice to Vendor, requests additional hours or unscheduled service, Vendor will make every reasonable effort to provide such service to ABC without any charge for overtime. However, if the additional hours of service can be provided only with overtime, Vendor will advise ABC of that fact, and the number of hours to which it will apply. The overtime rate will be charged at $_____.____ an hour.

Chapter 3

SECURITY DEPARTMENT MANAGEMENT AND OPERATIONS

In Chapter 2 we discussed the fundamentals involved in organizing security departments. However, once senior management decides to have such an organization, that decision is but a first step. Whether security managers are first establishing a department or assuming the leadership of an existing one, they have to be able to manage both the department and its operations and deal with a variety of issues that will be considered in this chapter.

THE BUDGET PROCESS

Regardless of whether a department is in formation or already in existence, personnel cannot be hired, trained, uniformed, or enabled to function unless there is money with which to pay people and support the department's activities. This means there has to be a budget, defined in *Webster's New World Dictionary* as "a plan or schedule adjusting expenses during a certain period to the estimated or fixed income for that period," or as "the cost or estimated cost of living, operating, etc." For managers a budget is a plan based on estimated costs for a fiscal year; it is not a precise instrument. Its purpose is to project expenses so funds can be allocated and to serve as a management tool for the control of those expenses on a period, quarterly, and annual basis. Simply put it is a financial plan for the department's operations.

Budget Preparation

Department heads prepare budgets, but this does not mean that they must do the job unaided. Their employers' finance departments provide both the format to be used and guidance on other financial factors that enter into budget preparation. Wise and experienced managers will also solicit input from subordinates who can contribute to the process. Furthermore, based on their experience with their employers, managers know about when they will receive "budget packages" from finance, and they will begin gathering data and working on budgets in advance of that date to minimize the risk of overlooking something under the pressure of submittal deadlines.

Formats are based on employers' fiscal years. While fiscal years may or may not coincide with calendar years, they nevertheless are divided into twelve periods (some of four weeks, others of five) and four quarters. The finance department usually sets the percentage to be added to labor costs to cover fringe benefits, percentages for pay increases based on performance, methods for calculating depreciation, and charges per period for occupancy (in employer-owned buildings the cost for electricity, heat, and general maintenance based on the amount of space occupied by each department).

Subordinates should be asked for data that they can best provide. For example, since supervisors normally write subordinates' performance reviews and initiate wage increases, they are best positioned to know what percent increase they will recommend for each subordinate. If employers offer tuition reimbursement programs to employees, supervisors are likely to know which of their subordinates are attending school. Thus they know from whom to get reimbursement data. They know what replacements may be needed for uniforms or equipment. If they have business travel or plan on attending any professional meetings, they can provide information on the projected costs. Secretaries can anticipate office supply needs so funds therefore can be included in the budget.

To all of the foregoing managers add their own projections and enter complete data on budget sheets. Despite the lack of precision in budgets, figures should be realistic. In many respects preparation of the personnel segments are relatively easy. Paid holidays are known; therefore, holiday pay figures should be reasonably accurate. The same is true for projected increases. In contrast, the greater challenge lies in preparing the operational portion of the budget. For example, one cannot realistically anticipate telephone charges or equipment repairs; travel expenses are an educated guess at best. Directors for multisite organizations—whether multinational or not—should also allow for unplanned travel to respond to off-site emergencies.

Aside from periods and quarters, budget formats also show line items for which appropriate entries are made (Appendix 3A). When the budget preparation process has been completed, the totals for each period, each quarter, and the year, as well as for each line item, must agree. Care has to be taken to ensure that all entries reflect the differences between four- and five-week periods so funds can be allocated accordingly. If this factor is ignored, period playbacks may show both over- and underruns and thus indicate a management deficiency.

Budget Approval

Review processes differ. In some organizations department heads' superiors review budgets before they go to finance; in others they go directly to finance. Rarely are first submissions approved. Sometimes managers are asked to justify certain entries; sometimes line items are approved as submitted. Occasionally, finance may unilaterally lower amounts; however, it will not unilaterally increase them.

Following this review, budgets may then have to be submitted to the employer's executive or finance committee, or possibly both, for final approval. Only after all necessary approvals are obtained do department heads receive copies of the next fiscal year's budget. It constitutes their financial plan, and it will greatly influence departmental operations.

Budget Playback

Not uncommonly, finance provides managers with data showing funds budgeted for each line item per period, the amount actually spent, and if it was over or under budget. After the new fiscal year's first period, the data are extended to show totals spent and over- and underspending from the inception of the fiscal year through the period or quarter covered by the latest playback (Appendix 3B).

Although budgets are imprecise, they are a financial plan for a manager's use, and like any plan, an effort must be made to conform. However, this cannot be done unless department managers expend the time and effort needed to study budget playbacks upon receipt, and question any marked deviations from the approved budget itself. Prudent managers also see budget playbacks as an opportunity to avoid surprises in terms of monies projected as against monies spent. They should be prepared to justify significant variations. To merely look at each period's playback and file it serves no real purpose.

For instance, if in a given period $775 was budgeted for telephone use and $800 was spent, the variation is not unreasonable, but if $850 was spent, a conscientious manager will try to see if the overage was justified. Conversely, if a contract agency's bill for a period is considerably less than the amount budgeted, a manager needs to ask why. Is the lower figure due to a billing error or the agency's failure to fully staff the site?

On occasion some managers will review a playback and see that they are considerably under budget for one or more lines. Instead of comparing their original projections with expenses and looking for a logical explanation for the variances, they seek ways to spend the funds for other items. They do so out of fear that if they do not spend all of their allocated resources for this year, their budgets will be reduced accordingly for the next one. This attitude should be avoided. While there will be times when departments will close a fiscal year over budget, a mark of a good manager is the ability to close either within or under budget, and the playback is an invaluable tool for that purpose.

Capital Budgets

Suppose a need arises for a new access control, patrol tour, and alarm system. Instead of submitting a proposal limited to these items, a business-oriented, knowledgeable manager recommends a building management system that will both cover all of security's needs and result in energy savings for the employer. However, this will mean a major expense with a total installed cost in excess of $300,000.

For this a capital budget would be prepared. Capital budgets usually require more than an itemization of the expenses involved, and their approval cycle involves more than a superior and finance department personnel. Submitting managers must justify the proposed expense in terms of benefits and the time of payback. Parenthetically, the latter not only helps determine the reasonableness of the expenditure, but from a financial viewpoint it may also offer tax benefits.

As an example, a security director submitted just such a proposal. The benefits included minimal savings for the department but better staff utilization and energy savings. Inasmuch as the installer projected a three-year payback, and three to five years is considered acceptable, a capital budget was submitted. The approval cycle consisted of a review by the director's superior, the vice president for facilities and administration, the vice president and chief financial officer, the vice president and treasurer, and the executive vice president. In this case the capital budget was approved, the system was purchased, and payback occurred within nine months.

THE RECRUITING AND HIRING PROCESS

Whether a security director is organizing a new department or assuming the management of an existing one, some recruiting is almost inevitable. It can be avoided to a degree by using contract personnel, but even so managers most likely will have to hire at least some proprietary support personnel, if not a complete staff.

Although managers' advice will often be sought in terms of sources from which to recruit, normally human resources personnel do the actual recruiting and preliminary screening of applicants. Hourly paid staff can be recruited locally by advertising in newspapers, through current employees, or possibly by contacting universities or colleges with academic security programs, vocational high schools, or employment agencies.

Job posting, mentioned in Chapter 2 in connection with promotions, may also apply to security department openings before there can be outside recruiting. If so, since experience is not a factor for most hourly positions, viable candidates may come from that source. Some managers oppose such transfers, arguing that familiarity with their coworkers may hamper their effectiveness. Truthfully, the same can be said regarding all security personnel once they have been on the job for any time. Good supervision can minimize such risks.

If job posting exists, it should not be a problem. Where salaried positions are concerned, there are educational requirements and, for managers, the need for some security experience. While newspaper and professional journal advertising are used for these jobs, other means are campus recruiting and, depending on the position to be filled, outside executive recruiters (often referred to as headhunters).

Recruiting for any job can be expensive. It involves interview time, probably advertising, and for some positions even travel expense. Much depends on the jobs to be filled. Recruiting support personnel or security officers may mean advertising but no travel; hiring managers or supervisors may require some travel by recruiters, viable candidates for the job, or both. Because some expense is unavoidable, care should be exercised in selecting personnel. It is important to pick not only the best person for the job in terms of qualifications, but also one whose apparently compatible personality will decrease the risk of rapid turnover.

The human resources department recruits and initially screens candidates based on employment standards and job descriptions developed for any given position. To do less wastes time and money. Viable candidates are then referred to the security department for in-depth interviews. If the department is organized in such a way that the person who would be the applicant's immediate superior can be identified, he or she should do the first departmental interview. Otherwise, it should be done by the manager.

It is naive to assume that human resources did a thorough job and that therefore this interview is pro forma. Realistically, their initial interviews tend to consist more of telling applicants about the organization than of asking searching questions. Consequently, the security department representative must be the one who reviews applications and/or resumes in detail and gets satisfactory answers to otherwise unanswered questions. This includes explanations for unaccounted gaps in time, reasons for job changes, and information about other experience, whether security-related or not. There should never be any discussion of matters prohibited by law. This also is the time to explain more fully to applicants the nature of the jobs for which they are being considered. By the end of this interview, both applicants and interviewers should be satisfied with each other if an offer of employment is to be made.

Assume that as a result of the recruiting process there are several viable candidates. Are more interviews needed or can a decision now be made with regard to an offer? In most organizations protocol dictates a meeting with the department interviewer's superior before an offer can be made. For example, if the interviewer was a supervisor, the manager would interview before an offer was made. However, in other cases, depending on the position to be filled, there may be still more interviews. An applicant for a corporate security director's job with a multinational corporation was first interviewed by a human resources manager, then by the vice president for human resources, the vice president and general counsel (to whom he would report if hired), the vice president for administration, and the president and chief executive officer. Of course, this may not be true of all organizations, but even if it is not, the courtesy of at least asking superiors if they want to meet the most promising candidates should be extended to them.

Once recruiting has been completed, all applications have been examined, and all apparently qualified candidates have been interviewed, the person for whom the applicant will work decides whom to hire, subject to whatever other approvals may be needed. Human resources is then informed and makes the job offer. In many organizations written offers tell the person for whom they will work, their starting salary, and their starting date. The offer letter also asks for a written acceptance. It is not unusual for offers to say that a preemployment physical examination must be taken before starting work; if the examination is passed, the person reports for duty. We discussed the nature of and reasons for physical standards in Chapter 2.

TRAINING, SUPERVISION, AND DISCIPLINE

In many respects training, supervision, and discipline are interwoven. Effective training makes supervision easier and less time-consuming; effective supervision reduces the need for discipline, and the most cost-effective way to discipline personnel is through additional training, not punishment. Furthermore, effective training and supervision also reduce the risk of lawsuits arising from malfeasance or nonfeasance on the part of security personnel, or the risk of liability when there are allegations of such behavior.

Training

Recognition of the importance of and need for training is not new. The results of a study published in 1972 noted that "The majority of the private guard forces in the United States do not have any formal training program, or any specified curriculum."[1] In 1976 the *Report of the Task Force on Private Security* observed that "Training is a vital determinant of job performance. Yet, every major research project reviewed and every study conducted for this report point to a serious lack of personnel training at all levels of private security."[2] Fourteen years later *The Hallcrest Report II* stated, "For at least 20 years, lack of training has been a matter of great concern not only to people employed in private security but also to public law enforcement officials and to the clients of private security organizations."[3] It also reported that participants surveyed at a 1989 International Security Conference said they considered a lack of security training the foremost challenge facing private security.

Nevertheless, existing legal requirements for training of private security personnel are not uniform. Historically, in states where at least some training has been mandated the laws have tended to apply to contract rather than proprietary security officers. However, there are increasing signs of change in this respect. Some states now either have or are considering legislation that would mandate minimal training standards for all security personnel, which obviously means that security managers must familiarize themselves with any such laws in those states in which they have operations in order to ensure full compliance.

The subject of training also acquired new meaning in 1993 with the introduction of H.R. 1534 in the U.S. House of Representatives. Called "Private Security Officers Quality Assurance Act of 1993," it will, if enacted, "require States to ensure the quality of private security services, and the competence of private security officer personnel." It is based on the combined likelihood of people having more contact with private security officers than with public police and the absence of even minimum training standards.

As introduced, the act would apply to both proprietary and contract security officers, setting certain employment standards and requiring a minimum of eight hours of basic classroom instruction and four hours of on-the-job training for all unarmed personnel. Fifteen additional hours would be required for armed security officers. Certain subjects would have to be included for both groups; security officers would also have to take annual refresher courses.

The mandated topics for unarmed and armed officers, upon which they would be examined, are:

- ❏ Legal powers and limitations of private security officers
- ❏ Law of arrest, search, and seizure
- ❏ Use of force as related to security operations
- ❏ Safety and fire detection and reporting
- ❏ When and how to notify public authorities
- ❏ Techniques of observation, incident reporting, and preparation of incident reports

- ❏ Patrol fundamentals
- ❏ Deportment and ethics

Of course, nothing in the act would prevent covering other subjects, such as those that are peculiar to an employer's activities. For example, hotels and hospitals have much in common, but they also are different and clearly distinctive from manufacturing. Computer, automobile, and clothing manufacturers are different from each other, as are their security needs. Nor would the act prevent spending more time than mandated for classroom instruction.

Professional security managers would agree that all of their employees should learn about public and employee relations, how their work is to be performed, and the basics of investigation. First aid and cardiopulmonary resuscitation (CPR) training deserve consideration. Both armed officers, who should use their weapons only as a last resort, and unarmed personnel need training in the fundamentals of defensive tactics. Everyone should know the employer's history, the organization's nature, and its applicable policies and procedures.

Realistically, eight hours is not enough time to cover thoroughly all of the required material. The legal powers and limitations of private security officers and the laws of arrest, search, and seizure alone, based on federal and state constitutional provisions and court decisions, can be complex for the uninitiated and could easily consume four or more hours of instruction. For example, while the commonly referred to *Miranda* warning does not apply to private security personnel, the need for and value of giving persons in custody a modified version of it, depending on circumstances, might require at least an hour's instruction. Most assuredly, something of this sort would be helpful to security personnel in states where admissions of guilt made to private persons must be voluntary before the courts will admit them. As an example, in New York, for a statement obtained by security personnel to be admissible, it would have to be shown that it was made "freely, voluntarily, and without compulsion or inducement of any sort."[4]

Regardless of any federal or state-legislated requirements, employers will be better served if security managers, knowing their employers' needs, decide on other subjects to be taught and how much time is needed to properly train their personnel. Basic and refresher training should be based on departmental objectives, the type of employer organization, and how the program can best protect and conserve the employer's assets.

Instruction often is given by those most familiar with the environment in which personnel will work, presumably their managers. However, regardless of topics and time, for the best results subjects should be taught by persons with both the requisite knowledge and ability to hold students' attention. Not all instruction has to be given by the security staff. For instance, labor relations issues are best discussed by a human resources representative rather than someone from security.

Regardless of whether H.R. 1534 or state laws are enacted, reality challenges security managers' creativity in developing programs. Contract agencies may hire enough new employees at one time to justify classroom training. However, this usually is not the case with proprietary personnel unless new departments are being organized. Otherwise, classroom training for only one or two new persons can be expensive and ineffective. The same is true with respect to refresher training. Therefore, ways need to be found to provide meaningful structured basic and in-service training, regardless of the number of new hires at any given time.

Another challenge for today's security managers, and one that can be met only through proper training, is a redefinition of the role of security officers. In other words, what should the job of security officer really be? For far too long the stereotype of a security officer has been that of a relatively uneducated, possibly older person or retiree in a police-type uniform either making patrol rounds or sitting behind a desk checking parcels and identification badges.

Some ideas on this subject were discussed in Chapter 2 in connection with staffing and opportunities for promotion. However, with suitable training there is no reason why security personnel cannot be made more productive and their jobs more meaningful. At the same time, to further expand on what security officers should be, one cannot ignore the importance of employment standards, also covered in Chapter 2, and the need to recruit people of a caliber that will enable them to be trained to do more than what has been accepted for so long as their traditional role.

Based on the premise that security managers have been successful in staffing their organizations with qualified people, and remembering that security's role is to protect and conserve the employer's assets, security officers must be encouraged to be always alert for things that represent an actual or potential threat to the employer so corrective or preventive measures can be undertaken. They should not feel, or be made to feel, that they are restricted to pure security issues or that they will get into trouble for reporting on other matters of importance to the employer's well-being. To limit their observations or comments is inconsistent with the very purpose of a sound security program.

It is with this thought in mind that they first must be trained in terms of how to look and for what to look. This is particularly true for patrol personnel, but by no means is it limited to them. In many respects they really are, and should be, the employer's eyes and ears. However, in too many cases training for patrol personnel emphasizes the need to complete tours instead of the importance of careful observation. As a result, anxious to make certain that every station on the patrol tour is clocked, some patrol officers look but do not see; matters that should be brought to the security manager's attention are overlooked.

To illustrate, suppose a security officer on tour, in hurrying to ensure that he or she clocks every station, fails to notice a tear in a carpet, a leak from a drum containing a hazardous substance, or a confidential document lying next to a copying machine. This failure obviously will either prevent or delay corrective action, yet all three examples constitute potential problems for the employer. The first example may result in a fall, injury, and liability; the second example may constitute a violation of environmental law and lead to a possible citation and penalties; the third example may allow information to be compromised. An example of this principle's application to other security officers might be a situation where one assigned to a shipping dock fails to carefully monitor activity to ensure that only authorized personnel are in the area. This failure contributes to an environment that almost encourages thefts.

Of course, training in what to look for and how to look must be accompanied by training not only in how to evaluate conditions, but also in to whom their observations should be reported. The first of these can have a bearing on the second since the evaluation process helps determine priorities. Under certain conditions this may require more direct and immediate action on the part of security officers than the standard procedure of reporting to one's immediate supervisor, and through him or her to the security director or manager.

For instance, that all of the illustrations in the preceding paragraph warrant corrective action does not necessarily mean that all are of equal value in terms of setting priorities for that action. The risk of employee exposure to a hazardous substance would get the highest priority. In this case directly notifying a person in the employer's organization who can expedite containment and cleanup and informing the security supervisor of the action taken would be proper. This does not mean the other examples are less important or that they do not need attention. It simply means that there is not the same sense of urgency, and reporting them through departmental channels would be proper. The security manager would then make the necessary referrals to those department heads of whom corrective action would be required. In other words, security officers should be trained in how to determine the relative importance of what they see. That, in turn, will ensure proper and effective reporting.

As part of their training, they also should be encouraged to help coworkers and visitors, as long as they can do so without neglecting their primary duties. By extension this also benefits the employer. Some police departments have adopted the motto "to protect and to serve," and there is no valid reason why properly trained security personnel cannot and should not be seen in this same light.

One security director met this challenge by using a combination of films, textbooks, occasional lectures, computers, and examinations for both basic and refresher training. In this particular case all security personnel had computer access so that certain training materials and all examination questions were made available via computer. Although not in a formal classroom setting, this structured format proved to be relatively inexpensive and very effective in terms of lessons learned. The result was improved training and morale for the security officers and a better and more professional image in the eyes of other employees and visitors.

At one time or another all security departments are faced with the need to investigate either actual or alleged incidents. Some may be criminal in nature; others may involve policy violations or other administrative concerns. It is not all that unusual to find criminal investigations conducted by security departments in cases where the offense is relatively minor, the resources for their being handled internally exist, and the employer prefers to dispose of the matter administratively. Despite this, there are few departments with such heavy case loads as to justify employing full-time investigators. Under such circumstances it is often the department head or a supervisor who does the investigating.

In this respect experienced security managers are conscious of three things:

1. All allegations of incidents must be investigated, especially those made by employees.
2. Failure to conduct an investigation, regardless of the likelihood of success, can be extremely damaging to the department and the security program.
3. Even the least complicated investigation can be time-consuming. Since investigations are fact-finding functions, they must be conducted to determine the truth or falsity of the allegations.

Suppose, however, that an employee alleges that some loose change kept in a desk drawer as coffee money was stolen, and nothing more is done than to record the information.

The security supervisor or manager, knowing that the chances of a recovery are virtually nonexistent, feels that an investigation would be a waste of time. Later the victim observes suspicious activity leading to the belief that a coworker may be selling drugs. Unfortunately, as an outgrowth of the victim's first encounter with security, it now is unlikely that a report will even be made. The employee feels that nothing would be done anyway.

Again, in terms of what security officers should or can be, training in the fundamentals of investigations, interviewing techniques, and investigative report writing will enable them to undertake inquiries in cases where the department's best interests merit a response but the investigative experience expected of a security supervisor or manager is unnecessary. Furthermore, even in more complicated cases being handled by a security supervisor or the security manager, security officers could with direction do some of the more time-consuming work that does not necessarily require a great deal of experience.

Aside from training given for the development of security officers, there should be basic and refresher instruction for all departmental personnel, including those at supervisory and managerial level. Regardless of experience, all new hires in these categories need to learn the employer's story, its policies and procedures, and how the security department head wants work done, if nothing else. Refresher training often can be done through conferences.

A multinational organization provided such training by holding two conferences a year. At the conclusion of each, the corporate security director, to encourage the involvement of those attending, designated an agenda committee charged with the task of suggesting items of interest for the next meeting. New internal issues and new developments in security were discussed. Regional and site security managers were assigned topics and expected to lead the discussion. Outside speakers, some from other departments and some from outside the company, were invited to make presentations when the security director felt they could make a significant contribution to a conference's effectiveness.

In addition to self-contained programs, supervisory and managerial personnel should continue their own training by going to seminars when the subject matter is appropriate and attendance would be consistent with company policy. Allowance should be made for attendance when preparing budgets. Department heads also need to consider attending themselves if the topics will further enhance their own skills. The criterion to be used in deciding on either attending a seminar or approving attendance by subordinates should be whether the nature of the subject and the faculty's qualifications will benefit the employer. Location should be a factor only as it relates to costs. Despite denials by some security directors, on occasion their attendance, instead of that of a subordinate for whom it might be more helpful, has been influenced by the climate or the proximity of tennis courts or golf courses.

Supervision

Businesses and institutions of any size have hierarchies with personnel rankings (and responsibilities) descending downward. Supervisors are often the lowest level of managerial employees. All management personnel are responsible for overseeing subordinates' work to ensure quality performance; however, persons in such positions sometimes fall into one or two traps of which they need to be aware and for which they need to strike a balance. One is confusing supervision of subordinates with micromanaging their activities. The other is failing to understand that just as they supervise their subordinates, so too are they subject to supervision by their superiors. Some managerial employees find these precepts difficult to remember.

These principles call for reporting mechanisms to ensure that all work is done according to departmental standards and employer policies and that appropriate levels of management are kept informed of what goes on. This is as it should be, but being kept informed by subordinates does not mean doing their work, nor should they be led to believe that that is the case. Good supervisors, knowing subordinates' abilities, should be able to assign work without worrying about proper and timely completion. Nevertheless, some become so involved with their subordinates' work that the latter tend to abandon their responsibilities to their supervisors or managers. Should this occur, supervisory personnel are forced to take over if the work is to be done. Not only does this practice add to managerial work loads, but it also adversely affects subordinates' morale.

Equally dangerous is an approach so lax that subordinates feel superiors either are disinterested in or unappreciative of what they do. This, too, can adversely affect morale. It can also cause disciplinary problems if subordinates interpret this seeming disinterest to mean that they are unaccountable for their job performance. From a management point of view, it is immaterial whether problems are caused by micromanagement or inadequate supervision: the results are unacceptable.

The nature of security work is such that officers must keep supervisors informed of all activities, but as reporting ascends through the hierarchy subordinates must also remember that superiors' increased responsibilities often prevent their becoming immersed in minutiae. Thus passing information upward becomes more selective. Ordinarily, it should relate to unusual rather than routine activities. To illustrate, officers should report everything that occurs on their tours of duty, including the completion of patrol tours, but their supervisors need not report that to managers. However, supervisors would report that in making rounds an officer found unsecured confidential documents and took them to the office for safekeeping. Security managers would discuss this with the manager of the responsible department without reporting it to their own superiors. In contrast, they would inform their superiors of a bomb threat, a fire, or evidence of a significant loss of assets.

While these reporting principles apply because of increased time constraints on those in management positions, this does not signify a lack of interest or concern. Consequently, to avoid problems department heads must set reporting standards to ensure proper oversight of subordinates and the provision of information. At the same time they should grant subordinates some degree of discretion, both in job performance and reporting, commensurate with a person's position in the organization; the higher the position, the greater the discretion. Doing this shows confidence in and support for subordinates. Properly administered, this approach is good for morale and improves job performance, thus reducing the need for possible disciplinary action.

Discipline

One definition of *discipline* found in *Webster's New World Dictionary* is "treatment that corrects or punishes." Persons who think of security departments as private police or quasi-military organizations might tend to reverse the order and put punishment first.

Treatment and punishment are not mutually exclusive, but managers whose first reaction is to punish ignore the humane and business considerations.

Discipline usually is prompted when a mistake is made, often in the form of a wrong decision. Managers intolerant of mistakes either are unrealistic or simply prefer that subordinates make no decisions. They also tend to micromanage. Playwright George Bernard Shaw was more realistic when he wrote that "A life spent in making mistakes is not only more honorable but more useful than a life spent doing nothing."[5]

Therefore, since it is impossible to avoid mistakes completely, managers must ask themselves whether subordinates can learn from their mistakes. If they can, using discipline to teach rather than punish is both more humane and better from a business viewpoint. Most employees can learn from their mistakes, and they often will show overall improvement. One security director used to tell all new employees that he had made, and probably would continue to make, mistakes. Consequently, he would tolerate first-time errors but not their repetition.

Those who repeat the same mistake usually are unable to learn, or they are disinterested. In either case this cannot be allowed to continue; some punishment is needed, possibly even discharge. Admittedly, this is easier said than done. Since disciplining people is unpleasant at best, some managers avoid taking action, or they look to others to act for them even when the need is obvious. Unhappily, tolerating either repeated mistakes or disinterest tends to breed contempt. It also adversely affects operations and conscientious employees' morale. Consequently, distasteful though it is, good managers must be prepared to discipline when the need arises, whether by teaching or punishing. However, it is equally important to remember that to enjoy disciplining subordinates is not the sign of a good manager.

Regardless of what form discipline takes, it must be prompt so errant employees can relate the action to its cause. Furthermore, because it is inherently unpleasant, it also must be administered in private and in a calm, courteous way. Do not add embarrassment to an employee's anguish.

Discipline staff objectively, whether by teaching or punishing. Do not discipline two employees guilty of the same offense differently. A word of caution: human resources policies and procedures may say little if anything if "treatment" is involved since it is an informal practice, but prudent managers still will make entries in their personal employee files for future reference. For example, company policy may allow a verbal warning in instances of first-offense discipline. Even so, the person who gives it should note the warning and the basis for it in their file on the employee. In any event, all disciplinary action, regardless of its leniency or severity, must conform with the employer's personnel policies and procedures.

LEADERSHIP AND MOTIVATION

Leadership and the ability to motivate subordinates, like good training and effective supervision, help to reduce the need for discipline and improve job performance and operations. Leadership begins at the top. Good leaders lead by example, not by orders. They recognize that in reality motivation and morale are inseparable. Therefore, good leaders try to motivate subordinates and keep morale high.

Practically speaking, there are limits on what even the best leaders can do. Many factors that can contribute to good morale and motivation are within their purview; others depend on employers' attitudes. Treating subordinates fairly and with respect, complimenting them for good work, trusting them to do their jobs, providing opportunities to learn and encouraging them to do so, and issuing nice-looking uniforms that fit are clearly under a manager's control. Locating poorly furnished security offices in basements or near shipping/receiving docks next to dumpsters, paying officers less than all other employees, and using staff for menial jobs unrelated to security are all under an employer's control. These practices minimize security's importance in the eyes of other employees, damage morale, and demotivate officers.

To illustrate the manager's role, a large organization's personnel director warned a new security director of 200 unionized officers to expect frequent visits from their leaders alleging grievances apparently caused by low morale and little motivation. A discreet study confirmed this and revealed the problems' sources, which included:

❏ A manager who worked Monday through Friday, 8:30 A.M. to 5 P.M., leaving his office only for coffee breaks and lunch

❏ A manager who issued directives without ever explaining their logic, even to the three supervisors who reported to him

❏ A manager who would see subordinates only by appointment

❏ A staff that was untrained but nevertheless criticized for their mistakes

The serious lack of morale and motivation called for significant changes. Among them the new security director

❏ Made occasional site visits at odd hours on weekends to say "hello" and ask how things were going

❏ Visited all shifts on holidays to extend greetings and his thanks

❏ Required the security manager to visit each post on each shift at least once a month

❏ Had an open-door policy if subordinates wanted to see him

❏ Instituted a three-day training program for all personnel, followed by an annual half-day of in-service training

❏ Met with the union leadership whenever he planned changes affecting the officers themselves, making it clear that he was not asking permission to do what he proposed, but he wanted them to understand what he planned and why he planned it so they could answer union members' questions

Within six months the personnel director and the security director's superiors noted that grievances no longer were a problem; morale and motivation had shown noticeable improvement. In turn, relations between officers and other employees also reached an all-time high. As a result, the number of security incidents to which management had become accustomed dropped significantly thanks to the cooperation of other employees. This further boosted morale and motivation.

Some would argue that components of the job itself—responsibility, achievement, recognition, advancement, and growth—are what motivate employees, while so-called maintenance factors such as pay, status, benefits, and working conditions have no effect on motivation.[6] This may be more true in theory than in practice since it ignores human nature. In reality employees tend to think of the job itself as including the other factors. Low pay, poor working conditions, minimal fringe benefits, and lack of recognition or opportunities for growth all can adversely affect morale. When morale is low, there is no incentive to put forth one's best effort; performance is geared to the minimum level necessary to avoid being discharged.

Managers must carefully monitor all factors that can affect morale, and over which they have control, to ensure that they themselves are not contributing to subordinates' lack of motivation. They should also be alert for employer-controlled conditions that can have an adverse impact on morale and motivation. In those instances they should at least put forth an effort to try to effect changes for the better. Even if unsuccessful, the mere fact that subordinates know their manager cares will improve morale, motivation, and consequently job performance.

UNIFORMS AND EQUIPMENT

The types of uniforms worn and equipment issued are best determined by the employer's environment. In most cases managers are able to express a preference, and in so doing they should keep in mind their program objectives and the types of people with whom the staff has contact.

Uniforms

Of course, not all organizations have uniformed security officers; many retailers prefer plainclothes personnel. However, when uniforms are worn, the choice should be based on ease of identification and projected authority, factors that do not necessarily require a police or military look. Nor should officers be dressed in ways that are threatening since this often results in less rather than more cooperation from people with whom they have contact.

In selecting uniforms the nature of the employer's business cannot be ignored. The uniforms must be compatible with the employer's image, something that may be damaged if the authoritarian uniforms of police officers are chosen. Furthermore, in businesses and institutions where public access is a factor, such as retail stores, hotels, hospitals, or an office environment such as a corporate headquarters, police-style uniforms may even give invitees the impression that the premises are unsafe. This may also be true of a manufacturing plant's reception desk. Uniforms consisting of color-coordinated blazers and slacks or skirts, shirts, and ties can be worn with the employer's logo and the word "security" on the blazer pocket identifying the wearer and projecting his or her authority.

In some cases police-like uniforms may be preferred. This might apply to officers at shipping/receiving docks or gates controlling access to a site, or those patrolling parking lots.

If a security department is a private police force, such as a campus police force, police-type uniforms obviously should be worn. However, since some states have specific restrictions or requirements, police-type uniforms for a security department must conform to any laws dealing with private security uniform styles, colors, badges, cap ornaments, or other ornamentation.

Deciding on styles and colors is only part of uniforming personnel. The number of items to be issued per officer, the weather's influence, and whether it is better to buy or rent also must be considered. Since appearance is important for both public relations and morale, enough uniforms must be issued to allow for laundering and dry cleaning. If both summer- and winter-weight garments are needed, allowance should be made for the fact that in warm weather changes are made more often. These factors—in addition to the need for a good fit and the cost of replacements due to wear or personnel turnover—suggest exploring the possible advantages of renting rather than buying uniforms.

Thought also has to be given to officers with outdoor assignments who must be issued suitable foul-weather clothing. Some locations may call for nothing more than raincoats, rain hats, and boots. However, in cold climates overcoats, hats, lined gloves, and possibly lined boots will be needed.

Equipment

Personnel must be issued whatever equipment they need to do their jobs. The need for some items is obvious, yet others equally important may be overlooked.

Officers should have notebooks and pens with which to record observed security or safety deficiencies and any information given to them by other employees or invitees. Whether or not security is responsible for safety, the need to protect and conserve the employer's assets mandates that officers report such deficiencies so corrective action can be taken.

Flashlights also should be issued to those making patrol rounds during hours of darkness, whether indoors or out. Few will question their importance for outdoor patrols, but it is unwise to think that indoor emergency lights operating off backup generators eliminate the need for flashlights. No matter how brief the interval between a power failure and generator activation, officers should not be exposed to risks that could cause injury.

Two-way radios are a must for patrol personnel. The ability to communicate directly with them gives management flexibility and facilitates proper and rapid responses in emergencies. Reliance on telephone communication under such conditions can waste precious time. For instance, if an incident occurs, radio-equipped personnel can get details while en route to the scene, report status upon arrival, or call for additional help or needed emergency equipment without having to look for a telephone.

At no time is the employer's environment more important than when assessing the possible need for protective clothing or apparatus to be used in response to emergencies. This does not necessarily require issuing individualized equipment. However, it does mean that suitable equipment must be provided if there are any substances on site that could affect the health or safety of responding personnel if leaked or released into the atmosphere. The substances present will dictate the types of protective clothing needed and whether other safety equipment such as respirators, hard hats, face shields, gloves, safety glasses or safety shoes should also be available to responding officers.

Any discussion of officers' equipment must consider the matter of firearms and such allied items as batons, handcuffs, or mace. As with uniforms, if a security department is actually a private police force with all that that implies, its members must be properly equipped for their own defense and that of third parties. However, since in most cases policing is not a security organization's main function, providing weapons or related equipment poses significant questions for managers with regard to licensing, training, use, image, and liability.

Security organizations are not exempt from a state's firearms licensing requirements. As with recruiting costs, if despite the best preemployment screening effort a person is hired only to be denied a license, an extraordinary expense is incurred.

No organization can afford to equip personnel with any weapons, not just firearms, without proper training in their use. One-time training is not sufficient protection for employers. Firearms can kill; so can an improperly used baton. Handcuffs or mace, incorrectly used, can cause injury. Consequently, added to the initial cost of such equipment are first-time and in-service training expenses.

Weapons cannot help but affect image and make people fearful; they also can affect labor and public relations. Their very presence often causes people to assume that the environment is unsafe. This reaction can be especially harmful to activities that cater to the public, such as hotels, retailers, museums, and banks, to name a few. It is worth noting that at one time bank security officers were armed; today even banks that still use officers at their branches rarely arm them.

Weapons also are dangerous since some armed officers may be less inclined to try to reason with people. Confronted with unruly or disagreeable persons, they first should try to defuse the situation through conversation. If that fails, they should call upon other officers or the police for help, depending on the circumstances. Equipped with any type of weapon as a symbol of authority, officers may feel it is unnecessary to calmly speak with people. If so, the level of disorder may be escalated, with possible injury to both the participants and innocent bystanders.

Death or injury to anyone from any form of weapon used by officers, no matter what their training, invariably raises issues of liability, litigation, and adverse publicity. Having insurance for just such eventualities does not automatically cover all liability that may result from litigation. In an unsuccessful defense, insured employers absorb both the amount of their policy's deductible and any amount in excess of their coverage. They also know that if a loss is substantial, or claims are frequent, future premiums probably will increase. Self-insured employers absorb the entire loss, including legal fees and court costs. Therefore, decisions about issuing any types of weapons should not be made hastily or without consultation with the general counsel and risk manager.

RECORDS AND COMMUNICATIONS

Records and communications exist in all security departments. Poor ones waste time and space; good ones contribute to efficient operations. On occasion they also may be helpful in avoiding or at least minimizing liability. Although communications eventually may become part of a records system, not all records are communications. For example, data on employee automobile registrations are records. A letter commending an employee is a communication that becomes a part of that person's record with the organization.

Records

In setting up records systems, managers should remember that retained materials whose only use is historical rather than as working tools serve no real purpose. Furthermore, regardless of the form of media, records occupy space and space costs money. While many businesses and institutions have records retention policies, department heads are often asked for opinions relative to their particular activities since, absent legal reasons for retention, they presumably know best what should be kept and for how long. For instance, in setting reasonable time limits for retaining records, managers may find it adequate to keep patrol rounds records and budget data for three and five years respectively, and investigative reports indefinitely.

Records and communications obviously must satisfy individual department needs. Nevertheless, the following, by no means the only items found in security department files, are among the most common:

- ❏ Departmental personnel records
- ❏ Records of identification badges issued to all employees, and of their recovery and disposition when employees are terminated
- ❏ Records of authorization to issue keys, to whom issued, and dates of loss or recovery
- ❏ Employees' automobile registration data
- ❏ Patrol rounds records
- ❏ Security incident reports
- ❏ All budget data
- ❏ Pending and closed investigative reports
- ❏ Data on all reported losses and recoveries, whether of assets or employees' personal property
- ❏ Comparative data based on annual losses and recoveries
- ❏ Information on all accidents involving company-owned or leased vehicles
- ❏ Security audit reports
- ❏ Copies of communications between security and other departments, outside organizations, or people
- ❏ Copies of all instructions to departmental personnel regarding such matters as duties, assignments, uniform regulations, and so on
- ❏ Inventory and location of all security equipment, supplies, and materials used in training
- ❏ Data on the issue and disposition of truck seals
- ❏ Authorization for individuals to remove property from the premises, the record indicating what was removed and by whom, return date if such is required, and if returned
- ❏ Personal data on employees and their families if participants in an executive protection program

Although much of the foregoing can be helpful in investigations if losses occur, other data can be useful in preparing and justifying budgets. However, access to records should be based not on security department employment but rather on a legitimate need to know, regardless of position. Whenever files are removed, they should be charged out and the place marked to show file name, who took it, and when it will be returned. This is due to the nature of the information and to ensure its proper use.

Communications

All communications, written or oral, should be clear, concise, and grammatically correct regardless of whether they are instructions to staff, internal memoranda, policies and procedures, or external communications such as letters. Communications that leave recipients with unanswered questions about their intent are of poor quality, often leaving an equally poor impression of both the originator and the organization by which he or she is employed or for which he or she is responsible. Avoid words that recipients will not understand, whether for technical or other reasons. If technical terms must be used, they should be explained. Good sentence structure and correct punctuation and spelling are mandatory for all written communications.

Clarity should not be sacrificed in the interest of brevity, regardless of to whom a communication is directed. Unclear communications to superiors frequently try their patience. They also raise questions about one's managerial skills and the clarity of communications to subordinates. Insofar as the latter are concerned, unclear communications to subordinates, who are often afraid or embarrassed to ask for clarification, can affect both operations and morale if they proceed on the assumption that what they are doing is correct when in fact it is not. Unsatisfactory results are operationally defective, subordinates are blamed, and superiors may even feel that disciplinary action is justified. If so, there is resentment, less respect for the superior, and an inclination to do no more than is necessary to keep one's job.

POLICIES AND PROCEDURES

Most organizations of any size have written policies and procedures applicable to all aspects of operations, not just security. It is immaterial whether there is one all-inclusive policies and procedures manual or a separate one issued by each of the employer's major functional departments or components. The fact remains that those related to security generally reflect one of two things. Either they will be based on how anticipated possible problems should be handled, or they will be in response to incidents that have occurred but for which there was no existing precedent for disposition and for which there is need for uniform guidelines in the event of a recurrence.

Security policies and procedures, regardless of the method of distribution, are written using the employer's format. (See Appendix 3C and Appendix 3D for sample texts.) However, each should include the following basics:

❑ Caption
❑ Issuing department

- ❏ Effective date
- ❏ By whom approved for issue
- ❏ Purpose
- ❏ Scope
- ❏ Policy
- ❏ Procedure
- ❏ Definitions (if needed for technical or otherwise unfamiliar terms used)

Although policies and procedures are issued by departments, not persons, they nevertheless should be approved by the executive to whom the security director reports. When operational integration exists, some policies and procedures may involve security and other departments. Consequently, they need two approval signatures. For example, an investigations policy indicating those that will be done by security and those to be handled by internal audit would need the approval of the executives to whom the security and internal audit directors respectively report.

The purpose section is a preamble. Both the purpose and the policy should be stated clearly. They also must be consistent with the employer's business objectives. Scope indicates to whom a given policy and procedure applies. It is of special importance to multisite or multinational organizations' department heads if confusion is to be avoided. To illustrate, in a multinational organization, scope might cover all facilities corporate-wide, including wholly owned subsidiaries, or it could be limited to all North American locations; or scope might apply to all manufacturing facilities but not to sales or services offices, depending on the nature of a given policy.

Procedures should be viewed as guidelines to help employees generally, and managers particularly, cope with known or anticipated incidents. They should be as flexible as possible. Security managers dare not assume that they are the only ones who can think or make decisions; others are equally capable of exercising good judgment. In addition, flexibility lessens the need for constant revisions, thus saving time, effort, and money.

Of course, under some circumstances there may be procedures that allow for either no or only limited discretion. An example of the former would be a procedure for so delicate an issue as searching employees' briefcases, purses, lockers, desks, or computer files. Here the potential for disaster in terms of an adverse effect on otherwise good labor relations, or the risk of possible litigation, is such that nothing should be left open to interpretation or chance. In contrast, local managers should be able to decide whether to evacuate in case of a bomb threat yet required to follow set procedures for notifying corporate headquarters.

In preparing policies and procedures, whether obligatory or not, prudent security managers will send draft copies of those proposed to all executives whose divisions may be affected to solicit their comments. If possible, security managers should incorporate these suggestions; if not, they should set up a meeting to explain the reasons for rejection. Such meetings may lead to acceptable solutions that will satisfy both the executives' concerns and those of the security manager. In any case, these meetings at the very least can gain support for the security program and help avoid resistance or implementation problems once the policies and procedures are finally approved.

LAW ENFORCEMENT LIAISON

While effective law enforcement liaison is important, security managers must remember two things: they are not law enforcement officers, and their relationships with public police or investigative agencies should be proper. Also, getting to know key personnel before their help is needed serves to dispel the impression that the main reason for liaison is to obtain favors.

Security directors or managers who consider themselves members of the law enforcement community tend to expect favors from public agencies, most often by asking for information to which by law they are not entitled. They also willingly do favors for public agencies, such as providing data from employees' personnel files without asking for a subpoena as a condition of its release. These are illustrations of pitfalls to which some security managers, and especially those who are former public police or investigative personnel, tend to be susceptible. They also illustrate good but improper liaison.

Legitimate cooperation is both needed and desirable. For instance, asking for police help with special events involving a lot of traffic or celebrities, investigations of crimes, lectures as part of security training, providing intelligence information about possible problems, or assigning officers to keep access open in case of a strike is quite proper. In contrast, it is improper to ask a police department to electronically search a metropolitan area's telephone records because an employer wants to try to identify those responsible for a suspected unauthorized disclosure of proprietary information.[7]

Certainly security should help the police when possible. Asking for a subpoena before releasing certain types of data is not being uncooperative. Providing information that is not confidential, possibly helping with some of their training, and alerting them to impending problems of which they might not be aware are other ways in which security can be of assistance.

Sometimes establishing liaison only with agency heads may be impractical. For instance, in large cities liaison with commanders of police precincts in which employers have facilities may be more helpful and important than relationships with commissioners or chiefs. In addition, although fire departments are not part of law enforcement, and safety may not be part of security, it is imperative to have good liaison with fire department officials who can contribute to the management of fire-related risks and add to the protection of employers' assets.

MANAGING HUMAN, PHYSICAL, AND FINANCIAL RESOURCES

Since no organization's human, physical, and financial resources are unlimited, they must be carefully managed. This is especially true of security departments inasmuch as their contributions to employers' successes cannot be readily measured, and thus they are seen only as adding to expenses rather than profits.

In Chapter 2 we said that managing human resources begins when a department's size is determined, either initially or during a reevaluation. Several factors are vital to effective human resources management: using physical security (some form of hardware or technology) in lieu of officers; using staff for multiple duties when possible; using small support groups; admitting the waste in having enough people to handle all possible contingencies; and realizing that personnel and operating expenses are related. Above all, needs must be balanced and bloated organizations avoided.

Vacations are one illustration of how not managing personnel can be costly. If there is no viable alternative to using officers, allowing them to take vacations only in summer with an unlimited number of weeks off at one time can mean excessive overtime payments for coverage. Another example is failure to accurately assess needed holiday coverage.

Failure to substitute physical security for officers wherever possible is equally poor and costly human resources management. In most cases personnel are the major security expense, becoming increasingly costly each year. Physical security is reliable, paying for itself over time. It can often be used for work officers find boring. When boredom causes inattention, human resources are poorly managed.

Physical resources are a department's tangible assets. Among them there may be office machines and furniture, vehicles, surveillance and access control equipment, intrusion detection and other alarm systems, training materials, and possibly a library. One aspect of their management is maintenance. If physical resources are allowed to deteriorate to a point where they cannot be used, or used effectively, it is inevitable that operations will be hampered. This also represents waste, both in terms of their original cost and the replacement cost. Obviously, therefore, all physical resources must be properly maintained.

Nevertheless, on occasion equipment can fail. This makes it important to do business with service companies that will lend equipment when on-site repairs cannot be made. One manager who failed to do this lost the use of two closed circuit television cameras for sixteen weeks. When asked how he had compensated for their absence, he knew that if he said that he had not he would be asked why the cameras had been installed to begin with. On the other hand, he also knew that if he said he had compensated by assigning officers, he would be asked who paid their overtime. Under the circumstances his superiors felt that not only did he fail to properly manage his physical resources, but he also failed to manage his financial resources by buying the cameras and monitors from this particular vendor initially.

Another aspect, especially applicable to multisite organizations, concerns managing surveillance equipment, training materials, and libraries. Rarely are surveillance equipment and training materials needed with such frequency as to justify each site's buying its own, even in decentralized organizations where each site has its own budget. While individual sites may have small libraries, the acquisition of more elaborate libraries and expensive equipment can be limited, yet all resources can be made available to sites in need. To illustrate, while plant security departments in a large multisite organization bought different physical resources over time, the corporate security director kept a complete inventory of all such assets by location. This enabled corporate security to manage all of the physical resources. If a particular site needed surveillance equipment or training materials, headquarters arranged for a loan by the owning facility. As a result, site operations and budgets benefited.

In discussing the budget process earlier in this chapter, mention was made of the importance of period playbacks. Budgets are financial plans for each department that, when consolidated, become an organization's budget. However, this does not mean that all funds allocated must be spent. To manage financial resources means being able to get a job done for the least amount of money but in ways that will not hinder operations. This involves close period-by-period examination of playbacks by managers to determine the reasons for over- and underruns. As a rule those who cannot successfully manage their human and physical resources will be equally unsuccessful in managing their financial resources.

THE LAW'S INFLUENCE ON SECURITY OPERATIONS

The law's influence on security operations is felt in two ways. First, despite differences among the fifty states, there may be various regulations governing private security activities. However, while these regulations may exist, there is not necessarily any degree of uniformity in terms of what each state may require. Second, there are substantive and more uniform legal issues of which managers also need to be aware. Both can affect a department, the scope of its operations, and the extent to which its employer may be liable for the malfeasance or nonfeasance of security personnel.

It is fair to say that all managers know that the law has some influence on operations, but not all appreciate to what extent. Agency managers tend to be more aware of regulatory issues than proprietary managers since most are directed toward their services. As for substantive law, both groups think of criminal and tort law and the rules of evidence, yet many ignore other facets whose effect on employers necessarily affects security operations.

Even though regulations primarily concern contract services, when the latter are used by proprietary managers, compliance should be confirmed before retention. When they also apply to proprietary personnel, compliance is mandatory. For example, all armed contract or proprietary officers must satisfy licensing, and possible firearms training, requirements. Any other training requirements must also be met. Security personnel must comply with regulations governing uniform styles, colors, badges, cap ornaments, and vehicle identification. In cases where security provides medical emergency services, including ambulance, the equipment used and training for personnel must conform to existing statutes. These are but some of the legal issues that bear on operations.

Failure to comply with regulations can mean penalties and embarrassment. However, to ignore substantive issues can prove even more costly and embarrassing to employers since it frequently breeds litigation accompanied by unwanted publicity, legal fees, and court costs. If a plaintiff prevails, there also are damages.

Regulations aside, few business functions are so affected by a wide array of legal principles as is security. To illustrate, purchasing and sales relate to contract law, human resources to labor law, finance to tax law. However, whether security managers realize it or not, in addition to criminal, tort, and evidentiary law, they may also be involved, even if only indirectly, with contract, agency, constitutional, labor, insurance, and real and personal property law. Furthermore, depending on the size and nature of the business, it is possible for large organizations' security managers to find themselves dealing with patent, copyright, trade secret, immigration, international, and environmental law. They also need to remember that government-issued rules or standards, such as those pertaining to safety, environmental protection, and the handling of hazardous materials, have the same force and effect as laws.

Other legal considerations, applicable to specific types of organizations, can also affect operations. Among them are the Bank Protection Act;[8] defense contractor obligations to protect U. S. Department of Defense interests; transportation industry conformity with U.S. Department of Transportation regulations; nuclear power plants' compliance with U.S. Nuclear Regulatory Commission security standards; and multinational companies' adherence to the provisions of the Foreign Corrupt Practices Act.[9]

Aside from an awareness of and familiarity with legal issues that influence operations, security managers need to understand that laws are not static. Whenever legislative bodies are in session, new laws can be passed, and existing ones amended or repealed; courts can interpret or invalidate them. Most managers are not lawyers; therefore, in order to properly manage the law's influence on operations, they must work closely with employers' attorneys and seek advice on pertinent legal issues whenever questions of either execution or interpretation arise.

INSURING SECURITY OPERATIONS

Security's role in protecting and conserving assets is to prevent losses wherever possible, and minimize the amount of those losses that are inevitable. Risk management buys insurance to cover losses in excess of a policy's deductible clause so the insured is compensated for those losses. Legal representation also may be provided if there is litigation. However, the need to insure security operations is often overlooked, or else such coverage is taken for granted even though it may be inadequate or nonexistent.

This can happen even when employers have risk management departments. Frequently the problem lies in poor communication between risk management and security department managers. The former do not always understand the risks inherent in security operations; the latter assume that the risks are covered or negligible. Unfortunately, sometimes neither security nor risk managers realize that existing coverage is inadequate until an incident occurs and the employer is served with a summons and complaint.

Some types of insurance can be taken for granted since they result from statutory requirements or awareness that certain risks exist: workman's compensation; automobile insurance in states where it is compulsory; coverage against losses from theft or fire, whether by insurance companies or self-insurance. However, insurance against losses linked primarily to security operations may be lacking or inadequate.

Among the more common security-related risks for which there should be coverage are assault and battery; false arrest and imprisonment; errors and omissions; and libel, slander, and defamation. Some are crimes, but all are torts with a high probability of civil litigation if such offenses or incidents occur. Victims usually are more interested in compensation for alleged injuries than they are in a security officer's incarceration. Consequently, they will sue employers who have the financial resources with which to pay a prevailing plaintiff, not the officers. If insurance is inadequate or nonexistent and a plaintiff succeeds, the defendant employer's loss is out-of-pocket and adds to the notion that security is a drain on profits. If risk managers are not fully aware of these possibilities, no matter how well trained officers are or how infrequently incidents may occur, they cannot buy insurance to protect employers against such hazards.

SUMMARY

More is involved in managing departments and operations than mere organization. Without adequate financing there can be no operations; without financial plans there can be no financing. Thus the budget process is a point of departure for obtaining the resources needed for effective protection. At the same time, knowing that despite the high cost of personnel staff cannot be eliminated, managers try to keep size small. This adds to the importance of recruiting, training, and supervising employees if the best are to be hired and retained.

Good organizations are disciplined, preferably with discipline used to teach rather than punish, although punishment is sometimes unavoidable. However, since poor communication or seeming disinterest often precedes disciplinary problems, good communication, leadership, sensitivity to subordinates' needs, and motivational skills lessen the need for discipline. This further reduces problems and expenses caused by high turnover.

Uniform and equipment selection should be based on the nature of the employer's organization, what personnel need to do their jobs, and the image the employer has created or wants to create. Some styles and equipment may be incompatible with that image. It is shortsighted to assume that police- or military-type uniforms and weapons must be issued without considering the image that the employer wants to project.

Records and communications, part of any organization, are of special import to security operations in general and to effective management in particular. Communications—whether written or oral, upward or downward—must be clear and concise. If they are either not understood or misunderstood, they create rather than solve problems: superiors may question managers' skills; erring subordinates may have to be disciplined. Records have many uses other than historical. They can help justify budget requests, plan personnel assignments, identify security deficiencies, and provide investigative leads.

Policies and procedures often result from incidents that ideally never should have happened. They are written to minimize the risk of recurrence, provide guidance and direction for dealing with security issues, and contribute to uniform program implementation. However, in preparing them security directors and managers should not forget their employers' business objectives; they must remember that rigidity is to be avoided if it will inhibit employees trying to do their jobs.

Whether limited or extensive, a need for law enforcement assistance exists and requires good liaison. At the same time the best relationships are those that are proper as well as good. Ignoring the need for propriety can become embarrassing and costly to everyone. It can also prove to be more damaging than if the relationship had been proper from the beginning.

One way in which all employers measure managers' skills is by their ability to provide optimum benefits for minimal cost. To do this managers must be able to properly evaluate and utilize all of their limited human, physical, and financial resources. They look for ways to substitute physical for human resources; they closely monitor expenses on the basis of approved budgets. To reduce the risk of poor performance reviews, they avoid overstaffing; buying excessive, expensive, and underutilized physical resources; and overspending.

Often overlooked is the extent to which laws (other than criminal and tort laws and the rules of evidence) influence operations, thus mandating contact with and the advice of counsel. Also frequently overlooked is the need to work closely with risk managers to ensure the sufficiency of insurance for security operations. Security managers, though neither lawyers nor risk managers, must think in broad terms to protect employer assets and avoid, or at least minimize, operating risks. This they cannot do without fully appreciating the law's influence and the need to insure operations.

REVIEW QUESTIONS

1. What is a budget?
2. What should the physical standards be for hiring new security officers?
3. In what ways are training, supervision, and discipline interwoven?
4. Who has primary responsibility for providing leadership and motivation?
5. What factors should be taken into account when considering uniforms and equipment, including weapons?
6. What purpose do records serve?
7. What do policies and procedures accomplish?
8. Law enforcement liaison should be both good and proper. Illustrate how it might be good but improper.
9. Discuss how a state's regulations can affect operations.
10. What aspects of security operations might call for insurance coverage?

NOTES

[1] James S. Kakalik and Sorrel Wildhorn, *Private Police in the United States: Findings and Recommendations,* Vol. 1; R-869/DOJ, U.S. Department of Justice, Law Enforcement Assistance Administration, National Institute of Law Enforcement and Criminal Justice, February 1972, pp. 34–36.

[2] The Report of the Task Force on Private Security, National Advisory Committee on Criminal Justice Standards and Goals, Washington, D.C., 1976, p. 87.

[3] William C. Cunningham, John J. Strauchs, and Clifford W. Van Meter, *The Hallcrest Report II* (Stoneham, MA: Butterworth-Heinemann, 1990), pp. 144–145.

[4] *People v. Frank,* 52 Misc.2d 266, 275 N.Y.S.2d 570.

[5] "Preface on Doctors: The Technical Problem," *The Doctor's Dilemma* (1913).

[6] Frederick Herzberg, "One More Time: How Do You Motivate Employees?" *Harvard Business Review,* January–February 1968, Vol. 46, No. 1.

[7] *The New York Times,* September 1, 1991, p. 18.

[8] 12 U.S.C.A. 1882.

[9] 15 U.S.C.A. 78.

APPENDIX 3A
An Example of a Security Department Budget's Line Items

LABOR

    Salaries and Wages
        Indirect Labor Hourly
        Indirect Labor Salaries
    Indirect Labor Sick
    Indirect Labor Vacation
    Indirect Labor Holiday
    Indirect Labor Overtime Premium
    Deferred Compensation
    Indirect Labor Salary Fringe
    Tuition
    Indirect Labor Nonexempt Fringe

TOTAL LABOR

NONLABOR

    Dues and Subscriptions
    Building Maintenance
    Equipment Maintenance
    Telephone
    Office Supplies
    Meetings
    Outside Services
    Travel and Expense
    Printing
    Security
    Indirect Support
    Training Direct
    Direct Material Usage
    Occupancy
    Intercompany Charges/Credits

SUBTOTAL NONLABOR

DEPRECIATION

    Office Equipment
    Building Improvements
    Office Furniture

TOTAL DEPRECIATION

TOTAL NONLABOR
TOTAL EXPENSES

NOTES FOR PURPOSES OF CLARIFICATION

Security department employees are considered as indirect labor, hourly personnel are nonexempt, and salaried staff are exempt, as noted in the text.

Despite separate line items for sick and vacation time, in budget preparation the percentage allocated for fringe benefits usually includes these items.

Overtime Premium represents double time paid for holiday work.

Deferred Compensation usually covers such things as stock options that may be made available to certain employees, most often at the exempt levels.

Outside Services might include such things as a handwriting expert in a suspected forgery investigation or a service to ensure that executive offices and/or telephones were not "bugged."

Security is the amount to be spent for contract (as opposed to proprietary) security services.

Indirect Support covers such things as postage.

Direct Material Usage includes materials other than office supplies.

APPENDIX 3B
Sample of a Playback Format

Q4 To Date - Budget VS Actuals
ABC Security (10722110)
September 1993

(UNFAV)	CURRENT PERIOD			4TH QTR-TO-DATE			YEAR-TO-DATE		
	BUDGET	ACTUAL	VARIANCE	BUDGET	ACTUAL	VARIANCE	BUDGET	ACTUAL	VARIANCE
LABOR									
182 S&W IL HOURL									
183 S&W IL SAL									
185 IL SICK									
186 IL VACATION									
187 IL HOLIDAY									
188 IL OT PREM									
190 DEF COMP RS									
205 IL SAL FRING									
206 TUITION									
208 IL NE FRINGE									
TOTAL LABOR									
NONLABOR									
229 DUES & SUBSC									
373 BUILD MAINT									
374 EQUIP MAINT									
375 TELEPHONE									
384 OFFICE SUPPL									
400 MEETINGS									
404 OUTSIDE SER									
406 T&E									
412 PRINTING									
611 SECURITY									
742 INDIRECT SUP									
793 TRAINING DIR									
795 DIR MAT USAG									
798 I.C. CHG CRED									
SUBTOTAL NONLAB									
DEPRECIATION									
910 DEPR-OFF EQ									
964 DEPR-BLG IMP									
967 DEPR-OFF FRN									
TOTAL DEPRECIATI									
TOTAL NON-LABOR									
TOTAL EXPENSES									
HEADCOUNT									
NON-EXEMPT									
EXEMPT									

APPENDIX 3C
Sample Text of Security
Policies and Procedures

PURPOSE

To provide a more effective loss prevention program through the consistent application and implementation of Corporate Security Policies and Procedures corporate-wide, maintain a constant awareness of existing or potential security weaknesses or deficiencies so that suitable measures can be adopted for improved protection and/or problem resolution, and provide meaningful information about the status of security operations to the appropriate divisional vice presidents and plant or site managers.

SCOPE

This applies to all manufacturing, research and development, and principal logistics facilities, and to such other (Company Name) facilities as may be specifically designated by an appropriate senior or divisional vice president at his or her discretion.

POLICY

It is <u>(Company Name)</u>'s policy to provide optimum protection for all of its assets, real and personal, and for all of its employees consistent with sound business practices and requirements.

RESPONSIBILITIES

A. Security Audits

1. The Corporate Director Security will:

    a. Conduct a security audit of each North American facility or site encompassed by the Scope of this policy at least once every twelve months, of selected European facilities or sites once every eighteen to twenty-four months, and of each Far East facility or site once every twenty-four to thirty months, unless it is deemed necessary to increase the frequency of audit for any location(s).

    b. Designate, on a rotating basis, one or more security managers or representatives from North American facilities or sites, other than that being audited, as a member of the audit team for each North American security audit to be made by him or her.

    c. Following the completion of each audit, prepare an audit report consisting of both observations and, where deemed necessary, recommendations for corrective action for submission to the appropriate manager and divisional vice president.

    d. Make certain that all facility or site self-audits are made, and reports submitted, in a timely fashion.

2. Site Security Managers or Representatives will:

    a. When designated by the Corporate Director Security as member(s) of an audit team, assist in the security audit of a designated North American facility or site.

    b. Not less than five nor more than seven months after the completion of a Corporate Security Audit make a self-audit of their respective facilities or sites using the same format as that employed for Corporate Security Audits.

    c. Following the completion of each self-audit, prepare an audit report setting forth their observations and, where necessary, their recommendations for corrective action, to be presented to their respective Plant or Site Managers, with one copy being forwarded to the Corporate Director Security.

3. Regional Security Managers or Representatives will:

    a. Assist the Corporate Director Security with security audits made of particular facilities or sites subject to their general oversight.

    b. Conduct self-audits of the facilities or sites for which they are responsible at least twice during each twelve-month period, other than when a Corporate Security Audit is scheduled, using the applicable sections of the Corporate Security Audit format.

    c. Prepare and submit security audit reports as set forth in Paragraph 2c above.

B. Security Conferences

1. Security conferences will be held twice a year, usually during April and October.

2. Attendance will be scheduled as follows:

    a. All North American Safety and/or Security Managers or Representatives will attend each conference.

b. Safety and/or Security Managers or Representatives repre-
      senting Far East Manufacturing Operations and Europe will
      attend the April conference each year.

   c. Safety Committee Chairpersons from all North American
      Manufacturing, Research and Development, and principal
      Logistics Centers will be invited to attend the April
      session each year.

3. Agenda

   a. At each scheduled conference the Corporate Director Secu-
      rity will appoint a subcommittee from among those attend-
      ing, selected on a rotating basis, whose responsibility
      it will be to plan the agenda for the next regularly
      scheduled conference.

   b. Each agenda developed by them will include two safety or
      environmental protection subjects.

   c. The nature of the agenda will suggest those persons best
      qualified to make presentations--e.g., Corporate Head-
      quarters personnel (not necessarily Security), Regional,
      Plant, or Site Security Managers or Representatives, or
      representatives of outside agencies--and invitations will
      be extended accordingly at the discretion of the Corpo-
      rate Director Security.

   d. At least thirty days before the next regularly scheduled
      conference the subcommittee members responsible for plan-
      ning the agenda will submit the agenda in writing to the
      Corporate Director Security so that copies may be sent to
      all scheduled attendees with the notice of the conference
      dates.

APPENDIX 3D
Sample Text of Security
Policies and Procedures

PURPOSE

In the course of conducting business, occasions may arise when losses of _(Company Name)_ 's property and assets are incurred or suspected, the cause of which may be either the commission of a crime or acts of negligence, malfeasance, or nonfeasance, or allegations may be made regarding employee conduct, not necessarily business-related but nevertheless considered detrimental to the Company's best interests. The purpose of this policy is to ensure that investigations requiring Corporate Security Department involvement are conducted uniformly in a way designed to develop and preserve evidence essential to either a successful prosecution and/or the taking of appropriate administrative action without violating the rights of those involved or suspected of involvement, and to help isolate and identify the conditions that allowed the losses to occur so that appropriate preventive measures can be adopted.

SCOPE

Applies corporate-wide to the reporting and investigation of incidents related to or affecting _(Company Name)_ 's best interests, and to _losses not related to accounting matters_, unless a crime has been committed or is suspected, i.e., accounting or allied transactions related to financial control variances (see Corporate Accounting Policy and Procedure #_____, Reporting Irregular Accounting Operational Activities). However, copies of reports dealing with losses or irregularities related to accounting matters sent to the Corporate Director of Internal Operational Audits should also be forwarded to the Corporate Director of Security in those instances where the losses are not clearly attributable to negligence, mistake, or similar circumstances. Furthermore, this policy also may apply, in whole or in part, to any irregularity where specific Corporate Security involvement is indicated as determined by mutual consent with the Corporate Director of Internal Operational Audits, or as deemed necessary by senior management.

POLICY

1. The Corporate Director of Security is responsible for establishing and communicating to the functional, general, and site managers all necessary procedures and guidelines for reporting and investigating nonaccounting losses or incidents occurring in their area of responsibility as required to implement the provisions of this policy in a timely manner.

2. The Corporate Director of Security is also responsible for the general supervision and coordination of such investigations. However, the follow-up and/or solution of loss-related or other problems remains the responsibility of the appropriate functional, general, or site manager unless or until specifically released from this responsibility by the Corporate Director of Security or senior Corporate Management (see also Scope above).

3. All investigations conducted in connection with this policy or related implementing procedures will be strictly fact-finding in nature and may not be construed as establishing rights between (Company Name)_____ and any department, employee, or other party.

4. It is the responsibility of each functional, general, or site manager to:

   a. Establish a reporting system to make certain the Corporate Director of Security is informed immediately and directly of any known or suspected acts of a criminal or negligent nature, or otherwise covered by this policy and affecting (Company Name)_____'s property or other assets, reputation included.

   b. Ensure the reporting system is used to communicate known or suspected losses or other incidents covered by this policy directly to the Corporate Director of Security by the most expeditious means necessary, depending on the circumstances and urgency, so that the reporting manager and Corporate Director of Security can jointly review and evaluate the facts and determine what further action appears to be warranted.

   c. Manage the investigation of the incident unless or until specifically relieved of this responsibility by the Corporate Director of Security or senior Corporate Management.

   d. Bring to the attention of the Corporate Director of Security real or potential weaknesses in internal controls, other than financial, that might contribute to an unacceptable risk of exposure of (Company Name)_____'s property and assets.

REPORTABLE ACTIVITIES

1. The loss or risk of loss of (Company Name)_____'s assets or other property that may be in its care and custody or for which it may be legally liable.

2. The theft or suspected theft of any (Company Name)_____ asset, including unauthorized employee conversion, diversion, or personal use of (Company Name)_____'s labor, facilities, proprietary or confidential information, or other property in

its care and custody and for which _(Company Name)_____ is or may be legally liable.

3. Activities in contravention of Company policy or other acts affecting _(Company Name)_____'s interest that appear to be dishonest or criminal in the considered opinion of senior management.

Note: The Location Controller or other financial representative, who traditionally acts as a clearinghouse for the reporting of all real, alleged, or potential losses and irregularities occurring within the facility or area of responsibility, should always be advised of loss reports that are submitted directly to Corporate Headquarters. The Location Controller or other financial representative will, conversely, advise the functional, general, or site manager of all nonaccounting irregularities as soon as these are reported to his or her office. Nothing herein relieves the appropriate functional managers (e.g., Sales, Systems, or Field Engineering at Area, Regional, or Branch level) of their direct reporting responsibilities to the Corporate Director of Security when incidents covered by this policy are involved and there is no Location Controller or other financial representative assigned.

4. All thefts, burglaries, and other known or suspected losses of _(Company Name)_____ property and assets, _other than those relating to accounting matters_ (see Scope above), or other incidents covered by this policy, must be reported immediately by the functional, general, or site manager to the Corporate Director of Security using the most expeditious and discreet means of communication available depending upon the circumstances. Initial oral reports should be confirmed in writing immediately.

5. Reportable losses will usually fall within or be covered by one of the following categories:

   a. Theft or loss of _(Company Name)_____ property.

   b. The unauthorized use of Company labor, materials, or facilities, if the aggregate cost of such use exceeds $50.

   c. Any falsification of group insurance claims data affecting a determination of the benefits payable with an intent to defraud.

   d. Any theft of property with a value of $50 or more belonging to employees, customers, vendors, or others if committed on Company premises.

   e. All known acts of a criminal nature committed by Company employees, whether or not business-related, while employed by _(Company Name)_____.

REPORT FORMAT

Initial reports, regardless of the manner in which they are transmitted, should include the following details at a minimum, to be repeated in any written confirmation if the first notification is made verbally:

1. The reporting date, Company location, and name and position of the individual making the report.

2. The nature of the known or suspected loss or incident and the date and time it first was detected.

3. The identity, including names and positions, of all persons whose involvement is known or suspected.

4. The circumstances leading to the detection or suspicion of the problem and by whom such discovery was made.

5. The dollar value of the known or suspected loss.

6. All others to whom a report is being made, including the police in the event of a crime such as burglary, robbery, etc.

INVESTIGATION PROCEDURE

1. Prior to reporting a real or potential loss or incident, the functional, general, or site manager first aware of the problem will review the circumstances and coordinate an initial fact-gathering inquiry only to the extent necessary to determine that a full preliminary or formal investigation is warranted. IMMEDIATE PRECAUTIONS MUST BE TAKEN TO IDENTIFY AND SECURE ANY ESSENTIAL OR POTENTIAL EVIDENCE. In no event, however, should reporting the problem to the Corporate Director of Security be delayed. If in doubt, the conservative course of action is to immediately report the incident orally, to be followed up in writing, rather than lose valuable time or essential evidence, or risk impairment of the investigation.

2. Once the pertinent facts are reported to the Corporate Director of Security, the functional, general, or site manager must await a reply before proceeding with the preliminary investigation. The reply will vary depending on the circumstances and facts of the case presented, and the judgment of the Corporate Director of Security. In some cases the Local Manager will be advised to continue the investigation according to standard implementing procedures; in other cases he or she may receive explicit special instructions. In still others the Corporate Director of Security, or his or her designee, may assume direct personal responsibility for the investigation.

3. The Local Manager and the Corporate Director of Security or their designees will conduct or direct the preliminary investi-

gation according to standard and/or special procedures and instructions, as the case may be, so that a maximum effort can be made to recover assets or determine the nature of the loss, identify person(s) responsible or involved, and isolate the conditions that allowed the incident to occur so that suitable preventive measures can be taken to minimize the risk of a recurrence.

4. The preliminary inquiry is to be conducted for the express purpose of determining if: (a) a more thorough investigation is warranted; and (b) if so, whether the nature and scope of such an investigation are within the capabilities of Company personnel and resources or if the matter more appropriately should be referred to a particular law enforcement agency with which the Corporate Director of Security will act in concert, in conjunction with the Local or General Manager.

5. If, in the opinion of the Corporate Director of Security, such referral to a law enforcement agency appears to be both necessary and in (Company Name)   's best interests, he or she will, in the absence of an emergency, first inform Counsel, or in Counsel's absence the President, to determine if they agree with the decision and if (Company Name)   is prepared to sign a complaint and proceed to prosecution if an arrest or arrests result from the investigation.

6. If it appears that a full investigation is within the scope and capabilities of Company personnel, the Corporate Director of Security will, in conjunction with the functional or general manager, delegate and assign responsibilities to Company employees as required for the completion of a thorough inquiry. Regardless of the department to which all or part of an investigation is delegated, it nevertheless is the final responsibility of the Corporate Director of Security to: provide overall direction, supervision, and coordination for full investigations, and to report the inquiry's results to those Directors and/or Managers whose areas of responsibility are affected thereby, or whose involvement with the legal, insurance, or personnel aspects of the inquiry necessitate their being informed.

7. In no event will the Corporate Director of Security be responsible for or participate in the initiation of any disciplinary or other administrative action to be taken against any employees involved or suspected of being involved in any matters subject to investigation by his or her department.

8. In accounting matter investigations conducted by the Internal Auditors, as set forth in the Scope of this policy, should it be necessary to interview any persons, within or without (Company Name)   or any of its subsidiaries, for purposes other than to confirm accounting or related records, the Internal Auditors will advise the Corporate Director of Security. If the losses under investigation by them are not

clearly attributable to negligence, mistake, or similar circumstances, interviews will then be conducted jointly by the Internal Auditor responsible for the investigation and the Corporate Director of Security.

RELATED POLICIES

Legal Notices and Potential Lawsuits

Reporting Irregular Accounting and Operational Activities

Chapter 4

Managing Emergencies and Disasters

Webster's New World Dictionary defines an emergency as a sudden, generally unexpected occurrence or set of circumstances demanding immediate action, and defines a disaster as an event that causes great harm or damage; a serious or sudden misfortune; or a calamity. No organization is immune from emergencies or disasters and the resulting loss or disruption, although its work or location may have a bearing on the subject.

Disasters invariably prompt an emergency response, but from a security viewpoint not all emergencies are preceded by disasters. For example, the February 26, 1993, bombing of New York City's World Trade Center was both a disaster and an emergency resulting in deaths, many injuries, and major business disruption. A bomb threat, on the other hand, is an illustration of an emergency that requires a response, although it is neither preceded nor followed by a disaster.

Although disasters and emergencies by definition generally are unexpected, they are not necessarily improbable. As a result, security managers cannot ignore the possibility of being confronted by them when examining all of the probabilities involved in setting loss prevention priorities. Even so, from a preparatory viewpoint security managers must be reasonable in making their assessments. However, since the times, places, and types of such occurrences are rarely known in advance, precise planning and preparation are not easy. Thus managers need to plan and prepare based on analyses of their environment. For instance, there is a greater likelihood of hurricanes than earthquakes in New England, and a greater probability of forest fires than tornadoes in southern California.

Effective planning and preparation require careful analysis of all of the types of incidents most likely to arise. In doing so it is only natural that security directors or managers will focus primarily on those that have security implications that, if not planned and prepared for, could adversely affect the employer's organization. Resources needed to cope with them have to be identified, located, and committed to a response. Since some emergencies or disasters arise from acts of nature, it is critically important for security managers to keep abreast of available forecast data so they can prepare progressively instead of waiting until disaster strikes.

No less important, security directors and managers have to remember that all plans and preparations must take into account the needs of the entire organization, not just of the security department. Failure to do so may play a significant role in the organization's inability to continue operations until the emergency has passed. Although the need for security's complete and successful integration into the employer's total environment will be discussed in detail in Chapter 6, nowhere is it more evident than in emergency planning and preparation (for example, advance selection of primary and alternate command posts from which senior management can operate, or close cooperation with management information systems to ensure uninterrupted computer operations should a disaster occur).

KINDS OF EMERGENCIES AND DISASTERS

Workplace disasters and emergencies can be many and varied. Most are the result of accidents, carelessness, negligence, or acts of nature. They can cause injuries, death, fires, and explosions. Natural acts produce hurricanes, tornadoes, earthquakes, blizzards, floods, forest fires, and major ice storms. Today politically motivated terrorism, homicides by disgruntled present or former employees, bomb threats, and incidents significantly affecting computer operations must be added to the list. Whether the result is a disaster, emergency, or both, security must be prepared to respond.

An increasingly serious problem is illustrated by an item in the February 14, 1994, *New York Times* stating that in September 1993 the National Institute for Occupational Safety and Health (NIOSH), a U.S. government agency, called on employers to examine their workplaces for ways to prevent homicides, which it referred to as "a serious public health problem." The same item said 1992 U.S. Department of Labor statistics showed that seventeen percent of all occupational deaths were homicides, reportedly prompting the Occupational Safety and Health Agency (OSHA), part of the Labor Department, to consider regulations to require employers to protect workers from threats of violence.[1] The Division of Industrial Safety and Health of Washington State's Department of Labor and Industry has issued a Late-Night Workers Crime Prevention Rule designed to protect retail workers.

From a security perspective a disaster might have been prevented in one case if a former employee's access code had been deleted immediately following termination so he could not use it to enter the workplace and kill several people. A security/safety relationship is exemplified by a December 1993 incident in an Oxnard, California, unemployment office where two employees were killed and four injured, prompting a complaint to be filed with OSHA charging a failure to provide employees with a safe workplace.[2]

As with all kinds of security risks, managers must distinguish between the possibilities and probabilities with which they may be confronted, and between those emergencies that may be preceded by disasters and those that may not. At the same time they need to recognize that in some cases the responsibility for plans and preparations may be a shared one rather than security's alone, and in still others it may not be primarily security's. Nevertheless, security managers should not assume that the absence of prior incidents guarantees that none will occur in the future, or that the need for communication and cooperation with other involved departments is unnecessary.

PLANS AND PREPARATIONS

Despite the many uncertainties, plans and preparations, which are not the same thing, need to be made for those situations most likely to affect employers. *Webster's New World Dictionary* defines the word *plan* as "to devise a scheme for doing, making or arranging," and the word *prepare* as "to make things ready." Consequently, to be able to plan and prepare for an effective response, security managers have to be familiar with all aspects of the organization's operations as well as acts of nature that might occur in those locales where their employers' have facilities. Without careful analysis of the likelihood of natural or human-caused emergencies there can be no plans; without plans there can be no meaningful preparations.

As examples, if manufacturers properly store materials that, if improperly mixed, could cause explosion or fire, security managers cannot assume that there is no risk of an incident being caused by employee carelessness. Those with facilities in New England cannot ignore the probability of hurricanes or blizzards simply because none have occurred for the last two or three years. Thus all possibilities that would constitute emergencies should they come to pass need to be evaluated before plans and preparations can be made.

Two examples might illustrate the difference between plans and preparations. If there is risk of destruction of a building that houses the executive offices, plans should include identifying primary and secondary sites from which the organization still could be run. Their selection would be based on location and the availability of those services (such as communications) needed for them to be fully functional. In a hurricane-prone area, preparations might involve getting a commitment from a supplier of plywood or plastic sheeting for window protection in advance of the hurricane season, rather than waiting until a hurricane is forecast.

Since plans cannot be made for all emergencies, they necessarily have to be based on probabilities. At the same time the very nature of emergencies is such that plans should be flexible enough to allow for adjustments as things progress. For example, an East Coast university's inauguration of a new president was to be outdoors. When asked about seating and related arrangements during a planning meeting, the buildings and grounds director was very precise. When asked about traffic and crowd control, the security director merely replied that the campus police anticipated no problems. At 3:30 A.M. on inauguration day, the buildings and grounds director called the security director, verging on panic because it was pouring rain. Rain was forecast for the day, and he was unsure as to whether alternate arrangements could be made in time for the ceremony. In contrast, a call to campus police headquarters was unnecessary; all assigned personnel had received alternate post assignments in advance in case of bad weather.

Preparations involving outside sources do not always require expenditures in advance. The relative ease with which many natural disasters and emergencies can now be forecast often permits arranging for necessities without expending funds before an occurrence. From a business viewpoint this is preferable as long as availability when needed is ensured. On the other hand, if there are persistent risks of relatively high probability, preparations may suggest the purchase and on-site storage of what might be needed to cope with the emergency and minimize downtime and other attendant losses.

TRAINING AND EQUIPMENT FOR AN EFFECTIVE RESPONSE

Plans and preparations for emergencies, whether or not preceded by disasters, provide the ability to respond when something happens. A response requires people and equipment. Despite calls to police and fire departments, the fact remains that the first response often is by security personnel or other employees, who obviously need to be trained. In this respect seven things should be remembered when planning training.

1. Since not all disasters are the same, dealing with each of the types most likely to occur may require specialized training and equipment.
2. Training should include the actual use of the different kinds of equipment that might be needed in a given situation.
3. Training should not be given only once or infrequently.
4. Certain types of incidents may require training all employees, not just security personnel.
5. Training must cover both what should be done and what should *not* be done.
6. All response team personnel should be trained to function in any assigned role.
7. Training must be given only by qualified trainers.

There are compelling reasons for the foregoing, not the least of which is the risk of adding to a problem's seriousness and possible liability if officers are inadequately or improperly trained. Hazardous material spills, assaults, executive kidnappings and ransom demands, injuries or deaths, and fires are all handled differently. For instance, fighting oil or electrical fires with water increases risks; ransom demands for kidnapped executives differ from the demands of extortionists who threaten to blow up a building.

Time is of the essence in emergencies. Therefore, those responding must be able to react spontaneously without having to stop and think about what to do or how to do it. They should know where OSHA-required material safety data sheets are kept, the recognizable symptoms when substances are ingested, and the recommended emergency treatment. These requisite skills are developed only with continuous training.

There is no reason why all employees should not be trained to deal with certain emergencies. For example, at least some in each of the organization's various departments should know how to use fire extinguishers, give CPR, and handle telephone bomb threats. Since security resources are limited, and since public safety officers responding to bomb threats often ask for employees' help with searches due to their familiarity with their work areas and presumed ability to detect the unusual, all employees, not just security officers, should be trained in search procedures.

Fire departments often respond to security emergencies and usually will help with training in their fields of expertise; the police will do the same. Employers' medical departments or occupational nurses can offer CPR and first aid training or arrange for qualified instructors to do so. It then becomes the responsibility of security directors and managers to provide or arrange for most of the other training that may be needed to ensure an effective response to any given situation.

Security officers or other employees should be trained to provide treatment, pending transportation to a hospital, for injured employees who need more than first aid in those instances where employers do not have their own medical departments or occupational nurses on site. Should it appear that movement to a hospital is called for, they need to know not only what accidents or injuries require OSHA notification, but also how such transportation is to be handled lest injuries be aggravated or liability incurred. For instance, allowing injured employees to drive themselves to a hospital, sending them by taxi, or having them driven by other employees conceivably could aggravate injuries and increase the risk of employer liability for not having called the police or fire department, or for not having provided for a licensed emergency ambulance service.

Employees must become familiar with the proper equipment and must be trained in its use. Aside from the personal equipment mentioned in Chapter 3, both security and purchasing managers should be aware of OSHA Standards and the range of safety-related equipment that they cover in terms of what is needed and the specifications therefor. For instance, there are standards for fire-fighting training and equipment, first aid supplies, fire hose and extinguishers, and breathing apparatus. Equipment must be in working order, and water pressure for hose use must be sufficient.

Parenthetically, both training and equipment needs can be influenced by employers' locations. This is particularly true with regard to fire fighting. Response time being critical, fire departments in congested areas, or those composed of volunteers, may encounter delays in getting to the scene. As an example, despite the fact that in a major city the nearest fire station was less than a block from a manufacturing plant, the constant congestion at the intervening intersection was so great that a response to a fire alarm often took as long as five to seven minutes. In the case of another plant in an area that relied on volunteer firefighters, it could take up to ten minutes for an adequate number to make it to a fire scene. Therefore, if conditions of this sort prevail at any location, employees may have to assume greater responsibilities for fire fighting at such facilities.

As for equipment selection, good equipment can be expensive and its purchase justified only when no reasonable alternatives exist. Therefore, before buying any equipment managers must consider the nature of the employer's activities, what risks exist, the potential for disasters (whether caused by nature or people), other types of emergencies most likely to befall their employers, the adequacy of what is already on site, and the closeness to equipped and trained public safety departments that would respond if called upon. Just as they cannot staff with enough people to handle all contingencies, security managers know that they cannot afford to buy equipment that will enable them to cope with all emergencies.

No matter how good the training or equipment, an insufficient amount of equipment can affect response. A good illustration of this can be found in the case of a major hospital that consisted of seven connected buildings. It had only one fire cart, located in the administration building's tunnel and equipped to control very small fires (such as might occur in wastebaskets) pending fire department arrival. No thought had been given to the risk of more than one small fire at a time, or the virtual impossibility of trying to suppress or contain what had been a small fire in another building that grew into a bigger one due to the lapsed time in getting there.

Emergencies may require evacuation, for which all employees must be trained. To prepare for such a contingency, easily seen and read evacuation routes, showing both primary and secondary ways out of a building, should be posted. Drills should be held at least semiannually. Since employees may not always be in their work areas at the time of evacuation, training should focus on their exiting via the nearest available exit rather than a specific one, unlike a major financial institution that assigned specific exits for each of its many departments.

In conducting drills security managers dare not ignore the possibility that in an emergency either primary or secondary evacuation routes could be blocked. With this in mind they should also make use of other nearby logical alternates. Drills should emphasize speedy evacuation, not collecting personal belongings or waiting for friends, going to preassigned departmental assembly areas at a prescribed distance from a building for purposes of safety, and having means by which to ensure that everyone is accounted for.

PLANS AND PERSONNEL ASSIGNMENTS

Just as some training should be extended to all employees, security managers should not limit emergency assignments to their own staffs. Emergency policies and procedures outline what is to be done; doing it requires people. If evacuation is necessary, assets must be secured, employees and invitees gotten out of the building and accounted for, disabled persons helped, and premature reentry denied. Bomb threats may necessitate searches, and if the police are called, someone should meet and direct them to the security office.

Security's key role is undeniable, but with limited human resources it obviously cannot, and should not, assume the entire burden of responding to emergencies. To further illustrate, if a bomb threat involves calling the police, evacuating, and searching the premises, security should meet and direct the police. Individual employees should secure the assets for which they are responsible; security should make a last quick check to see that this has been done before leaving the premises. Male and female employees should be assigned to inspect toilets as part of ensuring that everyone is out of the building. Allowing for their possible absences, principals and alternates need to be designated. The role of security managers is to let other department heads know what needs to be done and by how many people, and to see to their training. Security managers do not assign nonsecurity employees to emergency duties; that is done by the other managers.

The number of shifts worked must be considered when assigning other than security personnel to emergency duties. Emergencies can occur at any time. Nevertheless, some organizations tend to make plans and assign personnel on the basis of the mistaken idea that they only happen between 8 A.M. and 5 P.M., Monday through Friday. This obviously must be avoided. Even though there may be second and third shifts, emergency response assignments for those shifts often are not made. Then, when incidents do occur on those shifts, there is confusion, a lack of coordination, a waste of precious time, and a greatly increased risk of injury, death, or destruction of assets. While emergencies, whether they result from disasters or otherwise, are unpredictable, that does not excuse a failure to plan, including making personnel assignments.

Regardless of the number of shifts worked, or whether an employer's organization is centralized or decentralized, the need for flexibility in policies and procedures (see Chapter 3) applies equally here. Procedures for notifying key personnel, including security managers, must be strictly followed; however, beyond that the very nature of disasters and emergencies demands that rigidity be avoided. Senior managers at the scene are in a far better position to judge what has to be done to protect people and assets than are those physically removed and unaware of what is happening.

There must also be planning and personnel assignments for those employers who do not have their own medical or nursing personnel to handle on-the-job injuries, whether they only call for first aid or require hospitalization. The names, working hours, and locations of employees qualified in first aid, in CPR, or as emergency medical technicians should be listed with security as part of the planning process. If local public safety or hospital departments do not provide emergency ambulance services, companies that do should be identified and a relationship established with them in case of need. Planning should include locating the nearest hospital emergency rooms, preferably those with trauma centers, as well as assigning employees to accompany injured persons to hospitals, if that is to be done. The same is true of assigning employees who should inform victims' families and act as liaison with the news media.

THE CRISIS MANAGEMENT TEAM

Crises, like emergencies, are unpredictable, yet in both cases it is important for security managers to work as part of a team. Regardless of whether a situation is an emergency or crisis, they cannot properly discharge their responsibilities if they presume to do so without getting help from and helping other managers. Security managers should also understand that from a business viewpoint crises may differ from emergencies in that decisions that can affect an organization's very existence may have to be made. Therefore, crisis planning is different from emergency planning, as are the response personnel.

For instance, if there is a fire at a manufacturing plant, the plant manager normally decides on a proper course of action, and the local fire department responds. However, if the plant is critical and it is destroyed, it is senior management that decides if other plants can compensate or if there is an alternative. There are many other types of eventualities for which a crisis management team must plan. For example, a board chairperson is kidnapped and a million-dollar ransom is demanded, should it be paid? Who serves as chairperson in the interim? If four key executives die in an airplane crash, who handles their work?

Although crisis management teams are composed of key executives, security directors usually are included. Some may even feel that they are qualified to chair the team. If so, they are likely to be guilty of minimizing the very nature and possible complexity of the types of events that usually cause crisis management teams to be activated, and the impact of the team's decisions on the total organization. However, it is not all that unusual for a security director or manager to be the catalyst for a team's formation.

In any event, a crisis management team logically might consist of an organization's board chairperson or president, executive vice president, chief financial officer, general counsel, treasurer, and the persons in charge of human resources, public relations, risk management, and security. Of course, in the final analysis each organization must decide for itself on the composition of its own team. Regardless, since it would be naive to overlook the possibility that a crisis may result from an act related to one of the team's executives, alternates also should be selected.

Crisis management teams need to do more than react when crises occur; they should also try to minimize the risk of crises occurring. To illustrate, they can declare that key employees are prohibited from traveling together on the same aircraft, require the use of fire-retardant materials in all construction and furnishings, and have off-site storage for all backup computer files. Examples of reacting to a crisis would be to have key employees personally inform customers that a major fire will delay filling orders, or promptly recalling a defective product to prevent injuries or damage.

Since all crises affect assets, whether directly or indirectly, security is concerned. To deal effectively with such security issues as preventing further destruction or looting at fire scenes, protecting property against vandalism that may be caused by public reaction to defective products, threats to blow up buildings or injure people if certain demands are not met, or news stories about well-paid, high-profile executives that might lead to a kidnapping, security managers must be team members. Furthermore, insurance companies that insure against executive kidnappings and extortion generally require policyholders to have crisis management teams with their security managers as members.

PUBLIC SAFETY LIAISON

Chapter 3 discussed law enforcement liaison and the importance of ethical and proper relationships. Security managers are aware of the need for good relations with prosecutors, the police, and even federal agencies, whether for emergencies or otherwise. Regrettably, they sometimes forget the importance of similar relationships with fire departments, particularly since the latter respond to emergencies more frequently than the former. Fire department personnel obviously fight fires and respond to explosions regardless of cause. They may join the police in bomb searches, and they may even be called upon to assist with other disaster-caused operations. In some cities fire departments provide emergency ambulance services.

Developing relationships with public safety organizations should not be deferred until their help is first needed. Instead, relationships should be developed in anticipation of a possible need. This is particularly true for fire departments. While the police occasionally may get an emergency call, their familiarity with the premises and its contents rarely is crucial to their response. This is not the case with fire departments. More is called for than meeting fire department personnel. Their guidance relative to fire safety issues and fire prevention programs should be actively sought.

In responding to fires, regardless of cause, time is of the essence. Knowing a building's layout in terms of structural impediments that could delay access to any part and knowing if its contents could cause an explosion, hasten a fire's spread, or generate noxious fumes or deadly gases can be critically important. Would a fire have to be fought with chemicals or could it be fought with water? If with water, is there standpipe? (A standpipe is a large vertical pipe or cylindrical tube used to store water and ensure sufficient pressure when needed.) These are crucial questions that can best be answered when fire department personnel are invited periodically to inspect sites. Inasmuch as layouts and contents can change, this also gives them invaluable up-to-date information.

All bomb threats have to be taken seriously, and time permitting, all threatened premises have to be searched. If a search uncovers a questionable item, it must be handled only by qualified bomb disposal personnel, not by security or any other employees. Therefore, a facility's location may suggest a need for liaison with an Army Bomb Disposal Detachment or Alcohol, Tobacco, and Firearms field office, if nearby, even though they are not public safety agencies in a strict sense. For example, bomb threats occasionally were made against a large manufacturing plant in a small town with a very small police department and a volunteer fire department, neither of which had trained bomb disposal personnel. Fortunately, there was an Army Bomb Disposal Detachment nearby with which liaison was established.

EXTRAORDINARY SITUATIONS

Notwithstanding what has already been said about the unexpected and unforeseen nature of emergencies, two situations that may confront security managers might well be described as "extraordinary." The first can occur anywhere and any time there is an employee termination. The second is of importance primarily to those whose employers are multinational organizations.

Individual reactions to terminations can run the gamut from resignation to losing one's job through resentment and such bitterness that an act of violence will follow, whether in the form of vandalism to the employer's property or an attempted or actual homicide. Furthermore, these things can happen regardless of whether a layoff affects one person or many.

Minimizing the range of risks inherent in terminations requires the closest cooperation between the security and human resources departments. The way in which a person is told that they no longer have a job can help reduce levels of tension and resentment. This, in turn, can help reduce the risk of a violent reaction. In addition, performance reviews in employees' personnel files may contain information that conceivably could suggest a need for extra care in dealing with a particular individual. If so, this needs to be communicated to security in advance of the termination. Not only should such employees be escorted from the premises, but instructions should also be issued to deny them reentry to the premises. In some cases it may also be advisable to inform the local police department.

Multinational organizations must deal with the fact that even in politically stable countries they may have to cope with emergencies prompted by political dissidents who will resort to acts of terrorism in the hope of gaining publicity and causing government instability. Some, if not necessarily anti-Western or anti-American, nevertheless will target American businesses in the hope of getting a reaction from local governments and disrupting normal activities.

Incidents of this sort are not confined to underdeveloped countries; they occur in highly developed ones as well. Witness the terrorist activities of such groups as the Italian Red Brigade, Germany's Red Army Faction, the Irish Republican Army in Northern Ireland and England, Action Direct in France, and the Basque Separatist Movement in Spain. These have resorted to kidnappings, assassinations, extortion, and bombings.

Security managers confronted with comparable concerns at home normally seek assistance from law enforcement agencies with which they already have liaison. However, operating abroad there may be serious problems of language and customs, and such agencies may be lacking in terms of both their quality and integrity. This may mean that security departments must become self-reliant and develop internal programs to try to minimize some of the risks inherent in extraordinary situations. Doing so is consistent with security's proactivity and emphasis on and role in prevention.

Security managers are well advised to avail themselves of information that can be made available to the private sector by the U.S. Department of State. In a number of countries they also can get some guidance, particularly with regard to local law enforcement capabilities, from Federal Bureau of Investigation personnel assigned to American embassies as legal attaches.

By using these resources and being alert to world affairs, security managers can often reduce risks by issuing travel and other advisories to employees. As an example, they can provide information about countries, cities, airlines, and hotels that may be at risk on either a short- or long-term basis; the best modes of ground transportation; and types of restaurants and places of entertainment best avoided.

SUMMARY

While the nature, time, and place of the many and varied disasters and other emergencies that can befall any employer cannot be foretold, this does not excuse failure to prepare. Although virtually all organizations may be affected by either natural or human factors over which there is little or no control, security managers may have access to historical data, or be aware of other telltale signs that suggest the possibility of a particular type of occurrence. Therefore, to fully understand security's role and prepare for such eventualities they need to analyze those situations most likely to happen.

Without this analysis it is impossible to plan for a response or to know what supplies and equipment should be arranged for if not kept on hand. Fire extinguishers and hoses are normally found in all commercial and apartment buildings, hotels, hospitals, and schools. However, even in areas likely to have ice storms, one rarely finds large amounts of sand and salt on hand. Prudence suggests that sources for such materials be identified and commitments be made in advance for their sale and purchase as part of effective emergency planning.

When disasters strike or emergencies arise, there must be immediate action to minimize further injury to people or loss of or damage to assets. While public safety departments usually will be called, the initial response often is by security, whose human resources are limited, thus making it necessary to involve other employees. To respond effectively both groups must have not only access to the proper equipment but also constant training in what to do under any given set of circumstances.

Equally important to planning is the need for organization and an understanding that proper organization and planning can come about only when security is an integral part of an employer's total environment. In emergencies a rapid response is critical, but even the fastest and best-equipped response teams cannot function efficiently unless everyone knows exactly what their assignment is. If multiple shifts are worked, such as in hotels or hospitals, each shift must be covered and each must have a person in charge. Furthermore, the possible absence of any team members in an emergency means that alternates must be designated and trained.

Not all emergencies are crises. Some businesses and institutions may be more prone to crises than others, yet all hope they never will have to deal with any. Nevertheless, since the possibility always exists, the best organizations plan as they would for any other emergency. They have crisis management teams composed of key executive and senior managerial personnel who are authorized to make whatever critical decisions are necessary in the organization's best interests. Since some crises may require public safety departments' help, security managers logically are team members.

Despite uncertainties, and possibly even only slight probabilities, there is no reason why disaster and emergency planning cannot be proactive and seek public safety assistance, especially from fire departments. The latter can help assess fire-related risks in an effort to minimize the operational impact of a fire or explosion. This call for public safety liaison is a role for which security managers are well suited.

REVIEW QUESTIONS

1. Name the two principal kinds of disasters with which security may have to deal, and illustrate each.
2. Are all emergencies preceded by disasters? If not, give an example of one not preceded by a disaster.
3. Discuss ways in which security managers should plan for possible disasters and emergencies despite their uncertainty.
4. In developing training so employees can respond to emergencies effectively, what factors need to be considered?
5. Should at least some training be extended to employees outside of security? If so, what kinds of training?
6. What factors must be considered in deciding on personnel assignments?
7. To what extent are department heads other than security involved with emergency personnel assignments?
8. Discuss why crisis management teams are important, and illustrate conditions under which they are activated.
9. Why should security managers be part of crisis management teams?
10. What factors have to be taken into account in establishing liaison with public safety departments?

NOTES

[1] *The New York Times,* February 14, 1994, pp. A1, B5.
[2] *Corporate Security,* Vol. 20, No. 3, February 1, 1994, pp. 5–6.

Chapter 5

SECURITY'S ROLE IN RISK MANAGEMENT

In large organizations it is not at all unusual to have risk management departments that, as a general rule, are separate and apart from security. The roles of the two departments really are and should be complementary inasmuch as each of the department heads, in his or her own way, is involved with trying to manage those risks that pose real or potential threats that could result in some harm to the employer. True though this is, it is unfortunate that the heads of the risk management and security departments often see themselves as competitors instead of as collaborators. In organizations where this is the case, employers frequently fail to get optimum benefits from either of these functions. However, before one can better appreciate how the two should work together in managing risks, it is first necessary to understand the ways in which their respective approaches to the subject are different.

First, it is important to recognize that insurance is a factor not only vis-à-vis risk management, but it also has an indirect influence on security operations. Therefore, its place in the scheme of things needs clarification. To insurance companies whatever is insured is the "insured risk"; losses against which a policyholder is insured, such as fire, theft, dishonesty, and so on, are "hazards." Their underwriters take both risks and hazards into account in terms of whether policies should be issued to an organization and, if so, the amounts of the policy premiums.

Some organizations, however few they may be, are self-insured. This means that whatever losses they may suffer will have to be covered by their own resources instead of those of an insurance company. Organizations usually self-insure for one of two reasons. Some organizations may feel that they have the financial resources to cover any conceivable losses; therefore, they see no reason to pay premiums to third parties. In other cases it may be that an organization finds that it no longer can buy insurance due to the number of claims that it has filed with and received payment from its carriers.

However, of the overwhelming majority who buy their insurance, most find that the cost of complete coverage for their protection against all possible hazards would be prohibitive. Consequently, while trying to buy the best coverage and services, risk managers will also accept a deductible clause in the policy. In other words, they decide how large an out-of-pocket loss can be absorbed by their employers should a covered incident occur. For instance, since a $50,000 deductible per incident is not unusual for a large business, one incident resulting in a $100,000 loss would mean that half of the loss would be covered by insurance and half would be absorbed by the victim. If there were five separate incidents in one year, each representing a $49,999.99 loss, an employer's out-of-pocket loss would be $249,999.95 since each individual loss was within the policy's deductible.

Therefore, a principal difference between risk management and security lies in how they achieve their goals of managing those possible risks that may confront the employer. Risk management's goal is to try to *minimize* the amount of the employer's out-of-pocket losses by buying insurance to cover those losses that are in excess of a policy's deductible.

Security, on the other hand, has two goals in its approach to risk management. Its first is to *prevent* losses to the greatest extent possible. However, being realistic, security managers also know that some losses are unavoidable. As a result, security's secondary goal is to keep the dollar value of those losses as low as possible. To accomplish both of these objectives the methodology employed by security must emphasize prevention, which means security must be proactive.

WORKING WITH THE RISK MANAGEMENT DEPARTMENT

Since both department heads are trying to manage risks, despite the difference in their approaches, how can they work together in their employer's best interest? First, each needs to have a much better understanding of the other's role. Second, they need to improve their communications with each other. To protect and conserve assets, develop effective loss prevention programs, and make the best use of their resources, security managers must carefully and constantly examine and evaluate the vulnerability of all aspects of the employer's operations. In doing this they also must keep risk managers apprised of their findings. At the same time, risk managers must keep security managers informed with regard to what their insurers may see as possible sources of loss if not attended to. Each must lend support to the other in order to best serve the employer.

From a security viewpoint the constancy of examination and evaluation is a reflection of the fact that working environments not only are subject to change, but also that they do change. Some hazards may become more likely to occur, others less. If so, there may be a need for changes or other action in both the security and insurance programs. For instance, suppose security managers detect a loss potential in a behavioral area in which both they and their risk management counterparts have an interest, such as safety. In trying to prevent accidents and the subsequent filing of claims (both of which represent some form of loss), it can be far more effective if both managers jointly ask the human resources department to offer problem-specific training for affected personnel than if they approach the subject separately.

Nor should risk managers readily capitulate to insurance carriers' demands for changes because of perceived security-related losses or the prospect of such losses. Instead, risk managers should ask their security directors or managers to join them in meeting with the carriers to resolve such issues.

To illustrate, over the space of three years one organization had suffered losses of inventory attributable to burglaries at two out of more than 100 service offices' stockrooms. The claims filed with its insurance company for both totaled about $125,000 after deductibles. This prompted its insurer to insist on the installation of central station burglar alarms in each of its more than 100 service offices' stockrooms, all of which were in leased space. The initial cost would have been about $650,000; the annual costs thereafter around $175,000. The risk manager invited the security director and a representative of the insurance company to a meeting. At that time the security director convinced the insurer that a new local burglar alarm, which the company would buy, would be as effective as central station alarms, and the demand for the latter was dropped. This solution proved to be far more beneficial to the employer in two ways. First, in addition to protecting stockroom inventory, the total purchase and installation cost would be only $150,000. Second, in the event that any of the stockrooms were relocated, the alarms could be moved with them at no cost to the employer.

Another example of cooperation between security and risk managers occurs when risk managers buy insurance to protect against losses should executives or other specified personnel (or possibly their family members) be the victims of a kidnapping or assassination. Having crisis management teams (discussed in Chapter 4), and activating them in such an event, while crucial, is nevertheless reactive. Insurers and security managers, who want to try to prevent such happenings, are more interested in a proactive model.

To illustrate, in the case of a high-profile board chairman of a multinational, politically controversial organization, the security director worked closely with him and his family to increase their safety. The director not only surveyed the executive's home, but he also suggested and oversaw the purchase and installation of suitable protective measures. In addition, he recommended minimal but no less effective life-style changes in their personal habits in order to further reduce the levels of risk for the executive and his family.

Of course, in considering the many ways in which it is critically important for security and risk managers to work together, one must not forget the need for good communications and understanding that is required to make certain that security operations themselves are insured. As we discussed in Chapter 3, regardless of how carefully members of the security staff are screened, trained, and supervised, the very nature of their work subjects them to circumstances that could prompt third parties to file claims against the employer. There must be coverage for this, too,.

By no means are the previous examples illustrative of all of the many ways in which the two departments can and should work together. There are others to be sure, but suffice it to say that the employer's best interests demand that security and risk management departments, and especially their department heads, cooperate rather than compete with each other.

LOSS PREVENTION AND INCIDENT AVOIDANCE

It has already been pointed out that loss prevention from risk management's perspective is much more limited than it is from security's. This is due to the fact that while insurance can reduce the dollar amount of losses, insurance itself cannot prevent the occurrence of those incidents that lead to losses. It is in this respect that security has a more active role to play in incident avoidance to prevent losses.

Chapter 6 will discuss security's integrated role in detail. Suffice it to say for now that as security becomes more integrated in the employer's total environment so does its ability to reduce losses and incidents. This, in turn, can have an indirect but no less positive effect on productivity, morale, and profits. However, experienced security directors and managers are very much aware of the fact that for their departments to manage risks effectively and help avoid incidents, they have to be proactive. One of the many, and also one of the greatest, challenges facing security managers relates to their ability to detect potential sources of loss and take cost-effective steps to prevent their occurrence. They know only too well that all losses, regardless of insurance, mean an out-of-pocket loss to the employer.

Suppose, for example, that the theft of a computer terminal is reported at 9 A.M., and security finds the terminal at noon. To say there was no loss since, after all, the terminal was recovered ignores reality. Indeed, there was a loss. The employer lost the dollar value of the time spent by security in its investigation and search for the terminal. In addition, the employer lost the dollar value of the productive time of both the employee whose terminal it is and of the other employees who in turn depend on that person's work for their own. Of course, if the terminal was not recovered, there would be an additional loss of productive time until a replacement was obtained. Furthermore, because of the policy's deductible, this loss most likely would not be covered by insurance in any case. This is but one illustration of why security managers are expected to find ways to at least minimize risks if not actually prevent losses.

It is this effort to try to prevent losses and avoid costly incidents, or at least reduce their scope and magnitude, that makes it necessary for security managers to approach their roles in a dual rather than a singular way. When they focus on prevention, they will assess their surroundings, determine their employer's needs, and design programs to satisfy those needs. Rather than relying solely on security personnel and the use of physical protection, including high technology where applicable, they will also think in terms of procedural controls and accountability. These elements, in combination, are the cornerstones of effective security programs. However, despite management support and implementation of the program, some incidents resulting in losses will occur. When they do, security managers are faced with the challenge of preventing further losses, whether of the same or a similar kind.

While everyone would agree that an investigation is in order, the way in which it is undertaken may not necessarily be truly effective from a preventive viewpoint. Too often internal investigations conducted by security tend to focus on identifying the person or persons responsible for the incident so appropriate disciplinary action can be taken. Among police personnel the speedy identification, apprehension, trial, and punishment of criminals is thought to be an effective deterrent.

This idea is also endorsed by some security directors or managers, particularly those whose prior job experience has been as members of the law enforcement community. Regrettably, security managers who either do or would apply this theory to the private sector do not seem to appreciate fully the differences between policing and security. They fail to understand that in businesses and institutions, where the workplace environment is controlled by executive management, something more is called for than identifying and punishing errant employees. In reality, the effect of such action on other employees is no more likely to deter further attempts to commit the same or other offenses than is the apprehension, conviction, and punishment of criminals by the criminal justice system a guarantee that crimes will stop. In the workplace it is not unusual for someone else to be willing to commit or attempt an offense by gambling on not being caught.

Therefore, all investigations of security-related incidents must focus on accomplishing two things. First, every effort has to be made to determine who was responsible for what happened. Second, the conditions that allowed the incident to occur in the first place must be carefully and fully examined. Although these concepts are not mutually exclusive, if the security program's emphasis truly is on prevention, close scrutiny of the facilitating conditions is more important than identifying the perpetrator. Logic dictates that unless and until security managers isolate, carefully examine, and understand the conditions that contributed to the occurrence of any incident, they cannot even begin to think about adopting suitable corrective measures that are designed to prevent a recurrence. From the standpoint of prevention, if an employer is to enjoy both short- and long-term benefits, changing permissive conditions is much more effective than punishing an employee, no matter how severe the punishment.

SECURITY AUDITS

Properly structured, comprehensive security audits can also make a contribution to risk management. In fact, the very nature of security auditing lends itself to a preventive approach, which is what risk management is really all about. To make certain that audits are comprehensive, a format for their conduct should be developed. In this respect it is important to remember that one of the primary reasons for writing and issuing security-related policies and procedures, a topic that was discussed in detail in Chapter 3, is the institution and implementation of effective loss prevention measures. Thus in structuring the audit format, the threefold objectives of all security audits should be kept in mind. They are:

1. To detect any security deficiencies
2. To determine whether the audited facilities are complying with all applicable security-related policies and procedures
3. To enable security auditors to report audit results to appropriate personnel so action can be taken to correct all shortcomings

Unless all three can be accomplished, the format is ineffective.

Of course, there is much more to a security audit program than developing a suitable format and agreeing on its objectives; other considerations must be kept in mind. Of what should the format itself consist? If the audits are to be comprehensive, just how extensive should they be in terms of what they cover? Should the times for audits be made known in advance? By whom should they be conducted? With what frequency? Of what should the results consist? Who are the appropriate personnel to whom the results must be reported?

For ease in both devising a format and conducting an audit, an approach that is both logical and sequential is best. For instance, since asset protection includes real estate, a facility's physical security is a logical starting point. In turn, the examination of physical security should begin at a facility's property line regardless of whether that line encompasses landscaped grounds and parking areas or whether it merely consists of a building's outer walls.

However, because a building's contents also need protection, examining internal physical security should follow in sequence. This phase should cover the physical security of offices, laboratories, computer rooms, stockrooms, warehouse space, and so on. It should also look at the protection afforded to records (regardless of their form of media), machines and office equipment, the status of fire suppression systems, and the extent to which hardware and technology are used as part of the site's physical security program.

By no means is physical security the only way in which losses can be minimized, if not prevented. Well-run organizations also develop and issue policies and procedures that deal with administration and operations. Among other things they are intended to provide for controls and accountability that, in turn, can affect the protection and conservation of assets. Obviously not all policies and procedures are security-related. However, for those that are, controls and accountability can contribute to effective loss prevention, but only to the extent that those policies and procedures are implemented. Therefore, since the degree of implementation and compliance needs to be determined as part of the audit process, the adopted format should also have a section on administrative and operational security.

As an illustration, whether keys, coded cards, or combinations are used to control access to buildings, interior spaces, file cabinets, or safes, there must be a policy and procedure to control and account for the issue and recovery of keys and cards, and for combination changes when needed. Among the matters covered by the policy and procedure would be who approves access and under what circumstances, how to deal with reportedly lost or stolen keys or cards, their recovery or combination changes when individuals no longer need access, and how those to whom keys and combinations are given protect them when not actually in use. Some of this obviously entails record keeping; therefore, at least a random sample of those records should be examined as part of an audit. Examples of other records to be reviewed might include those kept on the issue and recovery of identification badges, shipping documents on which errors were made, or nondisclosure agreements signed by vendors. (See Appendix 5A and Appendix 5B for two sample security audit checklists.) Of course, as a practical matter record reviews need only go back to the time of the last audit.

The audit format should include a separate section for each facility at which there is a security department. It must also be comprehensive in terms of departmental operations. Normally this aspect of an audit would include, among other things, the type and frequency of training afforded the staff, the completeness and usefulness of departmental records, the adequacy and condition of uniforms and equipment, the site's security incident experience, and for multisite operations, whether those incidents have been reported to corporate security. For instance, the most complete records may be useless from an investigative point of view if they are filed in a way that would prevent or even hamper data retrieval.

From the foregoing it can be seen that audits should be as comprehensive as possible if they are to have a meaningful impact on security's role in risk management. If vulnerabilities are unobserved, they cannot even be minimized, let alone completely eliminated. At the same time, failure to act can mean continuing, and possibly greater, problems and losses for employers. Therefore, auditors must first determine whether there are any defects or weaknesses in the site's physical security, if there is evidence of either inadequate compliance or noncompliance with security-related policies and procedures in administrative and operational matters, and if there are any deficiencies in the security department's operations. Only after all of this has been done can auditors know to what extent there is need for improvement in the facility's security program. Those needs, in turn, will then enable them to determine and recommend appropriate corrective action.

Merely understanding the audit process and its objectives is not enough. Allied issues also warrant consideration. One of the first is whether or not sites or functions to be audited should be given advance notice of an audit. Arguments can be found in support of both positions.

Those who advocate the no-advance-notice theory contend that unannounced audits offer a truer picture of security, including whether there is compliance with security-related policies and procedures. They will argue that advance notice merely gives those locations to be audited a chance to review security, correct deficiencies, and ensure compliance with policies and procedures, at least for the duration of the audit. On the other hand, experienced security managers know that keen observers can always detect at least some deficiencies, whether in the course of audits or otherwise.

Therefore, there are questions that need to be asked. For instance, should the only purpose of security audits be to find weaknesses in the audited facility's security and shortcomings in its compliance with policies? Is it possible that they can serve other and equally useful purposes as well? Will the presumed benefits of not giving advance notice outweigh the potential harm that secrecy may breed?

In looking for answers to these questions, security directors and managers may find it helpful to remember that for their programs to succeed they need the cooperation of all employees, not merely of those who work in the security department. To achieve this, they must devote a good part of their time to educating and training employees generally. They should also understand that in many respects audits are like disciplinary action in that they can and should be used as a teaching tool.

Therefore, what is the harm if employees anticipate an audit? The advance notice will make them examine the site's security posture and increase their security consciousness. It is also an inducement to make a concerted effort to correct deficiencies and ensure policy compliance. However, this is done without the emotional stress that occurs when auditors suddenly appear on site ready to go to work. In addition, when program defects are found and corrective action is called for, there is no resentment against the auditors largely because of the openness of the audit process itself.

As security directors and managers become increasingly professional, many are beginning to feel that unannounced audits may do more harm than good. The unannounced audit puts the auditors in an adversarial position vis-à-vis the audited site's management. As a result, the very people whose help and cooperation they need for success in the area of program implementation are instead embarrassed and antagonized, regardless of whether the results of the audit are positive or negative. Nor will the results of an unannounced audit necessarily be much different from those of an audit when advance notice has been given.

Consequently, the principal difference lies in the fact that without secrecy there is little or no antagonism, embarrassment, or resentment of security on the part of those whose operations have been audited. This, in turn, contributes to a better appreciation of security's role in the total organization and fosters a better relationship between security and other departments or facilities, making them more receptive to working closely with security in the field of effective asset protection and conservation.

Regardless of whether these audits are unannounced or announced, other questions must be answered: With what frequency should the audits be conducted? By whom should they be conducted? The answers to both will be determined in part by an employer's size. For instance, if only one site is involved, semiannual audits by the security manager are not unreasonable. By the same token, if multiple sites are involved, and especially if the employer is a multinational organization, the expense and time away from headquarters would make a comparable schedule impractical. When such circumstances prevail, security directors are obliged to find other ways to ensure that designated facilities are audited regularly.

In this respect the security audit policy and procedure of a multinational corporation, dealing with both the frequency of audits and by whom they would be conducted, may be helpful. It stipulated the following:

1. All major U.S. facilities would be audited once a year by the corporate security director, assisted by a security manager from a site other than the one being audited. Canadian and Mexican facilities would be audited on the same basis, but by the corporate security director alone.

2. No less than five nor more than seven months following corporate level audits, site security managers would do self-audits using the corporate audit format. The results and recommendations for corrective action would be sent to corporate headquarters.

3. Principal European facilities would be audited every eighteen to twenty-four months. However, due to the number of sites involved, and their relative importance, certain key facilities would be audited on each trip; visits to others would be staggered so all would be audited within a reasonable time. The director of administration for European operations, who was also responsible for risk management, was the other audit team member.

4. Since the director of administration for European operations visited all facilities regularly, they would be audited by him or her semiannually other than when a corporate audit was made. The format and reporting requirements were the same as for U.S. operations.

5. Principal South American locations would be audited by the corporate security director with the same frequency as those in Europe. Semiannual audits were to be made by country general managers.

6. The program for European operations would apply to the principal Far East and Pacific operations, but with corporate security audits at twenty-four- to thirty-month intervals.

7. Because of the frequency and regularity with which internal auditors visited all sites worldwide, including those whose size did not warrant regular corporate security visits, they would be given a checklist of specific things affecting security, and risk management from a security perspective, to be examined as part of their own audits. Their findings would be reported to corporate security.

Lastly, to whom should the results of security audits be reported? A sound practice is to furnish the results to the person in charge of the audited facility as well as to the appropriate senior person with the ultimate responsibility for the functioning of the audited site. For instance, in a multisite manufacturing organization, a copy would go to the plant manager, another to the manufacturing division head, and a third to the security director's supervisor. Similarly, if the audited site is a sales office, retail store, or hotel, copies would go to the local manager and to his or her superior.

Regardless of the distribution, upon the completion of audits prudent security directors will discuss their findings with the individuals responsible for the audited locations before writing and disseminating the reports. This serves several purposes. As already discussed in this chapter, it helps avoid needless conflict with the very people without whose cooperation the security program cannot possibly succeed. Having advance notice of the deficiencies found saves them embarrassment should their superiors question the results.

Discussing audit findings with the appropriate people can also be helpful to the person who conducted the audit. The auditor's task goes beyond looking for shortcomings; it obliges him or her to recommend specific ways in which they can be overcome. However, in doing so no security director, regardless of how professional or astute, can hope to be thoroughly familiar with the in-depth activities of each audited facility. Consequently, his or her ideas for corrective action may not always be feasible without some modification. Frequently at these closing conferences site managers will share the auditor's concerns, but they also will point out that due to certain local conditions, of which the auditor is unaware, implementing the latter's precise suggestions will adversely affect operations. This, then, affords them an opportunity to search for and agree upon solutions that will satisfy both the security and operating concerns. In addition, should implementation of the agreed-upon approach possibly require funding not already budgeted for, both managers are much better positioned to support any such request.

The foregoing methodology proved to be an effective audit mechanism for this particular multinational organization. With help from the internal auditors, it also ensured complete coverage of all facilities regardless of size. Furthermore, it provided a learning experience for both the security managers who accompanied the corporate security director as members of an audit team and those who helped facilitate his work. Their exposure to the audit process increased their awareness of security's importance as well as their effectiveness in terms of being able to detect risks and recommend appropriate measures to prevent or at least minimize losses.

FEASIBILITY STUDIES

It is by no means unusual for large organizations, or even some medium-sized ones, that decide to either relocate or build new facilities to have feasibility studies made. Their purpose is to examine a wide range of issues that will be helpful in the decision-making process. They provide information as to whether the site or sites selected are suitable for the organization's purposes. For example, among the many factors examined are zoning requirements, building codes, tax structures, the condition of existing buildings or of the land on which new buildings will be erected, evidence of health or environmental hazards, water sources, availability of transportation for business purposes and personnel, and possibly the existence of a labor pool. However, rarely do these feasibility studies take security-related issues into account.

It is true that the presence or absence of real or potential security problems should not be the controlling factor in terms of selecting or rejecting a site, but to proceed without taking security factors into account is both shortsighted and potentially expensive. Prevailing conditions could conceivably affect insurance rates, employee morale, and construction or renovation costs (including the installation of physical security), all of which might influence a decision with respect to a particular project.

Consequently, when considering the acquisition of new locations, not only should security directors or managers be involved, they should also conduct security-based feasibility studies (Appendix 5C). These studies can serve a dual purpose for their employers. Obviously, they should highlight the extent to which a proposed site, if chosen, will have either a favorable or unfavorable effect on protection. At the same time they should be used to indicate what will be needed for security if a given location is selected. Checklists are used for security audits to ensure that all pertinent areas are covered. Therefore, prudent security managers should also develop a checklist for use when making a feasibility study. The question is, what should be included?

Certainly information should be obtained with respect to local police and fire services. While it is hoped that need for their services will be minimal, the fact remains that their location, size, and degree of professionalism can be important. For example, while police services provided by state police or a county sheriff's patrols, with the nearest barracks or station thirty miles from a proposed site, or a fire department composed only of volunteers, might not militate against a particular location, they assuredly would have an impact on a security department's size and training. In this same vein, what is the nature of criminal activity in the area, and how extensive is it? These matters have an undeniable relationship to the subject of risk management from both a security and insurance perspective.

Similarly, if contract security officers are used, the site under consideration may lend added importance to the criteria for agency selection discussed in Chapter 2. Location may be a factor in deciding whether to install central station or proprietary intrusion and fire alarm systems. Also, as discussed in Chapter 2, high technology properly applied often enables security directors to provide better protection with fewer security officers. If so, important matters to be considered would deal with the availability of such equipment, of qualified service personnel, and of prompt service when needed.

In addition to the various matters normally included in a security-related feasibility study, those made for multinational organizations must determine not only whether certain kinds of security practices are allowed, but also whether certain kinds of security equipment are readily available abroad or if they would have to be imported. If the latter, would the import duties be so great as to make the cost of using such equipment prohibitive? Even if cost is not a factor, can the desired items be used? Although the use of much equipment, and of certain practices, is perfectly acceptable in the United States, such equipment or practices are not necessarily equally acceptable in other countries. Consequently, these determinations must be made because of their possible impact on the loss prevention program. No less important is the possibility that in some places failure to fully consider these issues may not only result in embarrassment, but can conceivably lead to problems with the government that, in turn, might have an adverse effect on the entire proposed business operation.

To illustrate, in one country the size of a security department could have been reduced by approximately one-third and its operations made more effective and efficient if it had been equipped with two-way radios. However, since there was a government edict prohibiting the use of two-way radios by private organizations or persons, there was no reason to even look into the cost and service factors. A multinational employer with offices in another country had to use a modified version of its corporate-wide photo identification badges for its staff because the type of camera needed to make those badges could not even be used, let alone owned, by nongovernment organizations. Cost and service would not have been obstacles in this instance, but government regulation was. Insofar as security practices are concerned, in still another country local custom permitted employers to conduct rather thorough searches of employees, and whatever they might be carrying, whenever they left the premises. At the same time employees' lockers were considered private and not subject to search.

Consequently, feasibility studies can contribute to risk management and add another dimension to security's role in this area. In a broader sense, and perhaps of even greater importance, they also can be helpful to employers in avoiding certain pitfalls or minimizing some risks whenever expansion or relocation is being considered.

NEW CONSTRUCTION AND MAJOR ALTERATION PROJECTS

Feasibility studies generally precede new construction projects. However, once a decision is made to build, or undertake a major alteration for that matter, security's contribution to risk management through the use of physical protection should be neither ignored nor minimized. Despite this, too often security directors have little or nothing to say about physical security during a project's design and construction stages. This is true despite the fact that many architects have neither the requisite knowledge nor understanding of security to enable them to incorporate features that will help to reduce an employer's exposure to losses. Instead, architects, and unfortunately some employers as well, assume that the architectural plans will take security needs into account, or else they labor under a misconception that security is incompatible with esthetics and operating efficiency.

For example, front desk personnel at a luxury hotel were unable to exercise even minimal control over guest elevators because of a solid wall obstructing their view. A similar situation existed in a major hospital's new, circular-shaped patient care building due to the fact that the nursing stations on each floor faced 90 degrees away from the elevator bays. In a third situation the architect's failure to locate a security office on the building's first floor, where it also could be used as a reception function, obliged the employer to spend money for receptionists that otherwise could have been saved.

With proper planning and good communications among architects, engineers, employers, and security directors or managers, such problems need not happen. Once those responsible for a building's design or renovation understand that from a conceptual viewpoint esthetics, operating efficiency, and security are complementary rather than mutually exclusive, each of the three elements can benefit. The question is, when and under what circumstances should security directors or managers become involved with new construction or major alteration projects?

That involvement should begin when specifications are being written and the first set of plans come off the drawing board. If this is not done, and proper physical security is not incorporated, upon the project's completion one of three things may happen: the owner will (1) be unaware of the absence of adequate physical security until an incident occurs,

(2) learn of the problem and decide to do nothing, or (3) realize that risks exist and decide to retrofit. In the event of the latter, there may be more involved than just the extra construction costs associated with cutting, patching, and painting; conceivably there could also be a loss of revenue while the work is being done. For instance, suppose a newly built hotel decides to retrofit its guest rooms with a new electronic access control system. It may find itself unable to sell certain rooms until the work is completed. Therefore, it is evident that it is infinitely less expensive to make changes on paper than it is to start making them once construction has begun or been completed.

Perhaps three different illustrations will prove helpful. In the first, involving a multinational manufacturer, the corporate security director was asked to write the specifications for all security-related hardware, including locks, security and life safety alarms, and closed circuit television cameras and monitors, in addition to reviewing the plans as any modifications were made. This resulted in the purchase and installation of quality state-of-the art equipment for all planned new construction.

The second project was construction of a new luxury hotel. A security management consultant was retained from the project's inception to review all security-related specifications and plans and make recommendations. Everyone involved agreed that smoke detectors would be installed in all guest and public areas; sprinklers would be installed throughout the property. However, the consultant's advice was also sought regarding the installation of smoke and heat detection systems in the so-called "back of the house," including the laundry and certain storerooms. Installation costs had to be weighed against the impact on hotel operations should a fire occur; the decision itself would have no significant effect on insurance premiums. Inasmuch as the entire property was to be sprinklered, criteria were suggested to help the hotel owner decide. They were based on the extent of foreseeable but reasonable damage to assets, and access to replacements within twenty-four hours no matter the day of the week. In addition, the consultant regularly attended job meetings during the course of construction to ensure effective coordination of all security-related work with other aspects of the project and to provide for the expansion of certain security systems should that become necessary at a later date. This also helped avoid needless expense for the hotel's owner.

The third situation involved modifications for a 600,000-square-foot office building. A knowledgeable security director, whose role and department were fully integrated into the employer's overall business environment, recommended that instead of merely modernizing some parts of the physical security system, the project should be expanded to consolidate security and building management (heating, ventilating, air conditioning, elevator controls, and some electrical work) into a single system. The recommendation was approved. Once the work was completed, not only was security markedly improved, but security personnel were also used much more efficiently. Of equal importance was the fact that the integrated systems approach produced savings that resulted in the entire project's being paid for in nine months instead of the three-year period originally forecast by the vendor.

While the foregoing are examples of when security managers should become involved with new construction or major alteration projects, thought must also be given to the scope of their involvement. As a practical matter, if they are to help minimize risks and enhance the protection and conservation of assets, more is called for than writing specifications for security-related equipment and deciding on where it can best be used.

Some of a building's materials, and its layout, can also have an effect on security. Modern construction methods, building codes, and safety and environmental standards require the use of materials that are fire-retardant and that do not pose a threat to the safety and health of employees and invitees. At the same time, architects may not always think about using some materials that can improve security and provide savings to owners. For instance, a public school system was plagued with an almost constant need to replace windows broken by vandals. Although the initial installation of an appropriate glass substitute, such as Lexan, admittedly would have been more expensive than the regular window glass that was used, in the long run the board of education would have saved money by no longer having the labor and material expenses associated with the ongoing replacement program.

Since layout, including the location of various functional areas (and often of fixtures as well), tends to be considered during the design stage, the way in which it is handled can have a bearing on risk management from a security perspective. Therefore, security directors and managers rightfully deserve to have input on the subject. Once again, illustrations may prove helpful.

The location of functions to which the general public, or even some employees for that matter, should be denied access is a legitimate security concern. For instance, hotels do not want guests entering the "back of the house," hospitals do not want patients or visitors wandering into surgical suites, and retailers do not want customers to have access to stockrooms. At the same time, the need to locate a human resources office where it is accessible to employees is obvious. However, its location should be one that will also allow applicants to enter and leave, but without their having more access to the building than they really need. For instance, in the case of a human resources office, if location is not taken into consideration, it becomes relatively easy for people who enter for other than legitimate purposes (and who may be caught wandering about the building) to try to explain their presence by pleading that they must have gotten lost while looking for the personnel office.

Vendors' sales representatives do not sell to only one organization; they have other customers who may be your organization's competitors. Since information is a valuable asset, yours may be of interest to them; it is certainly of interest to their customers. To minimize the risk of organizations' needless exposure, purchasing offices should be near an entrance from the street so vendors' movements can be more easily controlled and effectively restricted to the purchasing department.

Executive offices should be placed where subtle but no less effective access control is possible. Not all visitors to the premises necessarily are there to see the executives, nor do all employees constantly have a need to enter executive office areas. Certainly offices in which considerable sums of money or other negotiable instruments, or other highly valued assets are handled or kept should be in relatively isolated areas. Hotel registration desks should be closer to the main entrance, and cashiers farther away. Hospital nursing stations should be located where nurses or floor secretaries can observe arrivals to and departures from patient care floors. In manufacturing, while finished goods should be located close to, but not at, shipping docks, they must also be protected. Regardless of the type of organization, storerooms for all materials, including foodstuffs, should be near receiving docks to expedite their movement to secure storage areas.

Layout in terms of overall design is one thing, but there are other more individualized aspects that should not be ignored, particularly in the case of retailing and the ways in which merchandise is displayed. For example, there are supermarkets where aisles, placed at right angles to checkout lanes, prevent cashiers from having even minimal deterrent value insofar as shoplifters are concerned. In other types of retailing, such as clothing stores, merchandise display racks are often placed in ways that make it extremely difficult, if not impossible, for salespeople to have a clear line of sight. This can do more than affect their ability to observe shoplifters; it also can adversely affect sales by making it more difficult for them to see and thereby help legitimate customers.

From these few examples one can easily see that the nature of each individual organization's activity, and the location of each of its facilities, if it has more than one, must be taken into account when thinking in terms of design and layout. Certainly there is nothing in any of the above illustrations that would detract from either the facilities' appearance or operating efficiency. Quite the contrary, operating efficiency would be enhanced.

Not to be forgotten is the fact that security's role in risk management warrants the consideration of other construction-related factors. No one would argue against the need for storerooms to help with both housekeeping and the protection of certain tangible assets. Nor would anyone disagree with the idea that to provide that protection the storerooms must be locked. Nevertheless, the construction of the storerooms themselves often leaves a good deal to be desired.

For instance, it is by no means unusual to find storerooms that consist of nothing more than chicken wire held in place by 2×4s instead of more substantial materials. Not infrequently storeroom walls, even when made of materials that afford better security, may be only six or seven feet high, despite the fact that there is a ten-foot ceiling. To make matters worse, some of the room's contents may be stacked both adjacent to and well above the outer wall's height so that the theft of inventory is relatively easy. There also are cases where storerooms are located within space that has hung or false ceilings and enough crawl space above them to accommodate a person, and yet there is no provision for the protection of their contents. Such exposure necessarily increases the risk of theft or damage, and consequently of loss.

There may be some who do not fully appreciate security's relationship to the whole concept of risk management, and as a result they feel that such concerns are of relatively minor importance. However, to those who are prepared to accept security's role in any organization—namely to prevent losses, or at the very least minimize the value of those losses that may be unavoidable—the previous illustrations should send all security directors or managers a loud and clear message: *Do not consider anything too small or unimportant for your attention.*

SUMMARY

Too often security's role in risk management is either ignored or misunderstood. When this happens, in the final analysis it is the employers who are the losers. In order for businesses and institutions to derive the greatest benefit from their security and risk management departments, not only the respective department heads, but also those for whom they work, must learn that these functions really are complementary, not competitive; they both have loss prevention as their ultimate objective. Inasmuch as few organizations carry, or can afford to carry, 100 percent insurance coverage for all possible losses, security's approach to loss prevention is based on the idea of incident avoidance by using a variety of techniques and tactics. Risk management, on the other hand, tries to minimize losses by buying the best insurance coverage for the least amount of money from companies that also offer policyholders programs to help prevent losses, and by processing and negotiating claims when losses do occur. Put another way, security's emphasis is on preventing losses; risk management's is on minimizing their financial impact on the employer.

In furtherance of their role in managing risks, security directors or managers are fully aware of the value of periodic security audits. These audits serve as a vehicle to detect deficiencies in all aspects of the employer's loss prevention program; they are also a means of ensuring compliance with security policies and procedures. Furthermore, if conducted in the right way, they can also be used to help educate other department heads in terms of security's importance in managing risks as well as to help train security department subordinates in the ways in which effective audits should be made.

If feasibility studies are to be made when relocation or expansion is being considered, they should be expanded to ensure that all of the various security factors are examined. This is not to suggest that they necessarily will or should be the deciding factor in terms of site selection. However, knowing what the risks may be once a location has been agreed upon will better enable the security director to plan for and provide the most appropriate and cost-effective loss prevention program. Doing this is yet another contribution to the employer's overall risk management program.

While there is nothing incompatible between esthetics and operating efficiency on one hand and security on the other, when new construction or major alterations are to be undertaken, security directors too often are precluded from even expressing their opinions on the subject, let alone being asked for them. When this happens, and the many security-related factors that should be considered are either ignored or placed in the hands of persons who are untrained or inexperienced in security, the element of risk for the employer, and cost of corrective action at a later date, are increased. At the same time, however, it is important for security managers to be able to expand their own horizons. They have to be able to go beyond pure security considerations in the design and construction of what are to be eye-pleasing and efficient workplaces, and better understand the employer's total needs if the organization is to succeed.

REVIEW QUESTIONS

1. What is the difference between an insured risk and a hazard?
2. What is meant by a deductible clause in an insurance policy?
3. In what ways are security and risk management complementary functions?
4. Why is it important for security and risk managers to work closely together?
5. What two things should investigations of security-related incidents accomplish?
6. What purposes do security audits serve?
7. What should security audits cover?

8. What is meant by a feasibility study?

9. Why should security-related factors be taken into account when feasibility studies are made?

10. Why is it important for security directors to become involved with new construction or major alteration projects from their inception?

APPENDIX 5A
Sample Security Audit Checklist
for a Manufacturing Organization

Facility Audited: _____ Audit Date(s): _____

Audited by: _____

I. Physical Security

  A. Exterior

    1. Grounds

      a. Perimeter protection is _____ acceptable
                                      _____ unacceptable

         If unacceptable, why? _____

         _____

      b. Lighting is _____ acceptable _____ unacceptable

         If unacceptable, why? _____

         _____

      c. Parking lot protection is _____ acceptable
                                            _____ unacceptable

         By what means, if any, is it provided? _____

         _____

    2. Storage Facilities

      a. Fuel
         Protection is _____ acceptable _____ unacceptable

         By what means provided? _____

         _____

      b. Other (Describe) _____

         Protection is _____ acceptable _____ unacceptable

         How provided? _____

         _____

B. Buildings (total number on site) _____ If multiple buildings, are they physically connected or separated?

_____

1. Ingress and Egress Controls

    a. Total number of employee entrances _____

    b. Total number of visitor entrances _____

    c. Do employees and visitors use the same one(s)?

    _____

    d. How is employee ingress and egress controlled?

    _____

    e. How is visitor ingress and egress controlled?

    _____

2. Doors Generally

    a. Are perimeter doors, other than designated entrances
       and shipping/receiving doors, normally locked? _____
       If yes, but there are any exceptions, explain.

    _____

    b. What means are used to secure perimeter doors?

    _____

    _____

    c. Are all key-operated door locks on the corporate sys-
       tem? _____ If not, explain.

    _____

    _____

    d. Describe the type(s) of shipping/receiving doors and
       how they are secured.

    _____

    _____

e. If shipping/receiving doors have automatic controls, how are the controls secured when not in use?

_____

_____

f. How are shipping/receiving docks protected when the doors are open?

_____

_____

3. Office area, office, computer room doors

a. Are those with locks secured after hours? _____ If not, explain.

_____

_____

b. If secured with combination locks, how often or under what circumstances are combinations changed, and by whom?

_____

c. How is computer room access controlled?

_____

_____

d. Do computer rooms have door or window openings for the passage of work? _____ If not, how is this handled?

_____

_____

e. Do computer rooms have security alarms? _____ If yes, describe.

_____

_____

4. Communication areas

    a. Are the mail and TLX-teletype rooms and copy centers consolidated into a single area? _____ If so, how is the space secured both during and after working hours?

    b. If not, describe how each separate area is protected, both during and after normal working hours.

Mail Room

TLX/Teletype

Copy Center

    c. How is the Telephone Switchroom protected?

5. Stockrooms, Tool Cribs, Warehouse Space

    a. Is access to each controlled, and if so, how?

    b. If not, explain.

c. Do those equipped with other than sliding doors have exposed hinges, and if so, how are the hinges secured?

_____

_____

d. Is there overhead protection? _____ If not, is the security afforded the contents of each _____ acceptable or _____ unacceptable? Explain.

_____

_____

e. Describe the physical protection, if any, provided for IOS materials.

_____

_____

6. Records and miscellaneous storage

a. If in storerooms, do doors have locks, and are they secured after hours? _____

b. If in file cabinets, how are the cabinets secured when not in use?

_____

_____

The protection is _____ acceptable
                   _____ unacceptable

c. If stored in locked file cabinets, how are the keys protected after hours?

_____

_____

d. How is petty cash protected during the day and after hours?

_____

_____

e. How are traveler's checks and blank check stock secured?

_____

_____

f. If the site has a check signing plate, how is it protected?

_____

_____

g. If any check stock and/or check signature plates are kept in a safe, how many people have the combination? _____ When and under what circumstances was the combination last changed, and by whom?

_____

_____

h. Where are computer backup tapes stored, and is their protection acceptable or unacceptable? Describe.

_____

_____

II. Operational and Administrative Security

A. Access Control Generally

1. Employees

a. Do photo ID badges conform to the Corporate Communications Manual and Corporate Safety/Security Policies and Procedures in *all* respects? _____ If not, explain.

_____

_____

b. Are badge requests properly completed? _____ If not, explain.

_____

_____

c. By whom are badges issued? _____ Recovered? _____ Do these conform to policy? _____ If not, explain.

_____

_____

d. Do nonresident employees require escorts? _____ If so, explain.

_____

_____

e. How or by whom are employee IDs, resident and nonresident, verified at point of entry?

_____

_____

f. Are key authorization requests properly completed in *all* respects? _____ If not, explain.

_____

_____

g. By whom are keys issued, recovered, and records thereof kept?

_____

_____

h. Are keys transferred from one employee to another without an actual recovery and reissue? _____

2. Contractors

    a. Are contractors issued identification badges, and if so, do they conform to the Corporate Communications Manual and Corporate Safety/Security Policies and Procedures? _____ If not, explain.

      _____

      _____

    b. By whom are they issued and recovered?

      _____

      _____

    c. Are written requests required for initial issue, renewal, or both? _____ If not, explain.

      _____

      _____

    d. Are keys issued to contractors? _____ If yes, explain.

      _____

      _____

3. Visitors

    a. Are visitors issued identification badges, and if so, do they conform to the Corporate Communications Manual and Corporate Safety/Security Policies and Procedures? _____ If not, explain.

      _____

      _____

    b. By whom are they issued and recovered?

      _____

      _____

c. Are visitors required to sign in and out? _____

d. Do visitors require escorts? _____ If not, explain.

_____

_____

B. Access to Sensitive Areas (Computer Rooms, Stockrooms, Tool Cribs, Shipping/Receiving Docks, R&D Areas, Marcom, etc.)

1. Are administrative as distinguished from physical security access controls used for protecting sensitive areas?

_____

2. If so, describe briefly the measures used for each such area.

_____

_____

_____

C. Protection of Assets

1. Are all contractors required to execute a Nondisclosure Agreement before starting their work? _____ If not, explain.

_____

_____

2. If yes, where are copies filed?

_____

3. What policy, if any, is followed regarding the use of cameras and picture taking on site?

_____

_____

4. Does the site comply with *all* provisions of the Corporate Safety/Security Policy and Procedure entitled Protection of Assets in Transit, including those relating to Property Passes? _____ List deficiencies or evidence of non-compliance.

_____

_____

5. Is the site in compliance with the Corporate Safety/Security Policy and Procedure entitled Loan, Use, and Recovery of Company Assets? _____ If not, explain.

_____

_____

6. Are personnel through whom Property Passes clear provided with current lists and sample signatures of authorized signatories? _____ How are sample signatures protected when not actually in use?

_____

_____

7. Have all managers and supervisors received copies of the Corporate Policy and Procedure entitled Protection of Company Confidential Information, and is the site in compliance? _____ If not, explain.

_____

_____

8. Describe how proprietary information is disposed of when not needed, whether destruction is witnessed, and if so, by whom?

_____

_____

9. Are accountability records kept on engineering or similar notebooks? _____ If so, are they audited to ensure their preservation and need for retention by the employee to whom charged? _____ With what frequency?

_____

_____

10. Is the need to protect proprietary information discussed at the site manager's staff meetings? If so, how often?

_____

11. If Inventory, Obsolete and Surplus materials are disposed of locally, what is done to ensure that those to be destroyed are in fact destroyed?

_____

_____

12. If truck drivers, other than company employees, are not restricted to the immediate vicinity of shipping/receiving docks, how are their movements controlled?

_____

_____

13. Are they allowed to load their own vehicles other than under direct supervision? _____ If so, explain.

_____

_____

14. Are all quantities—whether being shipped or received—checked, counted, and/or weighed by company personnel? _____ If not, explain.

_____

_____

III. Emergencies

A. Bomb Threats

1. Are switchboard operators and security personnel familiar with the procedure to be followed in the event of a bomb threat? _____ If not, explain.

   _____

   _____

2. Have they been made aware of the details of the call and about the caller for whom they should be alert? _____ If yes, how? _____ If not, explain.

   _____

   _____

3. Does a local bomb search procedure exist? _____ If not, explain.

   _____

   _____

4. Have any bomb threats been received since the last (corporate or self) security audit? _____ If so, were they reported to Corporate Safety/Security? _____ If not reported, explain.

   _____

   _____

B. Evacuations

1. Are evacuation routes conspicuously posted? _____ If not, explain.

   _____

   _____

2. Does a local evacuation procedure, including the designation of preselected departmental assembly points, exist? _____ Are all employees familiar with it? _____ When was it last reviewed with them?

_____

_____

3. If none exists, explain.

_____

_____

C. Fires

1. Are employees trained in the use of fire extinguishers?

_____

2. If yes, by whom has training been provided, and with what frequency?

_____

_____

3. Have there been any fires, regardless of size or possible loss, since the last corporate or self security audit?

_____

4. If yes, were they reported to Corporate Safety/Security? _____ If not reported, explain.

_____

_____

IV. **Security Administration/Operations**

A. Safety/Security Personnel

1. To whom does the site's safety/security manager, supervisor, or representative report directly?

_____

_____

2. Does the site's safety/security manager, supervisor, or representative attend the site manager's staff meetings? _____ If not, explain.

_____

_____

3. What percentage of his or her time does the site safety/security manager, supervisor, or representative devote exclusively to safety/security matters?

_____%

4. Does the site safety/security manager, supervisor, or representative regularly attend the scheduled Corporate Safety/Security Conferences? _____ If not, explain.

_____

_____

5. Are other safety/security personnel employed at the site? ___ If yes, for how many shifts per day, hours per shift, and hours per week?

_____

_____

6. If guards are employed at the site, are they proprietary or contract personnel, or a combination of the two?

_____

7. Are guards uniformed? _____ Armed? _____ If armed, by virtue of whose authority?

_____

_____

8. How much training, both initial and refresher, is given to guards, and by whom?

_____

_____

9. If no training is provided for guards, explain.

    _____

    _____

B. Operations

    1. Are patrol rounds regularly made both inside and outside
       the facility? _____ If yes, with what frequency?

       _____

       _____

    2. Are rounds made using a Dextex or similar device? _____

    3. Are patrols randomized both as to route and time? _____
       If not, explain.

       _____

       _____

    4. Are patrols made on foot, in a vehicle, or a combination
       of the two? _____

    5. If no patrol rounds of any sort are made, explain.

       _____

       _____

C. Incidents and Investigations

    1. Are incidents reported to Site Safety/Security recorded? ____

    2. How are all reported incidents followed up? Describe the
       procedure.

       _____

       _____

3. Does the site comply with the Corporate Safety/Security Policy and Procedure entitled Security Incident Reporting? _____ If not, explain.

_____

_____

4. Has the site encountered any "reportable activities" as defined in the Corporate Safety/Security Policy and Procedure on Investigations since the last corporate security audit? _____

5. If so, have they been reported to Corporate Safety/Security as required by and in conformity with that policy? _____ If not, explain.

_____

_____

D. Records and Communications

1. Of what do security records consist?

_____

_____

2. For what purpose(s) other than historical are they used? Describe.

_____

_____

3. Are security personnel duties and responsibilities in writing? _____ Are specific post instructions in writing?

_____

4. Are security patrol personnel equipped with two-way radios? _____ If not, what means of communication are used to maintain contact?

_____

_____

E. Liaison

   1. Is the site safety/security manager, supervisor, or rep-
      resentative personally acquainted with the locally appro-
      priate ranking law enforcement and fire service
      officials? _____

   2. Identify by title who those officials are for the audited
      site (e.g., police chief, sheriff, precinct commander,
      fire chief, fire battalion chief, etc.).

      _____

      _____

   3. To what extent, if any, is contact maintained with the
      respective officials?

      _____

      _____

   4. In the event of a bomb threat, how close is the nearest
      bomb disposal unit, and by what agency is it operated?

      _____

   5. In the event of an accident or emergency, other than bomb
      threat or fire, how close is the nearest rescue squad or
      similar unit?

      _____

      _____

   6. Is the local fire department a full-time paid unit, a
      volunteer unit, or a combination of the two?

      _____

      _____

APPENDIX 5B
Sample Security Audit Checklist for an Office Building

Office/Remote Location Audited: _____

Audit Date(s): _____ Audited by: _____

I. Physical Security

  A. Location

    1. Urban or suburban _____

    2. Structure

      a. Office building _____

      b. Office or industrial park _____

      c. Type of construction _____

      d. Sprinklered? _____

    3. Floor(s) on which located _____

  B. Exterior

    1. Grounds landscaped? _____

    2. Note window/door exposure _____

    3. Type(s) of door(s) and locks

      a. Leading into space _____

      b. Within space _____

      c. If unacceptable, why? _____

    4. Lighting is _____ acceptable _____ unacceptable

      If unacceptable, why?

      _____

      _____

    5. Parking protection is _____ acceptable
                         _____ unacceptable

      How is it provided? _____

6. Type(s) of window/door glass _____

C. Building Security

   1. Ingress and Egress Controls

      a. Total number of entrances to space? _____

      b. Do employees and visitors use the same one(s)? _____

      c. How is employee ingress and egress controlled?

         _____

      d. How is visitor ingress and egress controlled?

         _____

      e. Are perimeter doors, other than designated entrances and shipping/receiving doors, normally locked? _____

      f. What means are used to secure perimeter doors?

         _____

         _____

      g. Describe the type(s) of shipping/receiving doors and how they are secured.

         _____

         _____

   2. Office Area, Office, and Computer Room Doors

      a. Are those doors with locks secured after hours? _____ If not, explain.

         _____

         _____

      b. If secured with combination locks, how often or under what circumstances are combinations changed, and by whom?

         _____

         _____

c. How is computer room access controlled?

_____

_____

d. Do computer rooms have door or window openings for the passage of work? _____ If not, how is this handled?

_____

_____

e. Do computer rooms have any security type alarms? _____ If yes, describe.

_____

_____

f. Are terminals and computers physically separated? _____

3. Communications Areas

a. Are the mail room, TLX/teletype room, and copy centers consolidated into a single area? _____ If so, how is the space secured both during and after working hours?

_____

_____

b. If not, describe how each separate area is protected both during and after normal working hours.

Mail room _____

TLX/teletype _____

Copy center _____

c. How is the telephone switchroom protected?

_____

_____

4. Parts Rooms

   a. Is access controlled? _____ If so, how?

       _____

       _____

   b. If not, explain.

       _____

       _____

   c. Do those equipped with other than sliding doors have exposed hinges? _____ If so, how are they secured?

       _____

       _____

   d. Is there overhead protection? _____ If not, is the security afforded the contents _____ acceptable or _____ unacceptable? Explain.

       _____

       _____

5. Miscellaneous Storage

   a. If in storerooms, do doors have locks and are they secured after hours? _____

   b. If in file cabinets, how are the cabinets secured when not in use?

       _____

       The protection is _____ acceptable
                      _____ unacceptable

   c. If stored in locked file cabinets, how are the keys protected after hours?

       _____

   d. How is petty cash protected during the day and after hours?

       _____

e. How are travelers checks and blank check stock secured?

_____

f. Where are computer backup tapes stored and is their protection acceptable or unacceptable? Describe.

_____

II. Operational and Administrative Security

A. Access Control Generally

1. Employees

a. Is security discussed as part of new employees' orientation? _____ Is it ever discussed with employees generally at any time? _____ If so, at what intervals? _____ If not, why not?

_____

_____

b. Do photo ID badges conform to the Corporate Communications Manual and Corporate Safety/Security Policies and Procedures in *all* respects? _____ If not, explain.

_____

_____

c. Are badge requests properly completed? _____ If not, explain.

_____

_____

d. By whom are badges issued? _____ Recovered? _____ Do these conform to policy? _____ If not, explain.

_____

_____

e. Do nonresident employees require escorts? _____ If so, explain.

_____

_____

f. How or by whom are employee IDs, resident and nonresident, verified at point of entry?

_____

_____

g. Are key authorization requests properly completed in *all* respects? _____ If not, explain.

_____

_____

h. By whom are keys issued, recovered, and records thereof kept?

_____

_____

i. Are keys transferred from one employee to another without an actual recovery and reissue? _____

2. Visitors

a. Are visitors issued identification badges? _____ If so, do they conform to the Corporate Communications Manual and Corporate Safety/Security Policies and Procedures? _____ If not, explain.

_____

_____

b. By whom are they issued and recovered? _____

c. Are visitors required to sign in and out? _____

d. Do visitors require escorts? _____ If not, explain.

_____

_____

B. Access to Sensitive Areas (Computer Rooms, Storerooms, or Parts Rooms)

    1. Are administrative as distinguished from physical security access controls used for protecting sensitive areas? _____

    2. If so, describe briefly the measures used for each such area.

    _____

    _____

    _____

C. Protection of Assets

    1. What policy, if any, is followed regarding the use of cameras and picture taking on site?

    _____

    _____

    2. Does the site comply with the Corporate Safety/Security Policy and Procedure entitled Loan, Use, and Recovery of Company Assets? _____ If not, explain.

    _____

    _____

    3. Have all managers and supervisors received copies of the Corporate Policy and Procedure entitled Protection of Company Confidential Information? _____ Is the site in compliance? _____ If not, explain.

    _____

    _____

    4. Describe how proprietary information is disposed of when no longer needed, whether destruction is witnessed, and if so, by whom?

    _____

    _____

    5. Is the need to protect proprietary information discussed at managers' meetings? _____ If so, how often?

    _____

6. Are all materials—whether being shipped or received—checked, counted, and/or weighed by company personnel? _____ If not, explain.

_____

_____

III. Emergencies

A. Bomb Threats

1. Are switchboard operators familiar with the procedure to be followed in the event of a bomb threat? _____ If not, explain.

_____

_____

2. Have they been made aware of the details of the call and about the caller for whom they should be alert? _____ If yes, how recently? _____ If not, explain.

_____

_____

3. Does a local bomb search procedure exist? _____ If not, explain.

_____

_____

4. Have any bomb threats been received? _____ If so, were they reported to Corporate Safety/Security? _____ If not reported, explain.

_____

_____

B. Evacuations

1. Are evacuation routes conspicuously posted? _____ If not, explain.

_____

_____

2. Does a local evacuation procedure, including the designation of preselected functional assembly points, exist? _____ Are all employees familiar with it? _____

   When was it last reviewed with them? _____

3. If none exists, explain.

   _____

   _____

C. Fires

1. Are employees trained in the use of fire extinguishers? _____

2. If yes, by whom has training been provided, and with what frequency?

   _____

   _____

3. Have there been any fires, regardless of size or possible loss, since the last security audit? _____

4. If yes, were they reported to Corporate Safety/Security? _____ If not reported to Corporate, explain.

   _____

   _____

IV. Security Incidents and Investigations

A. Reporting Procedures

1. Are incidents reported to local managers recorded? _____

2. How are all reported incidents followed up? Describe the procedure.

   _____

   _____

3. Does the site comply with the Corporate Safety/Security Policy and Procedure entitled Security Incident Reporting? _____ If not, explain.

   _____

   _____

4. Has the site encountered any "reportable activities" as defined in the Corporate Safety/Security Policy and Procedure on Investigations since the last security audit? ____

5. If so, have they been reported to Corporate Safety/Security as required by and in conformity with that Policy? _____ If not, explain.

_____

_____

B. Liaison

1. Are any of the local managers personally acquainted with the local law enforcement and fire service officials? _____

2. Identify by title who those officials are for the audited site (e.g., police chief, sheriff, precinct commander, fire chief, fire battalion chief, etc.).

_____

_____

3. To what extent, if any, is contact maintained with the respective officials?

_____

_____

4. In the event of a bomb threat, how close is the nearest bomb disposal unit, and by what agency is it operated?

_____

_____

5. In the event of an accident or emergency, other than bomb threat or fire, how close is the nearest rescue squad or similar unit?

_____

_____

6. Is the local fire department a full-time paid unit, a volunteer unit, or a combination of the two?

_____

APPENDIX 5C
Security Feasibility Study Checklist

1. Is new construction planned or is an existing building(s) to be used?

2. Is the new location in an incorporated or unincorporated political subdivision?

3. If it is in an unincorporated political subdivision, what agency or agencies provide police services?

   a. Is there a local full-time police department?

   b. What is its size?

   c. Have its personnel attended a government-operated police academy? If so, for how long?

   d. What is the distance from the site to the nearest police station?

4. If the site is in an unincorporated political subdivision, is there a fire department?

   a. If not, who responds to fires?

   b. If there is a local fire department, is it full-time or volunteer?

   c. If volunteer, are there any full-time personnel in the department?

   d. How many firefighters are in the department?

   e. What is their level of training and by whom was it given?

   f. What is the distance from the site to the nearest fire station?

   g. What kind of fire-fighting apparatus does the department have?

   h. Would the apparatus enable the fire department to fight a fire at the new site if one occurred? If not, what is the estimated time for the arrival of proper equipment from the nearest fire department with suitable apparatus?

5. Regardless of whether the new site is in an incorporated or unincorporated political subdivision, what is the general reputation of the police and fire departments with respect to their training, efficiency, integrity, cooperation, and command structures?

6. What sorts of crimes are most prevalent in the neighborhood in which the site is located, and is their volume rated as high, average, or low for such an area?

7. Are there any legal prohibitions or other restrictions that would prevent using fire locks to secure exits?

8. Would it be possible to have fire alarms routed directly to the fire department?

9. Does the police department permit routing of privately owned intrusion alarms to its precincts or headquarters?

10. Are central station burglar and fire alarm services available in the area? If there are, what are their reputations for agency and systems reliability, service, response, and systems maintenance?

11. What is the nature of the contract guard services available in the area? Are the companies local, national, or both?

12. What are their reputations with respect to the following?

   a. The caliber, professional qualifications, and security-related experience of their managerial staffs

   b. The integrity of both management and line personnel

   c. Training

   d. Reliability

   e. Financial stability

13. What are the prevailing rates for contract security personnel?

14. Are there agencies with sufficient personnel to satisfy the new site's needs?

15. Of what does contract security officer training consist, by whom is it given, and what are the instructors' professional qualifications?

16. Do most other organizations in the area with security programs employ contract or proprietary security officers?

17. Is there a security officer labor pool in the area?

18. If the new site consists of one or more existing buildings, are they equipped with any kind of alarm systems? If yes, of what do they consist, how old are they, and when were they last tested?

19. If the proposed site is in other than a metropolitan area, what is the distance from the site to the closest companies with the ability to service alarm, closed circuit television, access control, or other high technology systems?

The following additional information needs to be obtained in connection with security feasibility studies pertaining to international operations:

1. Is it legally permissible to ask job applicants questions about arrest and/or conviction records?

2. Does the government prohibit or restrict the use of two-way radio communications, closed circuit television, or other high technology security equipment by private businesses or institutions? If the answer is yes, what are the prohibitions or restrictions?

3. Are there government prohibitions of or restrictions on the use and issue of photo identification badges or cards to employees?

4. If there are no prohibitions or restrictions with regard to any of the foregoing, are there local vendors or must any or all such equipment be imported?

5. If there are local vendors, what are their reputations for reliability and for having trained, skilled personnel capable of providing service and equipment repairs when needed?

6. If any permissible equipment would have to be imported, are the import duties high, average, or low?

7. Are there any prohibitions of or restrictions on an employer's right to search persons and parcels leaving an employer's place of business?

8. If not, can handheld or other magnetometers be used?

Chapter 6

Integrating Security into the Employer's Total Environment

In commenting on the role of security, Louis M. Spadaro, an economist and the former dean of the Martino Graduate School of Business Administration at Fordham University, observed that while detection and punishment are the primary focus of policing, they are not of central importance in a business environment since they add to costs much more than they reduce crime-related losses. He went on to say that both business and consumers are ultimately affected by such losses, and if allowed to develop along the trajectory as he then saw it, "industrial crime may become an intolerable social problem."[1]

There is much truth to what Spadaro says. It is both unrealistic and costly for businesses and institutions to rely on detection and punishment as the principal means of deterring wrongdoing, instead of instituting effective preventive measures; it is not unlike the cliche about winning a battle but losing a war. For instance, if assets are stolen, detection and punishment do not guarantee a recovery of the stolen goods. Nor is there any assurance that recovered goods will be in the same condition as they were when stolen so that they can be sold at the original price. Of course, if the wrongdoing involves a costly policy violation, no tangible recovery may be possible.

If the emphasis is on detection, apprehension, and punishment, and even if stolen assets are recovered, there will still be at least some out-of-pocket losses for employers based on the time spent investigating the incident, the time lost due to the inherently disruptive nature of investigations, the effect on employee morale when punishment is meted out, and the productive time lost by employees either directly or indirectly affected by the wrongdoing. Even if a loss is covered by insurance, the insured will not be compensated for any of the foregoing losses or for the amount of the policy's deductible.

By introducing the elements of economics and potentially serious social problems, Spadaro has focused on matters that both business and security executives have tended to neglect when thinking about the role of security. However, since his comments were made in 1977, one might well ask if Spadaro was overreacting or if he had foresight. While the magnitude of security-related losses cannot be ascertained with any degree of accuracy, it nevertheless is worth looking at some of the available data on business losses.

For the period from 1967 to 1976, the United States Chamber of Commerce, American Management Association, and Joint Economic Committee of the Congress of the United States had varying estimates of business losses due to crime ranging from a low of a little more than $3 billion a year to a high of more than $40 billion.[2] Less than twenty years later the projected annual business loss due to crime was put at $114 billion or more.[3] As further evidence of the difficulty in trying to accurately project losses, the *Lipman Report* of November 15, 1988, referring to "some experts," estimated that losses from computer crime alone would be $200 billion a year, a figure well in excess of the already cited total projected loss of about $114 billion. According to *The Wall Street Journal* of March 16, 1989, the International Trade Commission estimated that the value of stolen intellectual property alone was $40 billion a year.[4]

When businesses or institutions suffer losses of any kind, whether from the commission of crimes or because of other reasons, those in charge are concerned with their ability to maintain the organization's profit margins and viability. At the same time they also know only too well that their options are limited.

The initial reaction usually will be to raise the price for their products or services. However, they do this with the understanding that if the increases are excessive they can become self-defeating; it does no good to increase prices to a point where there are no buyers. If losses persist despite price increases, the next most likely step will be to downsize the organization. This will require a reduction in the number of employees and possibly in the number of facilities. Should options one and two fail to stem the tide of losses, those in charge now may find themselves faced with either having to file a petition in bankruptcy or go out of business. Despite our inability to determine the exact dollar amount that crimes can cost organizations, it is obvious that business losses attributable to crimes and other security-related issues can have an effect on the economy and, if large enough, on society. Therefore, Spadaro's predictions were not an overreaction; they were rather farsighted.

As security's role in relation to the needs of the many businesses and institutions that it serves continues to evolve, it is important to note that there is an increasing realization of the fact that the security function cannot and should not be limited to crime prevention. This is illustrated by the comments of Norman Bottom and John Kostanoski, who within a very few years following Spadaro's observations recognized that security had to do more than prevent crime; it also had to attempt to control waste, accidents, errors, and unethical practices.[5]

Notwithstanding the impact of business-related losses on the economy and society—whether the result of crime, waste, accidents, errors, or unethical behavior—the fact remains that the importance of integrating security into the employer's total environment is not yet fully appreciated either by many organizations' executives or by many security directors. In some respects this is just an extension of the problem encountered when employers fail to get optimum benefits from their security and risk management departments because the respective department heads see themselves as competitors rather than as collaborators, as noted in Chapter 5. So, too, are there times when employers enjoy less than optimum benefits from security because of their inclination to isolate rather than integrate it into all aspects of the workplace. Furthermore, this tendency toward isolation rather than integration is often aided by security directors and managers who either cannot or are afraid to clearly articulate the value of security's contributions to the organization.

This isolation is regrettable. It is more likely to occur when both senior management and their security department heads continue to think of security as but another form of policing. This misconception, of which both senior and security executives may be equally guilty, must be corrected in the best interests of all parties. To help make this correction can be one of the most challenging tasks that confront security directors or managers.

To achieve full integration security directors may find it necessary to educate their superiors with regard to what security's role really can and should be. However, an equally daunting task may be the need to educate themselves by developing a much better understanding not only of business but also of the relationship that must exist between security and all other business functions if security is to make a truly meaningful contribution to the protection and conservation of the employer's assets. In fact, security executives who do not fully understand their employers' business needs will find it virtually impossible to educate those same employers with respect to what an effective security program can contribute to an organization's overall success.

THE INTEGRATION PROCESS AND ITS IMPORTANCE

Without the meaningful integration of security as a concept, businesses and institutions tend to minimize rather than maximize the protection of their assets. But if integration is to occur, just what does this mean, and why is it important?

Of the various definitions of *integrate* found in *Webster's New World Dictionary*, the two that are most applicable to security's role in an organization's total environment are "to make whole or complete by adding or bringing together parts," and "to put or bring (parts) together into a whole; unify." To do precisely this in terms of security operations—in other words, to make security a part of the whole and bring it together with all of the other business functions—makes good sense and increases the benefits that can be realized by the employer.

For all practical purposes those employers who do not integrate security find themselves with a private police force. This, in turn, means that instead of having a department that is welcomed by other employees and contributes as do other legitimate business functions, their security directors and managers are effectively denied an opportunity to perform to the fullest extent of their ability. Equally important, this shortsightedness on the part of employers deprives their organizations of the benefits that could be derived from full integration.

One might logically ask what causes this far too prevalent isolation and lack of integration. As already noted, the cause can often be attributed to a combination of factors. On the one hand, executive management is often unable to distinguish between policing and security or to think of security as anything more than a form of policing. On the other hand, security directors frequently cannot appreciate that in many ways security is more of a business function than a law enforcement function. When these are the prevailing attitudes, who is to blame?

The blame must be shared by both employers and their security directors or managers, albeit not equally. As pointed out in Chapter 1, in the past, as increasing numbers of organizations saw a need for protection programs, and people to develop and manage them, they elected to recruit security managers primarily from among the ranks of retired or former law enforcement personnel. To both employers and their newly hired security directors, security's role was crime prevention.

As evidence of this approach to security, in a study published in 1972 in behalf of the Rand Corporation, James S. Kakalik and Sorrel Wildhorn reported that more than forty-three percent of security executives working for firms with 500 or more total employees, and almost forty percent of those with organizations having between 100 and 500 total employees, had backgrounds in either local or state police, the military, or federal investigative agencies.[6] They also observed that in 1960 the American Society for Industrial Security, the largest organization of its kind, estimated that of all in-house or contract agency security executives who were Society members, ten percent were former special agents of the Federal Bureau of Investigation (FBI), and another twenty-five percent had been trained by either the FBI or some other federal law enforcement agency.[7] Perhaps of equal note, in terms of the idea that security and policing were closely allied, is a footnote in the preface to the first volume of their series of five, which reads: "Throughout this study we have used the term *private police* to include all privately employed guards, investigators, patrolmen, alarm and armored-car personnel, and any other personnel performing similar functions." [8]

Because of the prevalent philosophy in policing, crime prevention by security personnel also emphasized a dual approach to deter crime in the workplace: the use of highly visible uniformed security officers on one hand, and the ability to quickly identify, apprehend, and punish those errant employees who committed crimes on the other.

Although this methodology was largely reactive, its supposed deterrent effect was thought to be the equivalent of crime prevention. As a result, it was adopted and accepted by employers who hoped that it would prove to be an effective preventive measure. Few saw a really proactive role for security. Furthermore, since acts of espionage were (and still are) crimes, and security as we have come to know it today really began in the post–World War II era when protecting government classified information in the hands of private sector defense contractors against spies was critically important, this seemed to be a logical approach.

This same very narrow view of security's role was also accepted without question by most newly hired security directors or managers for two reasons. First, many of them saw their new jobs as being little different from their old ones in policing. Second, even those few who might have been inclined to think of their new jobs in a somewhat different light understandably were hesitant or reluctant to disagree with their new bosses.

For example, one ordinarily did not expect a police chief to meet with a city purchasing manager to learn about the purchasing function in an effort to help reduce the risk of kickbacks to buyers. Consequently, one did not expect new security directors or managers to even consider that perhaps they might be able to contribute toward a reduction in the potential for such problems by meeting with the employer's purchasing manager. Nor did the idea that such a meeting might prove useful ever occur to their employers. By no means did this form of segregation or isolation cause security directors or managers any discomfort or lead them to feel that there was room for change in how they should undertake their work. On the contrary, it was precisely because they found a high degree of familiarity in their new roles that they were most comfortable with them.

One must also remember the prior training of many who entered the security field. Most came from police organizations, which by their very nature are highly structured and quasi-military; there the importance of discipline and unquestioned obedience to orders are emphasized. As a result, one did not expect them to disagree with whatever instructions they were given by their superiors. This readiness to obey assumed even greater significance for those whose backgrounds were in any government service, whether it was some type of law enforcement or the military, who soon discovered that the job security normally associated with being in government, and to which they had become accustomed, was not a staple of private sector employment.

As security's limited crime prevention role is challenged with increasing frequency, it will become obvious that both employers and security directors and managers must develop a better understanding of just what is required to satisfactorily, yet cost-effectively, protect and conserve an organization's assets. To be effective, security programs must be based on more than crime prevention, especially as the term is used in the traditional sense. To enjoy the greatest benefits both employers and their security directors or managers must be willing and able to adopt and implement a proactive approach. This includes looking for meaningful ways to prevent crimes as well as other kinds of incidents that can be costly to an organization and that can have a bearing not only on its profitability but also on its very survival. To do this with even a modicum of success calls for a better understanding of security on the part of general management personnel and a far better understanding of business on the part of security directors and managers.

Even those who may consider "the protection and conservation of assets" as too broad a definition of security cannot deny that many losses are security-related. In some cases, such as a known theft, the relationship is obvious. However, even in less obvious situations security eventually will become involved. For instance, should there be an unexplained shortage of any tangible asset, the very absence of a logical explanation for that shortage usually will result in at least some degree of security involvement.

Thus it is important for both senior and security executives to recognize and accept these realities, examples of which are found daily in a host of businesses and institutions. Clearly, there is no valid reason why security directors or managers who see any existing workplace conditions that could possibly contribute to losses should hesitate to suggest suitable corrective action to prevent or at least minimize loss. On the contrary, employers should encourage them to do so.

However meritorious the greater involvement of security directors or managers in the overall loss prevention program and the expansion of their roles, for them to succeed to the benefit of themselves and their employers they need to be realistic. In some cases this may require a change in attitude, in others a better appreciation of business practices and needs, and in still others, a combination of the two.

Some security directors need a change in attitude before they can improve the functioning of their department. The quality of an organization's operating systems and procedures and a security director's ability to get line managers effectively involved with the total loss prevention effort can have a greater effect on the security program's success than will the size of the security department's budget or staff. Unfortunately, not all security directors recognize this.

Some security managers tend to assume that complete cooperation is theirs for the asking simply because of who they are and what they represent. They do not understand that if they are to be successful in getting line managers involved, there must be a feeling of genuine trust on the part of those managers before they give their unwavering cooperation.

One way that security directors or managers can help to achieve this is to be open when dealing with their peers, not secretive. In policing, for example, the flow of information tends to be far more incoming than outgoing. However, it has to be more balanced and flow in both directions in an organizational setting. In businesses and institutions good communications are essential to effective collaboration among department heads and other managerial personnel. Security managers cannot expect other department heads to keep them informed unless they, in turn, reciprocate. As a retired FBI special agent turned security director once observed, "not being able to flash the tin" (show his badge) or display his credentials in order to get people to respond to his requests for help forced him to see how differently he had to deal with people in his new position.

In addition to this openness, to further good relationships with other managers, security directors' proposals for the protection and conservation of the employer's assets also must clearly indicate that they understand the needs and concerns of those department heads whose work may be affected by their proposals. Security managers who are so determined to forge ahead with what they see as solutions to their problems that they ignore the concerns of others about the possible impact on operations will only add to their problems. Self-assured security directors, who relate well to their peers and are willing to listen to their concerns, frequently find that when good conversation comes easily, agreement on modifications can be reached in ways that will satisfy both security and operating department heads' needs. This approach is not unlike the recommended circulation of proposed security policies and procedures to executives, as discussed in Chapter 4.

From the foregoing it becomes abundantly clear that security directors or managers may need more than a possible change in attitude. They have to bear in mind the fact that just as they must know and understand the employer's entire business if they are to develop effective security policies and procedures, so must they know and understand an individual department's operations and its place in the scheme of things if they are going to make practical proposals to other managerial personnel for the improvement of facility or unit protection. Those security managers whose interests are either parochial or limited exclusively to the subject of security shortchange themselves, their coworkers, and their employers in the final analysis.

To further illustrate the importance of learning about the employer's business or institution in the broadest sense, if security directors or managers are to function effectively in their expanded and integrated roles they must be able to ensure that whatever proposals they make are more than merely lawful. Of equal importance is the economic and operational feasibility of those proposals. Making certain that a proposal is lawful may be relatively simple; one discusses the matter with counsel. On the other hand, ensuring that it is feasible in terms of economics and operating procedures may be considerably more complicated.

If recommendations touching on either economic or operating factors are to be acceptable to executive management, when made by any directors or managers (security or otherwise), their feasibility and the benefits to be derived from their adoption must be incorporated into the proposal. However, if the recommendations are security-related, the opinions of those department heads directly affected frequently will be solicited by executive management before the recommendations are approved, unless the security manager's proposal itself indicates that this has already been done.

This methodology for approval is not designed to inhibit security directors or place obstacles in the path of meaningful loss prevention programs. Rather it is intended to ensure that all pertinent factors, not just those of a security nature, are taken into account. Thus security directors must learn about and understand the nature of the very activity involved if their proposals are to be accepted for implementation. This learning process is best and most easily done when the security function is integrated with all other operations.

To illustrate the importance of the integrated approach, there is ample evidence to suggest that even when one allows for the legal constraints imposed on applicant screening, the process is not always done as carefully as it might be. At the same time, by virtue of experience gained during the course of investigations, security managers may be able to suggest techniques that might help human resources personnel improve the applicant screening process. However, before security managers attempt to do so, they should first take the time to learn just how the human resources department handles this part of its work.

In a similar vein, security directors cannot intelligently discuss ways in which losses might be prevented or reduced in purchasing, manufacturing, sales, or service operations without first understanding how the various departments responsible for those activities normally function. For example, the very nature of purchasing makes those departments vulnerable to incidents that can prove costly to their employers in a number of ways. There may be some buyers who are receptive to the idea of either soliciting or accepting kickbacks from certain vendors despite the fact that in some states commercial bribery is now considered a crime. If even one buyer engages in this practice, the employer is victimized. Therefore, how to minimize the risk becomes a legitimate matter of concern to security as well as purchasing managers. However, as a practical matter unless security directors take the time to learn about purchasing and understand how the purchasing department operates and buying decisions are made, they cannot even begin to consider whether there might be ways in which they can assist purchasing managers in reducing such risks.

Of course, this does not mean that security managers invariably are able to make recommendations that will benefit operations, even if the real or potential concerns are only indirectly related to security. Nor should their efforts be dismissed on the theory that they are unable to contribute to the employer's overall success unless the issues involved are directly related to security.

No matter how worthwhile security managers' ideas may be, before those ideas are accepted other department heads must learn about and understand security's true role. Again, this much-needed mutual understanding and acceptance can occur only if the security function is openly and fully integrated into the employer's total workplace environment. For such integration to succeed, more than a mere policy statement from executive management is needed. Integration can be achieved in a number of ways, each of which will be discussed later in this chapter.

However, before entering into such discussion, it must be made abundantly clear that if the integration process leading to a comprehensive security program is to succeed, employers must recognize three distinct yet related concepts.

1. Without complete integration the resulting limitations imposed on the security program will minimize its effectiveness.
2. Integration cannot occur without the full cooperation of all of the organization's key personnel.
3. Security directors and managers must earn that cooperation by understanding the employer's total operation and learning to think like business people rather than as police executives.

THE SECURITY DEPARTMENT'S PLACE IN THE TABLE OF ORGANIZATION

If security is to be fully integrated into the employer's total environment, one of the first things that has to be done as part of the integration process is to look at the security department's place in the employer's table of organization. In this respect, to consider *place* realistically involves a good deal more than merely looking for where a block labeled "security department" appears on an organization chart, and how it is linked to other blocks by a series of lines on that chart. The security department's place in the organization also raises a number of other questions, the answers to which will have an effect on the department's image. Some of those answers will help create either a good or bad impression of security's relative importance not only for employees generally but also for members of the public who may have dealings with the organization.

However important these questions and answers may be in terms of integration, image, and their effect on the security program's success, the fact remains that while security directors and managers diplomatically may ask the questions, they have to remember that the answers are within the exclusive province of their employers. Therefore, unless the criteria suggested in this text already are met by employers, the diplomatic and sales skills of security department heads may be sorely tested.

It should be understood that there are several issues relative to the subject of security's place in the organization, each of which will be discussed separately. One, of course, is to whom security directors or managers report and their superiors' job titles. Another is the matter of salary, and in some cases fringe benefits. A third concerns not only the facilities made available to security directors, but also those for the department itself and its personnel, including the location of these facilities.

Each of these factors is important precisely because of their possible effect on the department's image. When security department personnel, from the department head down, feel that the department's image is a good one in the eyes of both other employees and persons who have business with the department, it boosts their morale and increases their pride in being part of the organization. This, in turn, adds to their productivity and effectiveness.

However, if they feel the department's image is poor, or even if they feel uncertain about its place in the organization, they have little or no pride or incentive to produce, and the department's effectiveness is markedly reduced. When this is the case, employers are the ones who have the most to lose in the final analysis, even though they may not realize it.

To Whom Should Security Report?

The rank of the person to whom a corporate level security department's head reports is a good indication of security's place in the organization. Security's importance to any organization obviously would be underscored if the department head reported directly to the chairperson of the board or president and chief executive officer, and if the security department head's title was vice president. However, in most cases, it is very unrealistic to expect to report to the board chairperson or president. As for job title, although employers certainly can call security department heads whatever they choose, finding security department heads who are vice presidents is far more of an exception than the general rule.

While reporting directly to a chairperson of the board or president might be a possibility, the probability is not very high even in a relatively small organization that occupies a single location. On the contrary, in most organizations, and especially those of any appreciable size (including many with only one facility), board chairpersons or presidents to whom the various vice presidents report are much more inclined to reduce or limit rather than expand the number of persons who report directly to them.

As a matter of fact, in some very large organizations it is not all that unusual for vice presidents to report through either chief executive or administrative officers, or executive vice presidents, rather than directly to board chairpersons or presidents. Consequently, even those board chairpersons or presidents who most appreciate the importance of security operations would tend to exclude rather than include security department heads from among those reporting directly to them. Therefore, the question as to whom they should report remains.

Realistically, the greatest opportunity for the security department to succeed in discharging its responsibility for the protection and conservation of the employer's assets in an integrated environment exists when the department head reports to someone at the vice president level. At the same time, however, in order to provide for an optimally effective security program, it is no less important to also consider to whom they should *not* report, even though from the standpoint of appearances the idea of integration might seem to be served.

Illustrations may be helpful to a discussion of this issue. For example, despite being responsible for security and safety on a corporate-wide basis, the security department head for a Fortune 500 manufacturing company, with the title of manager, reported to the director of administration. The latter, in turn, reported to the vice president for manufacturing, an arrangement that caused three significant problems concerning program implementation.

The first problem was due to the fact that the security manager reported to the director of administration. Title notwithstanding, since this person was really in charge of facilities engineering and maintenance, it caused employees to think of security as nothing more than another provider of housekeeping services. The second problem arose from security's placement under the manufacturing division's umbrella, which made it appear that whatever authority security might have was limited to that division. Consequently, other divisions felt that they were under no obligation to comply with security policies and procedures, and to make matters worse, for the most part they did not. The third, and potentially most serious, problem came at those rare times when the security manager had to have a prompt decision on a policy issue, which his immediate superior had no authority to make. This need to go through an intermediary caused delays, some of which were serious and occasionally resulted in a less than satisfactory outcome.

In this particular situation it eventually became evident to the organization's most senior executives that they were not getting the benefits from their security program for which they had hoped, prompting them to agree to make three very meaningful changes. The first step was to transfer the corporate security and safety department from the manufacturing division to the company's legal division. The second step was to upgrade the department head's title from that of manager to director. Last, but by no means least, the director would report directly to the vice president and general counsel without having to go through an intermediary. Within a matter of a few months the results of these changes were apparent in several ways. Among them was the vast improvement in the security department's image and morale. Equally noticeable, and of far greater importance from the employer's viewpoint, was the fact that with its improved image and morale the department's effectiveness, and its acceptance corporate-wide, meant heretofore unrealized benefits for the company. Security personnel got more respect from their coworkers and also found it much easier to get their cooperation in reporting questionable activities.

Important though the upgrading of the department head's position was, far more significant was the department's movement from the manufacturing division to the legal division, and the director's direct and easy access to a vice president, giving both the security director and the department stature that neither previously had. Above all, with security now part of a division that unquestionably had corporate-wide authority, security and safety policies and procedures were no longer subject to resistance, let alone challenge. This became especially evident when other department heads as well as other division vice presidents began to actively seek out the security director for discussion of a wide range of security-related concerns, and to ask for help in dealing with them.

This coordination between the security department and other departments also made it far easier for the security director to exercise authority in terms of developing and overseeing the implementation of security policies and procedures. It was now obvious that this was part of the job. Furthermore, the security director's ability to go directly to the vice president and general counsel on those very rare occasions when decisions on specific policy matters were needed did more than expedite the resolution of potentially serious matters. It also resulted in preventing what otherwise might have been substantial losses, thus adding to the program's overall effectiveness and its acceptance by employees generally. Another significant advantage of having the security function as part of the law department was the fact that with so many aspects of security operations affected by a wide variety of legal considerations, a matter discussed in Chapter 3, giving the vice president and general counsel responsibility for the general oversight of the security department was a sound move.

The foregoing example underscores the wisdom of having security directors report directly to vice presidents who, like the security directors themselves, head units that cut across all of the employer's divisional or departmental lines. Of course, law departments are not necessarily the only divisions with corporate-wide authority, and some organizations may not have even their own law departments; therefore, security will not always be part of the law department, notwithstanding the many advantages when they are. Certainly a vice president and chief administrative officer or a vice president and chief financial officer would have broad authority comparable to that of a vice president and general counsel. In fact, there are some organizations with unified security and internal audit departments that report directly to the organization's chief financial officer.

Just as consideration must be given to those to whom security directors and their departments should report, some thought should also be given to those to whom they should not report. Logically, security departments should not be part of limited-interest divisions, such as manufacturing or sales. But what about their being under the general supervision of a division, other than those already mentioned, with a corporate-wide role, such as human resources?

Although unfortunately this is the case in some businesses and institutions, placing the security function under an organization's human resources department, even if headed by a vice president, is unwise and can lead to a conflict of interest. After all, in the lives of businesses and institutions conflicts between employees and their managers do occasionally occur. When these conflicts involve relatively minor, day-to-day matters, an effort is usually made to resolve them at the departmental level. However, if they cannot be resolved to the satisfaction of the parties, the employees will then voice their complaints to their human resources department, which tries to serve as a mediator. Knowing that on occasion a member of the security department may do something that prompts an employee to complain to human resources, it becomes easier to understand how those who decide to have security as part of a human resources department have overlooked the potential that exists for a conflict of interest. When those conflicts move from potential to real, they can only be harmful to the employer.

Two illustrations, both in organizations where security was closely allied with human resources, are worth examining. In one case where the security manager reported to human resources, a low-level supervisory employee was suspected of selling marijuana to his coworkers. Confronted by the security manager, he gave permission for a look in his jacket pocket. Even though only a minuscule amount of marijuana was found, this was a violation of both law and company policy. An investigative report, accompanied by the evidence and the employee' freely given admission of wrongdoing, was submitted. Nevertheless, human resources decided that since the amount was so small and the individual's overall record was good, the only disciplinary action would be a written warning against repeating the offense. While the employee told his coworkers that he no longer could supply or sell to them, he also bragged about his light punishment—not even a short suspension, let alone being terminated or turned over to the police. Without questioning the propriety or impropriety of the decision, the end result was that employees came to the conclusion that since security was a part of human resources (which was interested in keeping employees happy so they would be less inclined to want to form or join a union), there was no need to worry about security. Shortly thereafter the human resources manager admitted that failure to support the security manager, combined with the inadequacy of the punishment, had contributed to an increase in security problems caused by employees.

The second example involves a person who functioned as both the human resources and security manager but whose interest in security often overrode what should have been his equal interest in good labor relations. Just as there was a tendency toward laxity in the first example, there frequently was overreaction in this case. Errant employees faced severe disciplinary action even for relatively minor infractions. Unlike the first illustration, this did not have a particularly adverse effect on the security program but did have a very bad effect on labor–management relations. The employees were convinced that because of security's relationship to human resources, if they were suspected of any wrongdoing, the burden of proving their innocence was paramount to the need for security to offer evidence of their guilt.

These two examples illustrate what under other circumstances would be considered conflicts of interest. Realistically, one cannot serve two masters equally well, yet that is precisely what may be expected when human resources also has security oversight. In those cases where employee complaints are prompted by some form of security activity, and decisions favoring the employees are made, the security program will suffer. However, if the decisions are favorable to security and unfavorable to the employees, labor–management relations will suffer. In either event, it is the employer who ultimately has the greatest loss. It finds itself with either a handicapped security program or poor employee relations.

Thus far we have focused on the subject of to whom security should report at a corporate level. However, many organizations have multiple locations with a security manager at each site. In such cases, to whom should the individual site security managers report? As discussed in Chapter 2, the answer to the question in a centralized organization is an easy one; site security managers report directly to the person in charge of the corporate security department. However, the answer can become infinitely more complex in organizations that are decentralized.

In discussing the security department's place in the table of organization, it already has been pointed out that as a practical matter those in charge of security departments at a corporate level must be prepared to accept both the titles given to them and the persons to whom they are to report, regardless of whether they agree or disagree with executive management's decision on the subject. At the same time this does not mean that they should hesitate to try to use their powers of persuasion if they disagree with site security managers' reporting lines in decentralized organizations. However, in the event that they elect to do so they must be prepared to support their arguments for change in a logical way.

As mentioned in Chapter 2, it is incumbent upon corporate level security directors who propose changes in site security reporting lines to avoid even the appearance of either trying to build a new corporate level bureaucracy or of enhancing their own positions by virtue of the number of people reporting directly to them. At the same time they should be mindful of the fact that they may not be able to convince executive management that a centralized model for security is preferable, and their proposals may be rejected. If this happens, they should be prepared with alternate proposals that will still upgrade local security operations in ways that will benefit the employer. In either case they must be able to show the organization's decision makers the benefits to be derived if their recommendations are accepted.

The case studies used to illustrate this subject in Chapter 2, while based on a manufacturing organization, nevertheless indicate how problems can arise, and losses can be incurred, when individual security managers in multisite organizations must depend on local management for their performance reviews, salary increases, and opportunities for promotion. In their wisdom the authors of the Constitution of the United States and the constitutions of the fifty states saw fit to make the federal and state judiciaries independent of the executive and legislative branches of government in order to ensure objective interpretations of legal issues. Similarly, organizations with multisite operations, regardless of the nature of their activity, can benefit when site security managers are able to administer their local security programs objectively without having their futures dependent on the whims of local plant, hotel, or store managers.

This issue of independence can become even more important when managers of individual cost or profit centers know that their own futures with their employers depend in large measure on their ability to operate "in the black." Consequently, managers who are determined to maximize profits yet fail to appreciate security's indirect contribution to those profits may elect to reduce the scope of the site's security program. While it is impossible to avoid all security-related problems and prevent all losses, this willingness to accept the risks that accompany a watered-down security program most assuredly is not in an employer's best interest.

Employers can derive the greatest benefits from their security programs when two key elements are present, both of which are most easily accomplished when the security function is centralized. The most practical approach to the protection and conservation of assets requires a combination of independence for local or site security managers, who report directly to corporate security directors and only indirectly to local site managers, and objectivity in their being able to uniformly implement corporate security policies and procedures.

Notwithstanding the logic of a centralized model for security operations, there are still occasions when executive management nevertheless prefers decentralization. Although the decentralized model for security activities deprives an employer of many of the benefits of centralization, corporate security directors for multisite organizations must be prepared to accept this practice as a fact of corporate life.

In the final analysis, since effective implementation of the overall security program for multisite organizations is determined largely by the program's acceptance at site level, it now becomes obvious that with decentralization site security's place in the organizational chart can be critically important. The impression that employees at each site have of security's importance will be based on the answers to the following questions: To whom does the site security manager report? To what extent does he or she participate in the site's general management?

These two questions are interdependent. Therefore, the answers to them can have a significant and direct effect on the success or failure of the local security effort, and indirectly on the corporate security initiatives. Unquestionably, the position of the person to whom the site security manager reports, and his or her presence at or absence from the local plant, store, or hotel manager's staff meetings, will indicate to other department managers the degree of importance attached to security by local management. The department heads' impressions, in turn, will filter down to the employees for whom they are responsible, whether the process is done consciously or not. If the message conveyed by local senior management is one of security's importance, the program will succeed. If, on the other hand, the impression conveyed suggests that security is either unimportant or only tolerated because it is a function required by corporate policy, the program will fail.

To help illustrate the point, it may be useful to look at the results achieved at two different locations within the same organization. In both cases the successes and failures of the local security programs were due largely to plant managers' attitudes and where they placed security within the plant's support structure.

Plant A's manager saw security as more than a management responsibility; he saw it as a management function. At this location the site security manager reported directly to the plant manager and was an active participant in all of the plant manager's staff meetings. This served to further the corporate security director's integration philosophy, with which the plant manager agreed. In addition, the site security manager's presence at staff meetings was a reminder to other department heads that security was important, and also encouraged a free discussion of security concerns. The entire security department and its work were respected. The resulting relationships among all of the department heads, including the security manager, meant that constant attention was being paid to loss prevention matters. Security-related incidents of any magnitude were rare; deficiencies noted during corporate security audits were negligible and were corrected immediately.

In contrast, Plant B's manager considered security unimportant. Its presence was tolerated only because security was required as a matter of corporate policy. The plant manager, who chose to call the site security manager the "site security representative," had him report to the site human resources manager. As previously noted in discussing placement at the corporate level, this was a mistake in and of itself. To make matters worse, the plant human resources manager was supposed to represent security at the plant manager's staff meetings, but for the most part other department heads never thought of him as having anything to do with the plant's security. On one of those very rare occasions when another department head remembered the human resources–security connection and asked a security-related question, the best the human resources manager could offer was to suggest that the question be asked directly of the "security representative." The plant manager's lack of interest in security was obvious to his staff. Unfortunately, it also soon became a matter of common knowledge throughout the plant.

In this case the absence of any meaningful relationship between the site security manager and other department heads detracted from the former's effort to prevent losses. Security-related incidents occurred with such frequency, and the number of deficiencies observed during corporate security audits were so noticeable and so many, that the corporate security director found it necessary to visit the site more often than should have been necessary. Among other things, the need for more frequent site visits by the corporate security director represented a loss to the employer in the form of his time and unanticipated travel expenses.

Consequently, while the centralized model for security operations is preferable, the foregoing examples of decentralization make it clear that effective local security programs require the support and cooperation of local plant, hotel, or store managers. Just as corporate attitudes toward security are evidenced by the title of the security department head and the position of the person to whom he or she reports, so must local management take into account these same factors when executive management decides to use the decentralized model. While executive management needs to understand that without integration it is difficult to achieve a truly effective security program, they must also recognize the importance of both reporting lines and job titles.

Salaries and Fringe Benefits

One might ask what salaries and fringe benefits have to do with the security department's place in the table of organization, especially since they are matters over which security department heads have no control. However, just as the title of the security department head and to whom that person reports have a bearing on the department's place in the organization, what employees receive in wages and fringe benefits can also be construed as a reflection of their relative importance to an employer. This is not merely a question of what security managerial personnel are paid; it also applies to the wages paid other members of the department. And despite the supposition of uniformity in fringe benefits, there can be some differences depending upon one's position in an organization.

It is highly probable that as security departments were being established, the decision to recruit former law enforcement, military, or government intelligence agency personnel for jobs in security management was influenced in part by economic considerations. Although many employers undoubtedly would deny it, instead of basing salaries on the job's duties and responsibilities, they tended to factor in (and some still do) what their new security directors might be getting in the way of pensions from their previous positions.

The rationale went something like this. Suppose an organization, where the average corporate level director's annual salary was $75,000, decided to hire a corporate security director. Its universally applicable fringe benefits were figured at twenty-five percent, or $18,750. This meant that the combined salary and basic fringes for a corporate level director would cost the employer a total of $93,750. Suppose, too, that it could recruit someone from government who had been making $80,000 and who now had a pension of about $53,000. If the employer offered that person a salary of $50,000 and the offer was accepted (as it often was), the company's total cost for salary and fringes would be only $62,500, or an annual saving of $31,250. From the prospective employer's point of view, it was providing an opportunity for a retiree to do work that was somewhat familiar, and at the same time the individual would enjoy an annual income that would be $23,000 more than he or she had earned in government.

While it is true that most organizations of any appreciable size classify all jobs by grade, and grades have a bearing on salaries, it does not necessarily follow that all job titles are graded the same. For example, in one company the corporate directors of administration and internal audit were at grade 15; the corporate security director was at grade 13. The inequity existed despite the fact that the security director's responsibilities were as great or greater than those of the other named directors, all three reported directly to vice presidents of equal rank, and executive management considered itself quite supportive of security. The sole justification was based on the fact that the security job initially was at manager level (grade 10). Therefore, as far as human resources was concerned, the new title and upgrade were a sufficient adjustment; nothing else was taken into account.

When disparities in salary or job classification occur they generally are a direct result of senior management's reliance on human resources personnel, who too often attempt to grade jobs of which they have little or no understanding. In this organization similar disparities existed with regard to the security department's nonexempt employees, for whom a job family had not yet been created. Here, however, the security director was able to convince human resources to establish a job family for the department and to recognize the true value of each position in terms of assigning grades.

Inequities in grades and salaries can affect not only security management personnel, but they also can have an impact on the grades and wages of nonexempt employees. When elements of unfairness exist in these categories they adversely affect morale and become a disincentive for members of the security department, both of which may be evidenced by a change in security employees' attitudes toward their work, their coworkers, and their employer. When these circumstances prevail, they do more than discourage productivity; they also tend to encourage turnover. The possibility of this happening should not be dismissed as something of minor importance. On the contrary, in combination these factors ultimately can be costly to employers. They undeniably cause a weakening of the overall loss prevention effort.

Since inequities affecting security department personnel, other than the director, can have a bearing on the latter's ability to manage the department's human resources, it is only logical to ask whether under such conditions security directors can do anything to effect favorable changes. In Chapter 1 we said that among other things security directors or managers now have to be salespersons. This, then, is an opportunity for them to use their sales skills for more than simply selling the idea and importance of security to their peers and employees generally. Although grades and salaries are matters beyond the control of security directors or managers, if appreciable differences exist between members of the security staff and relatively comparable positions, they should make every reasonable effort to persuade those who set grades (and by doing so affect salaries and wages), to take a more balanced approach in looking at the security department. They may not always succeed, but putting forth the effort in behalf of their subordinates is the sign of a good manager nonetheless.

Facilities

The facilities made available to the security director or manager, and for the department's operations, are linked to security's place in the organization by virtue of the fact that they have a bearing on image. Within the security department itself, they also have a bearing on morale.

This is another subject over which security directors or managers have no control and, in all likelihood, little influence. The allocation of space for all of the organization's functions is usually the responsibility of a facilities or engineering department. Nevertheless, while the choice of facilities assigned to security directors or managers and their departments is not necessarily determined by their superiors' positions, it would be naive to disregard the latter's ability to possibly influence the decision. If that superior happens to be a corporate officer who is interested in and fully supportive of the department's efforts, and he or she offers suggestions to those who do the allocating, those recommendations will be considered even if they cannot be implemented in their entirety.

Before entering upon a more detailed discussion of the subject, it should be said that there is nothing that requires having the department head's office and the rest of the department located in the same general space or next to each other. In fact, in many organizations circumstances may dictate that there even be some distance between the two. While it is only logical to have the security director or manager and the department's support staff together, it may be more advantageous from an operating viewpoint to have the rest of the department in a different location, something that will be discussed later.

At the same time, when security directors report directly to corporate officers, which is highly desirable in any organization, having them located near the latter is preferable if at all possible. While this is good for the security department's image, of far greater importance is the fact that it vastly improves communication between the security director and his or her superior.

In one Fortune 500 company, where all of the corporate officers were grouped together in an executive area, the vice president to whom the security director reported was able to arrange for the latter's office to be located just outside the executive area but adjacent to his own. The fact that the security director was the only department head at director level whose office was close to the executive area was not lost on either other employees or visitors. In a large financial institution where the corporate officers' offices were in their divisional areas, the security director's office was next to that of the vice president to whom he reported.

While these examples illustrate the preferred locations of security directors' office space, unfortunately they are not necessarily typical. The less desirable locations are more often found in relatively small single-site organizations rather than in large organizations, and more is involved than the mere distance between the offices of security managers and their superiors. Occasionally, the very placement of the security manager's office conveys the impression, whether done intentionally or not, that neither the job itself nor the job holder have any appreciable stature or are of any particular importance to the organization.

As an example, if the office is not too far from a dumpster and a garbage storage area in a dimly lighted basement—as was the case in a large, first-class hotel—one might well conclude that the security director's job was unimportant. Even if this is not necessarily true, if the security manager's office is difficult to find because it is in a hard-to-reach part of a building, it only serves to further isolate rather than integrate that person's position and what it represents. In locating this office employers should remember that it is in everyone's best interest—the employer's, security director's, and those who may need or seek his or her help—to have the office in decent and easily accessible surroundings.

Once the location of the security director's office has been determined, other factors that relate to image, and consequently place in the organization, are the size and furnishings of the security director's office. In many businesses and institutions, particularly those of any size, it is common to have a policy that dictates the size and furnishings of all offices depending on the occupant's position. In other words, all vice presidential offices are the same, the offices of all persons with the job title of director are uniform in both size and furnishings, and so on.

If this is not the case, while the office need not be huge or elaborately furnished, at the very least it should be large enough to accommodate a desk and one or more bookcases and file cabinets as well as a minimum of two or three side chairs and possibly even a small conference table to make meetings with security personnel, other employees, or visitors more comfortable and thereby more productive. Needless to say, the quality of the security manager's furnishings should be of the same standard as those found in the offices of others of comparable level. Whether that means gray metal desks or wooden executive-type desks, all directors of departments, including the director of security, should have office furnishings of equivalent quality.

As stated earlier under this section, it makes sense for the department head and support staff to be in the same general area, but there is no compelling reason why the entire department must be kept together. Such separation does not diminish the security department's place in the total organization as long as the space provided is adequately furnished and suitably located.

While security directors or managers rarely have any control over the location of their own offices, they often can and do have input regarding the location of the security department's operating space, which usually exist as control rooms or something comparable where closed circuit television and various alarm and other systems are monitored. When security managers are in a position to influence the location of the department's operating space, they should remember the lessons of Chapter 3 with respect to the management of their resources.

By strategically locating control rooms, they may be able to improve upon the quality of the department's service and conserve personnel simultaneously. For example, if the systems to be monitored are properly placed within a control room that is at or near an employees' entrance, it may be possible for security officers to control access and monitor the systems without reducing their effectiveness. The ability to do such things as this is evidence of good managerial skills on the part of security directors or managers. This, in turn, will do more than merely enhance and solidify their places, and that of security, in the employer's table of organization. It can also be immeasurably helpful in integrating security into the employer's total environment.

SECURITY ORIENTATION AND TRAINING FOR ALL PERSONNEL

At the outset of this chapter we set forth the basis for integrating security into the employer's total environment. Defining security's place in the table of organization and determining such allied issues as reporting lines, salaries, and facilities are only beginning steps in the integration process.

As was discussed in Chapter 4, integration is also facilitated by security's role in emergencies and disasters, and particularly by some limited training and personnel assignments for nonsecurity employees. There is a need for them to participate in order to help ensure a prompt and proper response when a business or institution is confronted with an emergency situation or disaster and its assets, including its employees, must be protected.

Helpful though this limited participation is, security directors and managers should be ever mindful of the fact that more needs to be done. If the security function is to be effectively integrated and the loss prevention program is to be a success, a way must be found to involve all employees, not just those whose exposure to the security department is limited, hopefully infrequent, and certainly not under ordinary conditions. Of course, for security department heads to know what needs to be done is one thing, yet how to get it done may be another.

The imperative for security directors and managers to learn and understand the operations of other departments has been made abundantly clear. However, they in turn have to find a mechanism that will enable them to get both their peers and all other employees to learn about and understand security's role in the organization. The answer to this problem lies in their ability to develop and offer two basic programs: (1) a security orientation program geared to all employees and (2) a training program for managers and supervisors whose help will be most needed in fostering the employer's security goals.

Obviously, suitable orientation and training programs must be developed before they can be presented; the responsibility for doing so rightfully belongs to the security director or manager. This is only logical. Surely the security department head is the person most familiar with what security really is and should be, the loss prevention goals of both the security department and the employer, and how these goals can be achieved in ways that are consistent with the organization's operations and business objectives. Nevertheless, developing programs is a waste of time and effort unless they are presented to the right audiences.

To ensure that the respective programs will be presented to the appropriate personnel, security directors have to work closely with their human resources departments. In some organizations they may also have to work closely with certain divisional vice presidents. While human resources departments are almost invariably responsible for both new employee orientation and management development programs, there are times when some divisions within large organizations may have technical or other needs that justify having their own programs to help with the development of managerial personnel.

As a result, if security-related programs are to be made available to all employees for the employer's optimum benefit, security directors or managers have to make every effort to ensure that allowance is made for a discussion of security whenever human resources personnel or others involved with training plan programs. In doing so security directors must also remember that although from their perspective both new employee orientation and management development programs represent opportunities to further security's successful integration into the employer's total environment, the fact remains that to be meaningful each calls for a different approach. New employees need orientation; management trainees need training.

New Employee Orientation

One definition of *orientation* found in *Webster's New World Dictionary* is "familiarization with and adaptation to a situation or environment." The purpose behind orientation for newly hired employees is to familiarize them with their environment and to make it easier for them to adapt to their work and surroundings. While one would like to think that new employee orientations would deal with all pertinent aspects of the job, even in a synopsized way, that is not necessarily the case. It is not unusual to find orientation programs that focus on some issues while at the same time ignoring others. For instance, a good deal of time may be spent discussing paydays, holidays, fringe benefits, and what the organization offers its personnel in the way of recreational activities. Little, if anything, may be said about security. This seems to be more prevalent when new employee orientation is conducted solely by human resources personnel.

Not being willing to spend some time on security can prove to be counterproductive. Needless to say, neglecting the importance of asset protection and failing to let new hires know that the organization has certain ground rules that they are expected to respect represents a risk from a loss prevention viewpoint. At the same time, the erroneous assumption that new hires will studiously read the employees' handbook may cause a labor relations problem. A new employee may inadvertently breech a policy that results in some disciplinary action by his or her manager. It also causes the employee to resent that discipline, however mild, because he or she never was told about the governing rules and regulations, even if only in an abbreviated form.

For the best all-around results, new employee orientation should be given by a security department representative. Its purpose should be to expose the new hires to the existence of the security program, the employer's ground rules, how they themselves can contribute to the protection of assets, and to whom they should turn if they have questions about security or security concerns. Perhaps an illustration will prove helpful.

With the foregoing objectives in mind, the corporate security director for a multinational organization, who also was responsible for safety, wrote an eight-minute script covering both subjects, from which a filmed presentation was made. Although intended primarily for new employees, the film made no mention of new hires. This meant that it could also be used periodically for refresher purposes for all employees. Copies of the script were sent to all overseas facilities so local languages could be dubbed in. The film, shown to all new employees, was followed by a five-minute presentation by the facility's security manager or representative covering any rules for the protection of assets unique to their location; questions from the audience were encouraged. Rarely did security's part of the orientation program take more than twenty minutes.

This did more than convey a message about loss prevention's importance and employee roles in the process. It helped to further integrate security by virtue of the relationship developed with human resources and to overcome possible misgivings about security personnel and the role of security. The film also had a positive effect on asset protection from which the employer benefited by ensuring a uniform approach to the subject company-wide.

Management Training

New employee orientation is usually offered in connection with a broader program given by the human resources department. In addition to introducing new hires to the workplace, in most businesses human resources is also involved with management organization and development (MOD) programs that are presented to newly hired or promoted managerial and supervisory employees. However, as noted before, the presence of technical or other factors in some large organizations may prompt certain divisions to develop and present their own training programs.

From the point of view of security directors it makes no difference which set of circumstances prevails. It is incumbent upon them to establish good working relationships with those responsible for program development, whether it is human resources or another division, in order to make certain that sufficient time will be set aside in each instance for a discussion of asset protection, loss prevention, and the role that line management and supervision must play. Nor should security directors overlook the possibility of participation in programs conducted by divisional vice presidents who periodically bring their managerial staffs together for the purpose of discussing ways in which to improve performance.

Security's role in training managers and supervisors, both those who were newly hired or promoted and those attending divisional meetings, in order to ensure their active participation in the employer's asset protection and loss prevention efforts can be illustrated by looking at the methodology employed by a multinational corporation. In doing so it is worth noting that in this organization the security function was considered an integral part of the employer's total business operation. Three different programs provided training in security issues.

First there were the MOD sessions conducted by human resources for newly hired or promoted managerial and supervisory personnel, all of which were held at corporate headquarters. Whenever sessions were being planned, the MOD manager would arrange for the corporate security director to appear and discuss the organization's security program, security goals, how the security function could help managers and supervisors, and how they, in turn, could make a meaningful contribution to the loss prevention program.

These appearances accomplished several things, all of which proved helpful in terms of protecting the employer's assets. They let the new managers and supervisors know that the corporate security director was approachable. By discussing problems that managers might encounter in protecting assets for which they would be responsible and how they could prevent or at least minimize both losses and possibly embarrassing situations, the corporate security director demonstrated security's interest in helping them do their jobs. In turn, any preconceived ideas that they might have had about either the security director or the security function being the "enemy" were dispelled.

This particular organization had a service component. Although a condition of employment as a manager in this division was an understanding of the technical nature of the service offered customers, nevertheless it was necessary for new managers to be trained by divisional personnel in both the use of the employer's products and its operations. To ensure that service calls could and would be handled to a customer's complete satisfaction, it was important for each branch office to be adequately staffed and also to have on hand the tools, equipment, and spare parts that might be needed to do whatever work was needed. Some of the tools and equipment, and much of a branch office's inventory, ranged from relatively inexpensive to quite expensive. Again, those who planned and conducted the training always included a session on security and asked the corporate security director to make the presentation. The results were the same as those cited above in connection with the MOD programs.

In addition to service, the employer had a sales division. Aside from any formalized training such as that already discussed, once a year the vice presidents of the service and sales divisions conducted a joint meeting for all of their regional and branch managers. They invariably invited the corporate security director to make a presentation at each of these conferences. The benefits were the same as those achieved as a result of his participation in the formal training programs, but the fact that the divisional vice presidents included security on their conference agenda further emphasized security's integration into the total workplace environment as well as its role and contributions to the overall organization.

Employee Education

As part of security's integration, and in furtherance of its goal of protecting and conserving the employer's assets, the importance of security's role in orientation and training should not be minimized or ignored. It is also important for security department heads to develop a methodology to help educate employees about the need for loss prevention and asset protection, and what they can do to help, and to work closely with employee relations departments in implementing these programs. Various techniques can be used for this purpose, such as posters, newsletters or similar company publications, films, and small group presentations.

However, in designing security education programs it is wise to remember three things. First, think in terms of the audience for which any program is intended. Second, avoid emphasizing only how losses affect the employer; find ways to show how losses affect employees as well. Third, for purposes of cost effectiveness explore the possibility of using materials that are already available and in use for new employee orientation.

Let's look at each of these principles more closely. While all employees need to be educated about security, as a practical matter not all of them have the same degree of education, or possibly even of understanding. Therefore, if the goal is to develop a single security education program, thought must be given to the terminology used and the program's level of sophistication. They cannot be such that one easily understands the program while another group has difficulty grasping the message. However, neither can the program be so simplistic that it serves a real purpose for one group of employees but is a joke to another.

To illustrate, a security manager whose employer was a U.S. Department of Defense contractor, and who thus needed to protect classified information, found some post–World War II era cartoon-type posters on the subject, felt that they would be ideal for his education program, and decided to display them. When he did, executives and managers thought they were funny and laughed at them. On the other hand, production employees took them quite seriously. Therefore, unless security directors can produce a single security education product that is neither too simple for one group nor too sophisticated for another, they are best advised to develop separate programs for each segment of their audience.

Another factor that relates to audience in the design and development of security education programs is language. If an employer is a multinational organization, the programs should lend themselves to translation into local languages with relative ease. Using expressions that are uniquely American or words that may appear in but have a completely different meaning in another language can only reduce or destroy an educational program's effectiveness. Language also merits consideration even for domestic organizations in those cases where a relatively large number of employees can speak, read, and write enough English to do their jobs but are not fluent.

Whether the employer is large or small, single-site or multisite, domestic or multinational, security directors who fail to take into account the several factors that relate to audience cannot hope to put meaningful security education programs in place. As we shall see later in this chapter, line management involvement and executive support are necessary for security's integration into the employer's total environment. However, without acceptance of and cooperation with security on the part of all employees, the task of effectively protecting and conserving an employer's assets can be extremely difficult if not almost impossible.

Even when the nature of an audience poses no particular problem for security directors insofar as the development of educational programs is concerned, their ability to translate security issues into a form to which employees can relate can help or hinder the quest for employee acceptance and cooperation. Understandably, security directors or managers are going to look at the employer's quarterly or fiscal year losses, but it may be futile to focus on those losses only from the organization's perspective in trying to educate its personnel. When this is the preferred format, even loyal employees may find it hard to understand how the losses affect them or to think of how they might help reduce those losses in the future.

Again, illustrations may prove helpful. The first case involved a large manufacturer that published and distributed a monthly newsletter to all of its employees. Executive management saw the newsletter as a way to try to teach personnel about the company's unexplained losses. At the close of every fiscal quarter, there would be an article reporting both the amount of such losses and what they represented in terms of the percentage of sales. To the overwhelming majority of employees the losses were regrettable, but nevertheless they saw the dollar amounts and sales percentages only in terms of impact on the employer. They saw no relationship between the losses and themselves until a business-oriented security management consultant suggested a different approach that, when implemented, not only got a much better reception from the employees but also resulted in a noticeable reduction in losses over time. The suggestion was a simple one: instead of reporting losses in relation to sales, report them in relation to different categories of jobs. In other words, how many research, manufacturing, sales, managerial, and secretarial jobs did the dollar value of the losses represent? Now employees had a much better appreciation of what the losses meant and a greater incentive to contribute to their reduction.

Another example involved a business whose very nature was such that its unexplained losses only could be attributed to employee misconduct; it also had a profit-sharing plan for its employees with a semiannual distribution. Despite profit sharing, employees still found it difficult to see how they were affected by losses reported to them. Their outlook changed with the receipt of their next profit-sharing checks. In addition to the checks, each envelope contained a photograph showing everything that had "disappeared" since the previous check distribution and bearing the caption "How much greater would today's check have been if this inventory had not disappeared?" This did not result in honest employees informing on those who were dishonest. Instead, the application of peer pressure was responsible for a marked reduction in losses.

Showing how losses affect employees' own interests is important when trying to educate personnel, more so in businesses or institutions of any appreciable size. The average employee in larger organizations is inclined to think of himself or herself as a very small cog in a very big wheel and sees little or no connection between billions or millions of dollars in sales and unexplained losses in the hundreds of thousands—that is, not until the losses have reached a point where reductions in force begin and they themselves are either victims or the friends of victims. By then it is too late to try to get them to understand that they have to be part of an integrated security program with a role to play in asset protection and conservation.

Security education need not require a constant search for new tools and expenditures. There may be materials already in hand or others that can be developed for repeated use at minimal cost. For instance, in discussing new employee orientation earlier in this chapter, we pointed out how one corporate security director wrote the script for an orientation film but made no mention of new hires. By deliberately leaving out any reference to new employees, the employer was able to use the same film periodically as an educational security refresher for all employees, regardless of their length of service. Copies of the script accompanied the international distribution of the film so the message could be translated for the benefit of employees in non-English-speaking countries.

Posters can also be used as part of a continuing education program. One corporate security director worked with the employer's marketing staff in the development of a series of eight posters, each focusing on a different aspect of security. Initially, one poster was distributed to all locations at the start of each fiscal quarter so that over a two-year period all eight posters had been sent out. Thereafter he would notify all locations of poster changes at the beginning of a new quarter. Having eight posters and rotating them quarterly allowed for an ongoing security education program without a lot of expense.

In another situation a corporate security director not only welcomed meetings with department heads in the course of security audits but also encouraged other directors at corporate headquarters to invite him to meet with their staffs to discuss security issues of particular interest to their spheres of activity. In addition, site security managers were encouraged to solicit invitations to meet with various department personnel at their respective locations for the same purpose. All of these meetings, both formal and informal, became an integral part of the employer's security education program.

No matter how much effort security directors or managers put into the integration of security into the employer's total environment, they cannot succeed until the very concept of asset protection and loss prevention finds acceptance on the part of both management and labor. This will not always come easily, but it will not come at all unless security directors, with their superiors' support, are ready and willing to invest in an all-out educational program to inform people about the many direct and indirect ways in which security can and does benefit employers and employees alike.

THE IMPORTANCE OF LINE MANAGEMENT INVOLVEMENT

In organizations where security is still considered as private policing, the security manager is the company police chief, and the focus remains on deterrence, detection, and punishment in lieu of a proactive preventive approach, line management's involvement with security tends to range from nonexistent to minimal. On the other hand, in organizations that think of security as the protection and conservation of the employer's assets (the definition of security used throughout this text), rather than in terms of a security director or even a security department, line management's involvement is of critical importance. In other words, it is the very concept of security as a management responsibility and function, rather than simply as personified by individuals, that must be integrated into the employer's total environment for optimum effect. With or without a security manager and a formally established security department, asset protection cannot succeed unless line managers and supervisors are participants in the loss prevention program.

Of course, in those businesses and institutions that both employ security directors or managers and accept and foster integration, it is important to distinguish between what security managers can do and what line managers can do, and how they can cooperate for the betterment of their employer and themselves. Unless they understand their respective limitations, each may be inclined to rely on the other for certain observations and corrective actions, a condition that by itself can pose risks for the employer. However, once these issues have been disposed of, it should be security directors or managers who take the initiative in getting line managers and supervisors involved.

As we already have discussed, successful integration requires that security department heads learn about the employer's total operations and other department heads learn about security's role in loss prevention and asset protection. In earlier chapters we also discussed the need for security directors to develop and sustain good working relationships with other department heads if their own programs are to succeed.

Good relationships and communications assume even greater importance when line management involvement is at issue. This is largely due to the fact that there are times when security directors will have legitimate concerns about certain operational matters that have security-related overtones. They will discuss their concerns with the appropriate line managers and supervisors, as they should, but the fact remains that only line managers, who are responsible for the operations, may be in a position to do anything meaningful in the way of corrective action. Thus their involvement is imperative since without it nothing will be done to correct a defective condition or prevent an incident's recurrence.

Consequently, two separate and distinct issues need to be considered. One is the matter of how to get line managers and supervisors involved. The other is what they can do to further integrate the underlying concept of security into the workplace. Security directors or managers bear a responsibility on both counts, that is, with respect to both involvement and integration.

In Chapter 5, in the security audit section, we discussed the wisdom of and benefits to be derived from security auditors having closing conferences with the managers in charge of audited sites. The very nature of these conferences is one example of how to get line management involved. This is true not just because the local manager is an active participant in the search for a mutually acceptable way in which to correct deficiencies. By coming to such an agreement, that manager, knowingly or otherwise, acknowledges that security can make a significant contribution to the success of his or her operation. At the same time, having actively participated in devising an agreement with the security director or manager, the local manager has recognized that what needs to be done is in fact doable and has also made a commitment to follow through in terms of implementation.

Another way in which to get line managers and supervisors involved arises when security directors participate in the educational programs discussed earlier in this chapter, particularly those for supervisory and managerial employees. Security directors should make their presentations in ways that help create an awareness of security and the roles that line management must play in security program implementation. For instance, in a manufacturing environment line management understandably tends to focus on productivity. However, in doing so it may not appreciate fully that if thefts of either components or time are tolerated, production itself may be adversely affected. Security directors who understand the production phase of the employer's business can help those managers see the connection between asset protection and the manufacturing process.

Educational opportunities notwithstanding, as a practical matter security directors may have little direct contact with some line management personnel unless and until the latter are confronted with a security-related problem. Even then, those managers may be reluctant to either recognize or admit that their own attitudes toward security may have contributed, subconsciously or consciously, to their difficulties.

As an example, in responding to just such a situation, one security director asked the complaining section manager why a rather obvious breach of security by a subordinate had been tolerated. The answer: because the word *security* was not even mentioned in his job description. When asked if the job description specifically mentioned writing performance reviews for section personnel, the section manager's answer was "no." The security director then pointed out that the section manager nevertheless wrote reviews because doing so was an integral part of a section manager's job, and notwithstanding the absence of any reference to security in the job description, the responsibility for protecting the employer's assets was no less a part of a manager's job.

These examples illustrate how security directors or managers can get line managers and supervisors involved in the security program. But how can line managers help integrate the security concept into the workplace, and how can security directors help them do so?

Once again, it is obvious that to make progress in this regard security directors have to do more than understand the employer's business operations. To be effective they need to call upon their diplomatic and communications skills. Not only must they identify real or potential weaknesses that can result in the loss of assets, they must also think of ways in which losses can be prevented, or the risks minimized, and have the ability to offer advice on the subject in a meaningful but inoffensive way.

In cases such as this, security directors should approach the task with a view to being helpful to the affected line manager or supervisor and thus to the employer. They must avoid any inference that line managers or supervisors are incompetent or disinterested in preventing losses. Instead, security directors can facilitate line managers' involvement by sharing their concerns and ideas about corrective action with those managers, much as they do with those in charge of facilities during security audit closing conferences. This approach has merit only when security directors have some ideas about how to solve the problems.

Of course, like all human beings security directors and managers have their imperfections. Consequently, there may be times when they have legitimate concerns but have little or nothing to offer in the way of problem-solving recommendations.

Despite their inability to suggest corrective action designed to forestall problems, it is no less important for them to share their concerns about possible sources of loss. This is particularly true in cases where initially the security interest, while legitimate, nevertheless is an indirect one and security officers lack the requisite knowledge or skills to deal with the issue, or where corrective action may call for some form of discipline for errant employees.

To illustrate, if manufacturing employees work inefficiently or produce goods of poor quality, their employers are the losers. Inefficiency can adversely affect production schedules, deliveries, reputation, sales, and ultimately profits. Poor quality affects reputation and sales; it also results in additional labor and material production costs which reduce profit margins.

A security director may have knowledge of either inefficiency or poor quality or both. However, aside from relaying that information to the appropriate line manager or supervisor, there is nothing security can do to prevent a continuation of these practices. Even if the security department's human resources were virtually unlimited, allowing security officers to be posted on the production floor at twenty-foot intervals, the officers would not have the training needed to detect employees whose work habits are inefficient or who fail to control the quality of their work, nor should they be expected to. These are matters for which line managers and supervisors are best qualified.

It is quite proper for security managers to help line management become aware of potentials for loss. In fact, they would be derelict if they did not. But having said that, how can security managers help line management integrate security into the workplace without line managers having to make examples of errant employees by resorting to disciplinary action? As with other measures that require individual participation if losses are to be prevented, the best method is education. A good example of how this can be done was discussed earlier in this chapter when photographs were used to help reduce losses in an organization that had a profit-sharing plan.

Certainly the effort to integrate security in the workplace should be overt, but this does not mean that it has to be so aggressive or obvious as to become self-defeating. An overly aggressive or blatant attempt to integrate security may backfire. With such an approach there is the risk that some employees, regardless of the level of their employment, may see the security program more as a challenge to find ways to circumvent the entire loss prevention initiative rather than as a way to protect and conserve the employer's assets.

Security's integration can be achieved in a variety of ways. Efforts to integrate security that are more subtle and focused on how effective security programs can be as beneficial to employees as to employers are often more readily accepted. Consequently, they are also more successful. Imperious security department heads, whose attitudes and programs imply that they alone know what is best and who feel that everyone else should obey their directives and follow their suggestions without question, will fail in their attempts to involve line management in the integration process. In doing so they will find that they have done as much disservice to themselves as they have to their employers.

THE NEED FOR EXECUTIVE SUPPORT

The most qualified security director, even if on good terms with other department heads, cannot hope to achieve an optimally effective, integrated loss prevention program without the support of executive managers. This support must be shown in a variety of ways. It cannot be limited to their willingness to hire a security director or manager and authorize the establishment of a security department. However, when such support is forthcoming, the entire process of integrating security into the total environment becomes much easier. The question is, how should the employer's executives show their support?

The mere willingness to authorize having a security department and department head is not enough. If there is to be a meaningful security program, there must also be a willingness to have the best one possible. That means that wages and fringe benefits have to be sufficient to attract and keep the best available people and to provide the department with whatever physical resources are necessary to do the job of protecting the employer's assets. Put another way, executives must show their support for the security program by responding favorably to department heads' reasonable and justified requests for the human, physical, and financial resources without which they cannot succeed.

As we have discussed throughout this chapter, employers cannot hope to obtain optimum benefits from their asset protection or loss prevention efforts unless the very concept of security is fully integrated into their total environment. That, in turn, requires security directors to learn about the operational side of the employer's organization. However, that cannot be done unless executive managers clearly indicate their confidence in their security directors' abilities to other department heads, and indeed to all employees.

Providing the necessary human, physical, and financial resources is one way of showing support. Another is by making it known to everyone that security directors have been granted the authority to ask questions and make appropriate and timely suggestions in all matters related to the protection of assets, regardless of the form in which those assets may exist. No matter how diplomatic or well intentioned security directors are, without such executive support and grant of authority security cannot and will not be integrated.

Security policies and procedures, discussed in Chapter 3, can also be a mechanism for gaining and indicating executive support. First is the value of circulating draft copies to division heads for their comments. This is helpful whether or not division heads, other than the security director's, will be involved in policy approval. The process itself helps integrate security. The integration aspect becomes even more evident in those instances where a policy is issued jointly by security and another department head and has the approval of two division heads.

There is another and equally important consideration regarding security policies and procedures. It relates to both integration and executive support, and depending on executive managers' personalities, it may also require the utmost tact on the part of security directors. It is the matter of executive compliance with those policies and procedures. Regardless of their willingness to provide resources and grant security directors the authority needed to implement the asset protection program, executive managers can seriously undermine the entire loss prevention effort if they themselves circumvent or simply refuse to comply with policy. In other words, they must show support for the security program by deeds, not merely by words. Doing so is a sign of their own commitment to the protection of assets in an integrated environment, and it soon becomes evident to everyone in the organization in ways that can only have a positive effect on security.

SECURITY DIRECTORS AS EFFECTIVE COMMUNICATORS

A thread common to both this and earlier chapters concerns the need for security directors and managers to be able to communicate not only with their subordinates, peers, and superiors, but also with those people and agencies with whom their work brings them in contact. Because the ability to communicate effectively can influence virtually every aspect of their work, it is of paramount importance. However, nowhere is that ability, or possible inability, more noticeable than when it can affect the integration of the security function into the employer's total workplace environment.

The security director for a Fortune 500 multinational organization, asked how he spent his time, answered that most of it was spent in the dual role of teacher and salesperson: teaching employees what security really was all about, and selling the idea that meaningful loss prevention programs benefit everyone, not just the employer. In other words, by passing on both ideas and information, he was communicating. He attributed his success in enlisting executive support and obtaining employees' cooperation—without which no truly effective program could be developed, implemented, and maintained—to his ability to communicate with his coworkers at all levels.

From a security director's perspective, executive support and employee cooperation are inseparable, but neither one is a gift that will be readily given to a security director. Both must be earned. However, for a variety of reasons, some of which have already been discussed in earlier chapters, this may not always be easy. Because so many of the early security directors or managers were recruited from law enforcement or military sources, the resultant image of security personnel, and of the security function itself, was not always conducive to good relations with coworkers. Consequently, cooperation was given grudgingly. Having come from highly disciplined and clearly defined organizations, security managers were inclined to be not only somewhat rigid but also intolerant of people whose attitudes were much more casual with respect to both their work and dealings with fellow employees.

Their role was not made easier by the fact that the public perceived security directors or managers to be authority figures, and in truth many people simply do not take kindly to those in positions of authority who can tell them what they can or cannot do. The very persons who might have been able to profit most from a cooperative spirit were inclined to think of security directors as adversaries rather than as coworkers. Regrettably, this view exists in some quarters even today despite the many changes that have occurred in the qualifications for and hiring of security executives. In any event, the resultant difficulties that stemmed from cooperation that was limited at best also made it much harder to achieve security's integration into the employer's total environment. These obstacles, to the extent that they still exist, must be overcome.

To help change this image, we must accept the idea that two of a security director's many tasks are to teach employees about security and to convince them and the organization's executives that protecting assets is a necessity, not a luxury. Of course, even this may not be enough. Security directors must also be able to persuade everyone in the organization that simply because they cannot produce hard figures to prove the loss prevention program's contributions to the employer does not mean that the security function made either very little or no contribution at all. However, to be able to do this, and do it well, security directors have to rely on their communications skills. This they can do, at least in part, by taking full advantage of the countless opportunities they have to use their oral and written communications skills during the course of their work.

We discussed the ways in which these skills should be refined and used in Chapter 3, whether security directors are looking for executive approvals or support; writing policies and procedures, departmental instructions, employment standards, or job descriptions; or making presentations at training programs for new managers and supervisors. Experienced and prudent security directors or managers will take advantage of every chance they have not only to enhance cooperation but also to advance the idea of how much greater security's contribution can be when it is fully integrated into the overall workplace environment.

Obviously, security managers who lack good communications skills will find it much harder to establish good relationships with their coworkers, particularly those whose help they need for the loss prevention program to succeed. This, in turn, will make it more difficult to win executive support, employee cooperation in preventing problems, and acceptance for the idea that security programs that are integrated into all aspects of the employer's business also are the ones that offer both employers and their employees the greatest benefits.

There are some directors or managers, whether or not in security, who see good communications skills as calling for nothing more than being able to speak or write clearly and concisely and in terms that will be understood by those for whom their communications are intended. Those who feel this way, and especially security directors, lose sight of the fact that much more is involved if communications are to be effective. They forget that the best communicators are those who are skilled in being able to make clear, concise, and easily understood statements *in ways that neither offend nor alienate those to whom they are addressed.*

For instance, other directors or managers are no less interested in protecting their own spheres of activity than are those in charge of security. Consequently, while security directors should be able to inquire after and make suggestions for the improvement of operations generally, they cannot ask questions or make recommendations in ways that appear to be threatening or that will antagonize other department heads. Such an approach will deter rather than enhance efforts to integrate security.

This can be illustrated by the reaction of various managers to two different security directors who worked for the same multinational employer, one succeeding the other. The first one was nicknamed "The Inspector General" soon after joining the company because of the way in which he spoke to and dealt with his coworkers. His visits to sites were unwelcome; while some of his inquiries and suggestions had merit, they were both resented and ignored. His successor, instead of merely asking questions, showed an interest in both operations and what other managers were doing and made recommendations by posing them in the form of an idea for managers' reactions rather than as simple solutions to somewhat complex problems. He and his ideas were welcomed, and he was urged to return. During his tenure the entire security function achieved its highest possible level of integration.

Thus security managers who ask questions and make recommendations, no matter how pertinent and valid, in ways that suggest either their own superiority or their peers' incompetence will not be received kindly. Regardless of their experience or professional qualifications, if they lack good communications skills, they will be ineffective and will alienate rather than befriend executives and other managers. This, in turn, will impede rather than help achieve integration, and without integration employers will be deprived of the many benefits that can and should be provided by their security operations.

SUMMARY

Those who question the need for security, let alone the importance of its integration into the employer's total environment, often either ignore or are unaware of the possible impact of its presence or absence on the employer, the economy, and consumers, who ultimately pay for business losses. Nor do they understand that if organizations—whether manufacturers, wholesalers, retailers, service industries, or institutions—begin to hemorrhage financially, more than just the economy is affected; the social fabric may be strained as well. Therefore, while the need for organizations to protect and conserve their assets is undeniable, they cannot do so in the most effective way unless the very concept of security is integrated into the employer's total environment. Organizations that elect to formalize their loss prevention programs by establishing security departments need to integrate them as well.

Most businesses and institutions of any appreciable size have security directors or managers and security departments, but not all have yet achieved a level of integration that will provide the greatest benefits. This is because some employers and their security department heads fail to understand that several components must be in place to achieve security's integration into the total workplace environment.

Before integration can occur, there must be acceptance. In the minds of many people, the degree of the security department's acceptance and its image are inseparable. In turn, the department's image will be influenced not only by its place in the table of organization but also by the person to whom the department head reports, the salaries and hourly wages paid its personnel, and the facilities made available for its operations.

The most desirable reporting line is to a person at least at the vice presidential level who, like the security director, has all-encompassing rather than limited authority, such as when the security director reports to a vice president and general counsel. Executive management obviously will make the reporting decision, but in doing so care should be taken to avoid placing security under someone, such as the head of human resources, where there is the risk of a potential conflict of interests.

Usually, all full-time employees, regardless of department, enjoy the same fringe benefits. Nevertheless, all organizations have gradations in pay. While there may not be other positions comparable to security's for payroll purposes, the fact remains that security personnel at all levels deserve to be treated fairly. The same applies to the facilities provided. For example, the offices and furnishings assigned for the security director's use should be neither better nor worse than those given to other employees at director level. Furthermore, the facilities for the department's operations should be large enough to accommodate both equipment and personnel comfortably. Equity in pay and facilities does more than contribute to a department's image; to employees both within and without the department it also is evidence of security's integration and relative importance to the employer.

In any organization security orientation for new employees is a logical time to introduce them to the fact that the employer has a loss prevention program. It is best done by security department representatives and is a way of letting new hires know that they are expected to play a role in asset protection and conservation. These presentations serve a dual purpose by integrating the very concept of security into the workplace and encouraging new hires to cooperate with security personnel.

One of the best opportunities for implementing security's integration is during in-house training programs for newly hired or promoted supervisory and managerial personnel. Allowing time for security presentations to those undergoing training means they can be given sound advice to help them protect assets for which they will be responsible, and it furthers the idea that loss prevention is everyone's responsibility, not just the security department's. Of course, it is naive to assume that introducing the subject of security to new employees or discussing it in management training is all that needs to be done. For continued success in protecting assets and integrating security, the security director must also be involved in an ongoing educational effort using both accepted and innovative means to reach out to everyone in the organization.

Whether or not employers provide in-house training for line managers and supervisors, it is imperative that security directors find ways in which to involve them in the loss prevention program. If assets are to be both protected and conserved, line managers must become involved. Remember, security is a concept; security departments help make it meaningful. As we have discussed in this and earlier chapters, there are various security-related operational matters that are necessarily more the province of line managers and supervisors than they are of security managers, at least initially. Therefore, by developing good working relationships with line managers, and eliciting their cooperation and assistance, security managers can ensure that the concept of security becomes integrated, thus benefiting both employers and employees.

The greatest impetus for security's acceptance and integration by line managers, supervisors, and other employees, must come from an organization's executives. Without their support no loss protection program can succeed. While one might rationalize that the very existence of a security department is evidence of their support, experienced security directors know that it must be shown in other ways as well. No less important to the program's success than executives' willingness to provide resources for departmental operations is the need for them to respect and maintain the program's integrity by complying with security policies and procedures. In fact, doing so can be the most telling way in which their support is shown.

Notwithstanding the critical importance of executive support, line management involvement, and security orientation and education, the responsibility for integrating security into the employer's total workplace environment rests primarily with the security director. While there are a number of factors over which security department heads may have little or no control, such as to whom they will report or where their offices or operating units will be located, they can have an influence on the extent of executives' support of and line management involvement in the security program.

Without executive support, line management involvement, and everyone's cooperation, there will be no meaningful integration. Without integration employers will not enjoy the full benefits that security programs can offer. Unfortunately, neither support nor involvement will become realities without effective communications skills on the security director's part. Security directors who cannot communicate in clear, concise, and understandable language and in ways that do not demand or antagonize may be technically but not necessarily professionally well qualified for their jobs. They may even find that their inability to communicate effectively is the greatest obstacle on the road to complete integration.

Suffice it to say that for optimum integration of security programs, security directors or managers must be effective communicators in order to get and maintain executive support, line management involvement, and employee cooperation in the protection of the employer's assets. Furthermore, they need to be aware of the fact that in many respects what they have to say and the way in which they say it, whether in writing or verbally, or to persons either within or without the organization, may also indicate the extent to which their efforts to integrate the security program have been successful.

REVIEW QUESTIONS

1. Explain the relationship between security and the economy.
2. From a practical point of view, to whom should security report?

3. If the security department reports to the human resources department, why might this arrangement pose a possible conflict of interest?

4. What is the relationship between security's image and its ability to become integrated?

5. Why is it important for security to participate in new employee orientation?

6. What is the best approach for security directors to take when they are invited to participate in management training and development programs?

7. Why is line management involvement in the loss prevention program important?

8. If security programs are to succeed, is it enough for executives to ensure that they are adequately funded? If not, what else must they do?

9. Explain the difference between security as a concept and security as a function.

10. Is it enough for security directors to be able to communicate clearly, concisely, and in understandable language, or do they need other communications skills as well? If other skills are necessary, what are they?

NOTES

[1] Harvey Burstein, *Industrial Security Management* (New York: Praeger Publishers, 1977), foreword.

[2] William C. Cunningham, John J. Strauchs, and Clifford W. Van Meter, *The Hallcrest Report II* (Stoneham, MA: Butterworth-Heinemann, 1990), p. 24.

[3] *Ibid.,* p. 17.

[4] *The Wall Street Journal,* March 16, 1989, p. 1.

[5] Norman Bottom, Jr., and John Kostanoski, "An Informational Theory of Security," *Journal of Security Administration,* Vol. 4, No. 1 (Spring 1981), p. 1.

[6] James S. Kakalik and Sorrel Wildhorn, *The Private Police Industry: Its Nature and Extent, Vol. II*; R-870/ DOJ (Washington, D.C.: Law Enforcement Assistance Administration, National Institute of Law Enforcement and Criminal Justice, U.S. Department of Justice, 1972), p. 76.

[7] *Ibid.,* p. 14.

[8] James S. Kakalik and Sorrel Wildhorn, *Private Police in the United States: Findings and Recommendations,* Vol. I; R-869/DOJ (Washington, D.C.: Law Enforcement Assistance Administration, National Institute of Law Enforcement and Criminal Justice, U.S. Department of Justice, 1972), preface.

Chapter 7

Employers as Beneficiaries of Security

Thus far we have considered ways in which security, both as a concept and as a function, can contribute to virtually every organization by protecting and conserving assets. Regardless of size, businesses and institutions first have to be receptive to the concept of security. If they are not, they will continue to be plagued by a host of problems, in many cases accompanied by unexplained or questionable losses. Therefore, to accept the concept means to recognize the fact that all of their assets must be protected and conserved.

However, recognition alone is insufficient. Executives will say that asset protection and conservation are fundamental to sound management, which is true. However, some also think of protection and conservation in a more traditional sense. To them good accounting practices, buying and selling at the best price, and holding line managers accountable for profits and losses all contribute to profits and therefore are at the heart of protecting assets. It may not occur to such executives that security programs, integrated into all aspects of operations instead of being relegated to a more traditional role of making patrol rounds, controlling access, and verifying the contents of outgoing parcels, can make significant contributions.

Once the concept is accepted and the organization's executive management recognizes that asset protection can be enhanced by security's involvement in a broad sense, the concept has to be transformed into a function. The first step in this process calls for designating someone as the focal point for the design, management, oversight, and implementation of the loss prevention initiative. In smaller organizations this role may be assigned to one person, possibly even in conjunction with other duties. In larger businesses and institutions, the responsibility for the functional phase almost invariably will rest with a security director or manager and an organized security department.

Regardless of which alternative is adopted, the person to whom the security responsibility is given will need resources with which to effectively discharge that responsibility. Whether those resources are only financial and physical, or financial, physical, and human, they still will have to be authorized by executive management. Obviously, the primary resource has to be financial, for without adequate funding the use of either physical or human resources is not possible.

It is incumbent upon those responsible for security to understand that in today's business environment getting the necessary authorization involves more than submitting proposals or budgets. From a business management viewpoint, approvals tend to be granted or denied on the basis of costs in relation to benefits. This does not necessarily pose a problem for those many functions that can offer tangible proof of benefits if their requests are approved. Unfortunately, this is not the case where security is concerned. Nevertheless, there must be evidence of benefit to the employer if a viable loss prevention and protection effort is to receive the support of the organization's executives.

In this chapter we shall discuss more specifically the benefits that can be enjoyed by businesses and institutions that both recognize the need for and are willing to initiate or support effective loss prevention programs. However, in doing so one must recognize that organizations whose security programs are integrated into the total workplace environment will derive the greatest benefits; those that isolate security or limit it to what really is a private police function benefit the least. Therefore, it is only logical to base what follows on the integrated model.

In what ways then can employers be the beneficiaries of security programs? Despite being unable to offer tangible proof, logic tells us that employers' operations generally can benefit from well-thought-out security programs in five different yet interrelated ways:

- ❏ Savings
- ❏ Improved operating efficiency
- ❏ Increased competitiveness
- ❏ Better employee and public relations
- ❏ Increased profits

SAVINGS

One of the most frequently heard arguments is that security is part of the employer's overhead. Therefore, it only contributes to expenses, not to savings, and certainly not to profits. This sounds reasonable to the uninitiated. But is it true? No. Nevertheless, since even today there are executives who must be counted among the uninitiated, those responsible for security have to be prepared to counteract this argument. The question is, how can this be done most effectively? Perhaps one way is to illustrate how security programs can and do contribute to savings.

Three possibilities, discussed in Chapters 4, 5, and 6, albeit from somewhat different perspectives, can be used to show concrete ways in which employers benefit from security. They are security's role in loss prevention, risk management, and emergencies and disasters; in each case we will see how integrating security both conceptually and functionally results in optimum effectiveness.

Loss Prevention

Security and policing share the goal of preventing crime. However, in a business or institutional environment the term *loss prevention* means a good deal more than crime prevention. It covers anything that can adversely affect profits. Losses can be caused by crimes committed by either employees or third parties. However, employees also can cause losses through negligence, conflicts of interest, or even honest mistakes. In this respect security, unlike policing, is or should be able to help prevent losses.

For example, while police departments are an integral part of a community's government, they really are not integrated into the employer's total environment. Of necessity their entire focus is on preventing crimes as defined by law. The very nature of the law, as it applies to policing, is such that police executives rarely, if ever, are asked for input into the work of other governmental departments with a view to possibly helping to eliminate or minimize losses.

In contrast, when security activities are integrated, the scope of security executives' work and authority are controlled primarily by their employers. Those to whom security responsibilities have been given are expected to be able to analyze their employer's total situation from a loss prevention point of view and suggest ways in which losses can either be eliminated or at least markedly reduced. This calls for consideration of all possibilities that can cause losses, not just criminal activity. What they can or cannot do in discharging their duties is ultimately determined by their employers based on whether recommended measures for the prevention of losses are lawful and economically and operationally feasible. They only need executive management approval to begin implementation, unlike their counterparts in policing who must deal with a host of statutes and jurisdictional and political issues.

Inasmuch as the primary responsibility for the protection of private property, both real and personal, continues to rest with the owners, security undeniably has a role to play in preventing workplace crimes. A security director's familiarity with the employer's overall activity puts him or her in a better position to assess vulnerabilities; it also puts him or her in a better position to look for ways in which to cope with them.

As an example, an employee, found to have submitted fraudulent expense reports totaling about $3,000, was fired; the matter was referred immediately to security for investigation. The day after his termination he called both his former manager and human resources offering to repay the amount if he could have his job back. Told that security had the case, he called with the same offer, and it was denied. The completed investigation determined that the actual total involved exceeded $18,000.

Had the $3,000 offer been accepted by the manager or human resources, regardless of the investigation's outcome, the employer most likely would have been barred from recovering anything more. This prompted the security director to suggest a change in the employer's termination-for-cause policy to the human resources director designed to prevent the acceptance of similar offers in the future. Furthermore, by working with the authorities, the security director also recovered the entire $18,000. Therefore, any action by security to prevent the theft of assets or assist in their recovery is a direct contribution to savings.

Another example of a direct contribution to savings occurred when evidence suggested that one or two telephones at a soon-to-be-closed facility were being stolen. Security policies and procedures for parcel inspections and searches at the site were activated immediately. No further losses were reported.

To illustrate indirect savings, in a manufacturing plant located in a semirural area where ownership of firearms was quite common, both the plant and human resources managers had reason to believe that one or two employees were the victims of spousal abuse. However, it soon became clear that the mere presence of security officers was a factor in preventing assaults against the employees who were suspected of having marital problems. Security helped protect not only specific employees and employee morale in general, but by reducing the likelihood of problems, it also helped protect the employer's reputation.

Another example of indirect savings is found in the case of two employees who were involved in a conflict of interest. Their outside business activities were neither criminal nor in competition with their employer, but nevertheless they were costly to the employer because they were engaged in on the employer's time. Company policy clearly stated that all employees were expected to devote all of their working hours to the employer's business. By not doing so these two employees were wasting the employer's money. The resulting investigation, in conjunction with disciplinary action taken by human resources and appropriate but legally permissible publicity within the organization, proved to be an effective deterrent against other possible conflicts of interest.

This same principle applies to employees who steal time from their employers by arriving late, leaving early, or taking more time than allowed for breaks and lunch. This can occur when a coworker either clocks a friend in or out or lies about a friend's whereabouts when asked. Employees who do not work in the most efficient way also steal time. Therefore, if time equals money, the theft of time is a crime, yet as a rule it is not one that causes employers to file criminal complaints.

While the comings and goings of employees or their work habits are not matters of primary concern to security, conserving and protecting the employer's assets are. Thus it is entirely proper for security directors to at least point out how such activities can prove costly when they have an opportunity to do so as participants in training programs for managers. Security directors should alert those managers to these and other problems that may confront them, and provide guidance to help them prevent losses. This, too, is a way in which security can contribute indirectly to savings.

To be sure, there are countless other ways of making such indirect contributions to savings for the employer's benefit. Among them are matters of quality control, safety, and environmental protection. Throughout this text we have said that to be effective those to whom security responsibilities are assigned must familiarize themselves with all aspects of the employer's operation. This does not mean that they are expected to become experts, but they should be able to detect potential problems and communicate their concerns to those managers who are directly responsible for specific functions.

For instance, in a manufacturing environment one would not expect a security director to judge quality. However, if during the course of moving about the plant he or she sees a production employee who often seems to be distracted or careless in handling assets of any kind, the situation should be brought to the attention of that employee's manager for closer examination. Distraction or carelessness in production can affect quality, in which case an employer has three choices: (1) spend more money for time and material to rework the product, (2) absorb the cost of scrapping it and making a completely new item, or (3) risk its reputation by letting a defective product go to a customer and later accepting its rejection and return. Regardless of the course chosen, the employer's profit margin is reduced.

In some organizations safety, and possibly even the responsibility for environmental protection, come under the security umbrella. Whether or not they do, our very definition of security makes it impossible to avoid at least some participation in both programs thereby making further contributions (albeit indirect ones) to savings. A company driver seen operating a vehicle in an unsafe manner may cause an accident. This, in turn, means damage to the vehicle and its contents as well as possible injuries to the driver and third persons. In such cases the company's traffic manager must be told if accidents are to be prevented. If a production employee in a safety glass area is not wearing glasses or if a materials handler improperly tries to lift a heavy box, their managers must be informed in order to reduce the risk of injuries.

Although the employee injuries will be covered by workman's compensation insurance, their severity and the length of disability may have an impact on both the amount of future premiums paid by the employer and the amount of money it has to set aside as a reserve. However, in the case of the driving accident, the employer may be faced with an actual out-of-pocket loss depending on the amount of the deductible in its other insurance, the damage to the vehicle and its contents, and the amount of damages awarded to a successful plaintiff who has sued for personal injury or property damage sustained as a result of the accident.

The person responsible for security can make a similar but indirect contribution to savings with respect to observed actual or potential violations of OSHA standards or environmental protection regulations. Again, while either or both of these functions may be the province of other department heads, this does not relieve security of its obligation to report unsafe or unhealthful conditions to those who are responsible so that appropriate corrective and preventive action can be taken. Even though taking such action may mean spending money, from the standpoint of savings this can prove far less costly than taking no action at all. There is ample evidence as a matter of public record that illustrates how costly OSHA or environmental protection violations can be to businesses and institutions in terms of civil and criminal penalties and adverse publicity.

Risk Management

In Chapter 5 we discussed how security works in relation to risk management and pointed out that in reality insurance does not prevent the loss of assets. It only provides for compensation in accordance with the policy's terms when losses do occur.

Suppose a department store's warehouse is burglarized; the insured values its loss at $250,000, a figure that includes overhead and what it had hoped to realize in the way of profits based on the selling price of the merchandise. Even though it has an insurance policy with a $50,000 deductible, the insurance company will not necessarily process its claim for $200,000. On the contrary, assuming that the burglary was a hazard covered by the policy, the fact remains that the insurer will make every effort to limit its liability to the amount paid by the store to its suppliers.

As a result, if after deducting the $50,000 the insurer concluded that the store paid its suppliers a total of $120,000 on the remaining $200,000 claimed, that would be the maximum paid by the insurance company. In other words, the store would absorb the other $130,000 reportedly lost. However, if in this situation the security provided at the warehouse had succeeded in reducing the amount of the loss to only $50,000 in terms of what the stolen goods actually cost (the amount of the policy's deductible), in real dollars the store would still be better off even though it got nothing from its insurer. Consequently, even in cases where losses cannot be prevented, to the extent that security can minimize the dollar value of those that do occur, it makes a real but indirect contribution to savings for the employer.

Emergencies and Disasters

Emergencies and disasters are another aspect of security that must be taken into account in relation to savings. If an emergency arises or a disaster strikes, some losses are inevitable. If there is any damage or destruction to either facilities or their contents, or there are injuries or deaths, there obviously is cost to the organization. However, even without damage, destruction, injuries, or deaths, operations invariably will be disrupted. At the very least this disruption leads to downtime, and downtime equals loss. In either event, the question is, how much of a loss?

As we discussed in Chapter 4, while one hopes that there will not be any emergencies or disasters, there is always the possibility that some untoward events will occur. As a result it usually falls to security department heads to develop suitable plans for dealing with those events in the most efficient and effective ways. The objective of these plans is to reduce, to the greatest extent possible, the threat of (1) death or injury to people, (2) damage to or the loss of assets, and (3) disruption to the employer's business operations.

Thus it is clear that security departments have a key role to play in minimizing the impact of emergencies or disasters and their attendant losses on their employers. This, in turn, calls for careful and thoughtful planning and preparation on the part of security directors or managers. Among the things included in the process are the writing and implementation of well-thought-out policies and procedures for such occasions, appropriate to the nature of the employer's business. Security department personnel must be well managed, properly trained, and suitably equipped. Security directors must also take steps to ensure total employee involvement in implementing these policies and procedures.

For example, if a fire breaks out and a combination of properly trained employees and the availability of the right kind of equipment results in the fire's suppression (or at least in its confinement to a relatively small area), and people can resume their regular activities with little disruption or downtime, the employer has saved money. In case of a bomb threat, if little time is lost in evacuating the premises, conducting a search, and getting people back to work in a safe environment, this also means savings for employers.

These few but varied examples make it increasingly evident that security can and does make multiple contributions to savings for employers who have chosen to adopt and implement loss prevention programs. Admittedly, in many cases where such contributions are made it is impossible to present tangible proof of savings, but in others security directors or managers, who have good records systems as discussed in Chapter 3, can use data that, on a comparative basis, indicate reductions in security-related problems, which, in turn, signify savings. Of course, regardless of whether security's contributions to savings are direct or indirect, the difficulty in proving actual savings still exists. However, to deny that employers do benefit from effective security programming simply because of the lack of tangible proof of savings flies in the face of reality.

IMPROVED OPERATING EFFICIENCY

A careful analysis of just a few of the many ways in which effective security programs can help employers realize savings inevitably leads one to conclude that they also can make a meaningful contribution to improvements in operating efficiency. As is the case with savings, these contributions may be made either directly or indirectly. In any event, they constitute a second benefit that employers can derive from their asset protection and loss prevention initiatives.

All businesses and institutions, regardless of the nature of their activity, use a variety of supplies and equipment. For instance, manufacturers need raw materials, machinery, and in most cases packing materials in order to pack and ship finished goods to customers. Sales organizations cannot sell to their customers if they do not have merchandise. Hotels and hospitals need a constant supply of clean linens and foodstuffs, and they must ensure that their heating and air conditioning systems are in good working order for the comfort of guests and patients. Medical centers must make certain that their pharmacy inventories are properly maintained.

Organizations that lose assets, regardless of the reason for the loss, tend to become less efficient. In turn, a decrease in efficiency can have an adverse impact on their financial well-being. Consequently, most business or institutional executives would concede that there is a relationship between operating efficiency and fiscal stability. However, these same executives might not see any connection between operating efficiency and an organization's financial health on one hand and security on the other, even though such a relationship does in fact exist. Certainly if in a business sense smoothly running organizations are considered efficient ones, and if one of security's roles is to minimize anything of a disruptive nature, the linkage among operating efficiency, financial health, and security should not be hard to understand or accept.

For example, suppose that in a manufacturing plant raw materials are stolen, thereby affecting work in process. Although the stolen materials can be replaced from on-site inventory, the fact remains that production has been disrupted, even if only for a relatively short while. Another illustration would be a situation where an order processor's computer terminal is reported missing. Even if found within an hour, its disappearance has an impact on other employees in the organization who depend on that person for their own work.

Each of these incidents is undeniably disruptive, even if only for a relatively short period of time. They interfere with the smoothness or efficiency of the plant's operations. Furthermore, there is a ripple effect; the impact of each incident travels to other parts of the organization. Therefore, to the extent that security could have prevented the theft of the raw materials or the temporary disappearance of the computer terminal, it would have made a direct contribution to the plant's operating efficiency.

Loss of assets can affect operating efficiency in other types of organizations as well. When retailers suffer from shoplifting or thefts by employees, they lose more than the stolen merchandise. They may also lose business because they do not have a particular product on the floor or in stock when a potential buyer comes in to shop. Put another way, customers cannot be served efficiently. Here, too, security's contribution can be a direct one.

When linens are stolen from hotels or hospitals, or employees do personal laundry using the employer's facilities in violation of policy, guests' rooms and patient beds cannot be made up, causing disruption and reduced efficiency. To deny that such abuses occur is naive. Certainly effective security can minimize the risk of theft. If the program has been integrated into the overall environment, it can also help reduce policy abuses by employees. Just as by preventing thefts security directly contributes to operating efficiency, its role in reducing policy violations contributes indirectly toward the same goal.

Another example of how security can make an indirect contribution to operating efficiency is in the field of applicant screening. Inadequate or lax screening procedures may result in incompetent or unqualified people being hired. This, in turn, may cause a high rate of turnover among employees, regardless of the cause. A high turnover rate is more than expensive; it is also disruptive and can have an adverse impact on operating efficiency. Consequently, to the extent that the turnover rate can be reduced, efficiency can be improved.

The primary responsibility for screening applicants rightly rests with the human resources department. In many, if not most, cases, security has little or no direct role to play in the process. However, in organizations where the security concept is fully integrated, security directors, by virtue of their investigative experience, are often able to suggest certain applicant screening methodologies that can be useful to human resources. To the extent that security directors can help human resources avoid some pitfalls, they contribute to the human resources department's operating efficiency. If this helps reduce turnover and the attendant disruption, they are also contributing to the overall operating efficiency of their employer.

Security, both as a concept and as a function, can benefit organizations by helping them to save and operate more efficiently, even though the benefits may not be tangible and do not lend themselves to measurement with any degree of accuracy. It is equally difficult to enumerate the number of ways in which these benefits are derived. So much depends on the employer's attitude toward security and the extent to which it has become integrated into the employer's total workplace environment. In some organizations integration has not yet taken place or is very limited. For such employers the benefits will be far fewer than they are for those businesses and institutions where loss prevention means a good deal more than the mere existence of a security department. The greatest benefits are enjoyed when security is recognized and accepted as an integral part of the entire operation.

INCREASED COMPETITIVENESS

In what ways does an organization's competitive position benefit from having an effective security program? The same persons who would argue that security does nothing for either savings or operating efficiency would also deny that it can contribute to an employer's competitive position. In all likelihood these are the same people who see no reason for security's integration into an organization. They persist in their belief that security is nothing more than private policing and therefore its role should be limited to what basically are police functions on private property—preventing crimes in the workplace and identifying, apprehending, and punishing those employees who do commit crimes. They believe that security should not be involved with any other aspects of the employer's operations. They fail to see any relationship between security and the business community's larger need to do more than prevent crime.

This attitude reflects a serious lack of understanding of what security can and should do if given a chance. If meaningful loss prevention programs contribute to both savings and improved operating efficiency, whether directly or indirectly, it defies logic to contend that they do not also contribute to an organization's ability to compete more effectively in the marketplace.

Consumers, whether they are businesses, institutions, or individuals, tend to take two factors into account when they are ready to buy a product or service. They are interested in quality and price—so much so, in fact, that there are some retailers who have earned national reputations for their ability to offer consumers name brand items at discount prices. Businesses and institutions must also look for ways to save on purchases by buying from organizations that offer them discounts if they buy in large quantities. Furthermore, businesses and institutions that can conserve rather than waste their resources, and whose efficiency is at the highest level, are often also known for the quality of their products or services. As a result, they are in a much better position than their competitors to satisfy consumers' demands on key issues.

It is important to remember that business-oriented security programs have as their mission the protection and conservation of all of the employer's assets. Consequently, it is only right that effective loss prevention programs should help employers conserve their resources, whether in the form of time or materials. In doing so they contribute to the organization's ability to be more competitive. In addition, since integrated security functions proceed on the premise that good controls and accountability are vital to loss prevention, they also contribute in that sound, well-thought-out controls and accountability can help increase operating efficiency. Certainly the more economically and operationally efficient organizations are, the more competitive they can be.

BETTER EMPLOYEE AND PUBLIC RELATIONS

One of an organization's most important assets is its reputation, something that too often is overlooked. To a large extent reputation is based on how a business or institution is perceived by its employees and on its image in those communities or countries where it has operations or is otherwise active. In some cases a good reputation simply is taken for granted; in others it gets less attention than it deserves largely because it is an intangible. Nevertheless, a good reputation frequently is a product of good employee and public relations. Evidence of its value often is found when a business is for sale. An item included in calculating the sale price, called good will, really represents the value attached to the seller's reputation.

In some organizations, such as manufacturing, reputation can be affected not only by the price and quality of their products but also by employee or labor relations. Others, such as retailers where employees deal directly with customers, must give equal weight to their labor relations and public relations. Providers of services, such as the lodging industry, mindful of the importance of good labor relations, are even more aware of the need to develop and maintain good public relations since their reputations with the general public will have an impact on their business.

Despite these shadings virtually every business or institution will find that as a practical matter its employee relations and public relations cannot be completely separated from each other. Certainly those of any appreciable size will find that employee relations and public relations can be enhanced through the medium of a sound security program. Once again the obvious question is, how can security help? In what ways can it be a factor in bringing about better employee and public relations?

Employee morale can affect more than productivity. If morale is good, savings, operating efficiency, and the quality of products or services tend to be good, and thus the employer's competitive position ultimately is strengthened. Conversely, poor morale more than likely will hurt savings, operating efficiency, quality, and the organization's competitive position. Furthermore, if employees do not belong to unions, poor morale may prove to be the catalyst that prompts them to organize. If they are unionized and morale is bad, it portends the development of labor problems. Obviously, then, morale is an important consideration. Assuredly it has a direct impact on the employer's labor relations, and it may well have an indirect impact on its public relations.

There is an important relationship between good security and good employee morale. Unfortunately, it is not always recognized. Employees are entitled to feel safe while at work and also to assume that what personal property they are permitted to have on the premises will be protected within reason. Therefore, if the employer's security program is deficient in ensuring safety and protecting personal property, morale will suffer. On the other hand, if employees feel safe in the workplace, morale will be good.

In Chapter 4 we learned that workplace homicides are a major concern to the U.S. Department of Labor—so much so, in fact, that there is consideration to possibly promulgating an OSHA standard to deal with this critically important issue. Obviously one cannot divorce the subject of workplace homicides, or of employees being injured or taken hostage during an incident, from the subject of security. OSHA takes the position that employers have a responsibility to provide their employees with a safe and healthful workplace. Needless to say, then, to the extent that security departments can help prevent incidents that result in losses or injuries to employees, whether those incidents are criminal in nature or not, it contributes to better employee relations. If in so doing it also helps the employer avoid adverse publicity in the news media, it contributes to better public relations.

As a general rule businesses and institutions also have at least some obligation to provide for the safety of invitees, even though the degree of protection to be extended to them may vary according to the laws of different jurisdictions. Consequently, when effective security programs can prevent incidents that are injurious or cause losses to invitees, such as retail store customers, hotel guests, or hospital patients or visitors, employers obviously benefit from better public relations.

However, in considering the importance of good labor and public relations, it also is important to be realistic. As a practical matter it is impossible to prevent all security-related incidents from occurring. Therefore, good security programs, at the very least, try to minimize the dollar value of unavoidable losses. This same approach makes it imperative for security programs to be implemented in ways that will help to minimize the impact of security incidents on employee and public relations.

It would be a mistake to think only of homicides when examining security's role in helping to better employee and public relations. While it is obviously preferable to be able to prevent homicides, it is important to remember that one of security's objectives should be to try to prevent all acts of violence from happening within the employer's sphere of responsibility. At the same time security directors and their employers must not forget that for the most part security personnel have neither the training nor the equipment needed to cope with situations of this sort.

Nevertheless, security need not be completely ineffective in this regard. First, if security officers are patient, alert, and properly trained in how to deal with people who appear to be agitated or otherwise disturbed, they may be able to help reduce the risk of violent crimes. Second, when such people create an incident, effective liaison between the security and police departments is imperative. In the event that a violent crime should occur, evidence of the security department's professionalism in terms of its response can at least help lessen the impact of criticism of the employer. Conceivably it may even help avoid or at least minimize adverse publicity.

Patience, the ability to calm the victims of any trauma, and projecting an image of genuinely wanting to be helpful can also help to improve both labor and public relations. Violent crimes aside, it is immaterial whether the trauma is the result of the theft of an employee's coffee money from an unlocked desk drawer or the theft of jewelry from a hotel guest or hospital patient; the victim feels violated. In such cases the behavior of responding security personnel can do one of two things. It can either add to the victim's distress or provide some reassurance that everything possible will be done to solve the problem.

Let us consider two possible scenarios, both involving a theft of money and a response by security personnel. In one case the security officer takes the report without comment and leaves. In the other he or she also takes the report, but this time expresses regret over the incident without in any way committing the employer from a liability point of view. In addition, while the victim is reassured that every effort will be made to effect a recovery, the officer also makes sure the victim's hopes are not unreal by taking the time to explain that since the loss was of cash, a positive identification of the stolen money for purposes of a recovery is highly unlikely.

In the first case the seeming disinterest, no matter how good the officer's intentions, can adversely affect the relationship between the employer and the victim. In the second, the officer's expressed concern and intention to investigate, coupled with his or her honesty in explaining why a recovery is unlikely, will help rather than hinder relations despite the loss.

In addition to security's contribution to savings when an employer is confronted with an emergency or disaster, security can also contribute to better employee and public relations when the unexpected happens. Security's role in emergencies and disasters was explored in Chapter 4, principally in terms of protecting the employer's assets. However, if security programs are designed to deal efficiently and effectively with such untoward incidents, and departmental personnel are well trained so as to minimize the impact of such events on their employers and to reduce the risk of death or injury to employees and invitees, such programs cannot but help to improve the organization's relations with both employees and the public.

As is true of so many aspects of security, its effect is rarely noticed when programs are sound and personnel do their jobs professionally. Under these circumstances security tends to be taken for granted. However, when security programs either are nonexistent or inadequate, the impact of such deficiencies is most often reflected in poor employee or public relations.

INCREASED PROFITS

Thus far we have examined the ways in which employers can benefit from security's contributions through savings, improved operating efficiency, increased competitiveness, and better employee and public relations. Whether those contributions have been made directly or indirectly is immaterial. The fact remains that comprehensive loss prevention programs, fully integrated into the employer's total environment, can have a positive effect on organizations, including the realization of increased profits, despite the fact that security's contributions are rarely recognized, much less acknowledged.

For instance, when security helps a human resources department save money by a reduction in employee turnover resulting from the use of perfectly lawful but more comprehensive preemployment screening procedures, it also helps the organization's profit picture. The same is true when security suggests ways in which to reduce the risk of kickbacks to buyers, the submission of fraudulent expense reports, or short shipments by vendors.

As a practical matter professional security directors or managers understand that a critically important part of an effective loss prevention effort is the quality of the employer's operating systems and procedures, which, of necessity, must incorporate good controls and accountability. Thus when security's ability to help prevent losses—whether of time, materials, or both—is coupled with a good system of controls and accountability, the employer benefits through improved operating efficiency. When any business or institution functions at optimum efficiency, its profit picture is improved.

Therefore, to the extent that security contributes to savings and efficiency, it can have an effect on the employer's competitive position. Not to be overlooked, however, is that by fulfilling its role in loss prevention, security is uniquely qualified to make a contribution to the employer's competitive position, both short- and long-term. In doing so it ultimately makes a contribution to profits. Perhaps this is best illustrated using two different types of businesses.

The first is a manufacturer with little or no security. It has received a sizable order for seasonal merchandise from an old and good customer, but due to a theft, whether of raw materials or finished goods, it finds itself in an awkward position. It cannot make a shipment to the customer within the time specified on the order. The customer is told. Because the product is seasonal, and the customer already has committed itself to an advertising and sales promotion campaign, it must look elsewhere to satisfy its needs.

The customer calls another manufacturer with whom it has done little or no business and is assured that its order can and will be filled. The original manufacturer obviously is embarrassed, but of greater importance is the fact that it has lost an otherwise good sale. Furthermore, it may also lose future business because its competitor helped a customer that faced an embarrassing and potentially costly situation. Thus the first manufacturer has lost what would have been a profit from the sale. Conceivably, it may also lose the profits that it otherwise might have realized from future business with the customer.

The second situation involves a corporate headquarters for a company in a highly competitive field. Here executive management and the security director see security's principal role as that of a private police force. Emphasis is on a highly visible presence, technology for access control and possibly surveillance, and a rapid response to reported incidents in the hope of identifying and apprehending those responsible. Since security is not fully integrated into the overall operation, the director sees no reason to consider or make suggestions to other departments that might help prevent or minimize losses. As a result, an unhappy employee with access to valuable, if not especially sensitive, information contacts a competitor and offers to sell it a customer list; the competitor accepts. The competitor then uses the list not only to contact customers but also to sell its products or services for less money. The difference in price is so attractive that it results in both the immediate and long-term loss of business and profits to the employer.

The embarrassment caused by the security deficiencies in this case may be more limited that in the first illustration. Nevertheless, this example highlights two major shortcomings on the part of the employer. First, there was a failure to educate employees about the importance of information, and about the fact that information may well be one of the employer's most valuable assets and that the loss or theft of information can prove to be costly. Second, the primary responsibility for protecting information rightly rests with line managers, but for this they need guidance and direction. They must be made aware of the importance of protecting proprietary information as well as of the methodologies to be used for that purpose. To do this employers must provide them with well-defined security policies and procedures, the authorship of which is a security director's or manager's responsibility.

SUMMARY

While the management of security operations can be challenging in any event, without doubt one of the greatest and most frustrating challenges confronting any security department head is the need to overcome the stereotypical image of security as an expense item that offers little to the employer in return. All organizations are the beneficiaries of their security programs, but not all organizations enjoy optimum benefits therefrom. The benefits to be derived are in proportion to the effectiveness of the loss prevention effort and the degree of security's integration into the employer's total environment.

Unfortunately, even when the programs are optimally effective, security directors may still find it necessary to overcome this false impression that sometimes seems to enfold all security operations in the eyes of those who do not understand them or who resent them. However, trying to do so may not be easy since so many of the benefits that can flow from effective programs are indirect, and rarely can security directors introduce tangible evidence, of even a limited nature, of those benefits.

Therefore, persuading executive management that organizations can benefit from effective security programs and showing how this can happen become exercises in logic and reasoning. For example, to the extent that security can prevent losses, it undeniably contributes to savings, even though it may be impossible to document the amount of those savings. Furthermore, when losses are prevented or at least minimized, employees lose little or no time having to wait for replacements, and so they, and others in the organization who depend on them, can proceed with their jobs. Thus loss prevention not only equals savings, but in this regard it also helps improve operating efficiency even though security's contribution to improvement may not be quantifiable in a monetary sense.

By extension, the benefits derived from effective loss prevention programs in terms of savings and improved operating efficiency help employers by enabling them to offer their products or services to consumers for less money and with better delivery schedules. Therefore, their ability to function more economically and more efficiently than other like businesses or institutions undeniably puts them in a much better competitive position.

Certainly employees look to security to help protect them and their property while at work. If they feel safe, morale tends to be good. Good morale contributes to better productivity, and productivity leads to savings, improved operating efficiency, and the betterment of the employer's competitive position. Organizations that serve the general public, such as retail stores or hotels, know that they need to make customers or guests feel safe and secure in order to encourage their continued patronage, and for this they must have security programs. In this respect it should be noted that for businesses dependent upon the general public, employee morale can have a significant impact on the employer's public relations. Consequently, effective security operations can contribute to better employee and public relations.

If effective, integrated security programs contribute to savings, improved operating efficiency, increased competitiveness, and better employee and public relations, then by extension these programs also contribute to improved profits for the employer. It is in these ways that employers with meaningful loss prevention initiatives can derive optimal benefits from their security programs. This is what those who either are skeptical of security or doubt that it really serves a useful purpose must be made to realize.

REVIEW QUESTIONS

1. Security programs can benefit employers in five ways. What are they?
2. What do some executives usually have in mind when they think about protecting and conserving assets?
3. Discuss how employers can realize greater benefits from integrated security programs than they can from those that are not.
4. What is the first thing that employers need to do once they accept security as a concept?
5. How does the question of employee safety affect security?
6. Security can contribute to savings in three ways. What are they?
7. Discuss how security can contribute to improved operating efficiency.
8. Explain how integrated security programs can help their organization's competitive positions.
9. What does the term *good will* mean, and how can security contribute toward it?
10. How can security contribute to an employer's increased profits?

SELECTED
BIBLIOGRAPHY

ALLISON, MARY ANN, and Eric Allison, *Managing Up, Managing Down.* New York: Simon and Schuster, 1984.

BLAIR, PETER M., and Richard A. Schoenherr, *The Structure of Organizations.* New York: Basic Books, 1971.

BLUMENKRANTZ, S., *Personal and Organizational Security Handbook,* 3d ed. Washington, D.C.: Government Data Publications, Inc., 1993.

BURSTEIN, HARVEY, "Beyond Cops and Robbers: A Note on Corporate Security." *University of Michigan Business Review,* Vol. 30, No. 2 (March 1978), pp. 30–32.

————, *Industrial Security Management,* 2d ed. New York: Praeger, 1986.

————, *Introduction to Security.* Englewood Cliffs, NJ: Prentice Hall, 1994.

————, "Security Problems? It Could Be Your Attitude." *Journal of Applied Management,* Vol. 5, No. 1 (January-February 1980), pp. 10–12.

BURSTEIN, HARVEY, and DIANNE ANDREWS HINDMAN, "Security's New Horizons." *Journal of Security Administration,* Vol. 8, No. 2 (December 1985), pp. 7–10.

CLINARD, MARSHALL B., and PETER C. YEAGER, *Corporate Crime.* New York: Free Press, 1980.

FEINBERG, MORTIMER R., *Effective Psychology for Managers.* Englewood Cliffs, NJ: Prentice Hall, 1966.

HERZBERG, FREDERICK, "One More Time: How Do You Motivate Employees?" *Harvard Business Review,* Vol. 46, No. 1 (January-February 1968).

KAPLAN, LAWRENCE J., and Dennis Kessler, eds., *An Economic Analysis of Crime: Selected Readings.* Springfield, IL: Charles C. Thomas, 1976.

RITZER, GEORGE, *Working Conflict and Change,* 2d ed. Englewood Cliffs, NJ: Prentice Hall, 1977.

THOMPSON, ARTHUR A., Jr., *Strategic Management—Concepts and Cases,* 6th ed. Homewood, IL: Irwin, 1992.

WHITE, WILLIAM H., Jr., *The Organization Man.* Garden City, NY: Doubleday Anchor Books, 1957.

INDEX